Writing Systems

Writing Systems

A linguistic introduction

Geoffrey Sampson

Stanford University Press

Stanford, California

Stanford University Press
Stanford, California
© Geoffrey Sampson, 1985
Originating Publisher: Hutchinson
& Co. (Publishers) Ltd., London, 1985
First published in the U.S.A. by
Stanford University Press, 1985
Printed in the United States of America
Cloth ISBN 0-8047-1254-9
Paper ISBN 0-8047-1756-7
Original printing 1985
Last figure below indicates year of this printing:
09   08   07   06   05

Sophie's Book

The above dedication, which reads *gadub ᵍᵉᵐᵉnam-igi-gál,* literally 'tablet-collection of Miss Wisdom', is written in 5000-year-old Archaic Sumerian script, the oldest form of writing known, and, in the view of some scholars, the ancestor of all other writing systems used on this planet.

Contents

Preface

In writing this book I have been heavily dependent on others' knowledge of fields in which I am not expert. A number of scholars have given me encouragement and advice which, in many cases, must have cost a great deal of their time. I should like to express my warmest thanks to the following: Andrew Ellis, Department of Psychology, University of Lancaster; Soo-nai Ham, Department of Linguistics and Modern English Language, University of Lancaster; James Hartley, Department of Psychology, University of Keele; William Labov, Linguistics Laboratory, University of Pennsylvania; W. G. Lambert, Department of Ancient History and Archaeology, University of Birmingham; Ki-moon Lee, Department of Korean Language and Literature, Seoul National University; J. D. McCawley, Department of Linguistics, University of Chicago; Anna Morpurgo Davies, Somerville College, Oxford; E. G. Pulleyblank, Department of Asian Studies, University of British Columbia; Michael Pye, Department of Theology and Religious Studies, University of Leeds; John Randall, Department of Classics and Archaeology, University of Lancaster; my wife, Vera van Rijn; J. F. A. Sawyer, Department of Religious Studies, University of Newcastle upon Tyne; D. G. Scragg, Department of English Language and Literature, University of Manchester; W. E. Skillend, Department of the Far East, School of Oriental and African Studies, University of London; Michael Twyman, Department of Typography and Graphic Communication, University of Reading; Valerie Yule, Department of Psychology, University of Aberdeen.

In interpreting their various expertises to the layman I have striven not to distort them, but I feel sure that there must be places where I have failed in this endeavour. If so, the faults are mine, not theirs.

I thank the Ford Motor Company Ltd and the Language Research Unit of Seoul National University for permission to reproduce copyright material.

Ingleton, Yorks
July 1983

1 Introduction

This book is offered in the belief that written language is a form of language. As such, it deserves to be treated with the methods of modern, scientific linguistic study which have been increasing our understanding of the spoken form of language for many decades.

To say that writing has as much claim as speech to be treated as language may strike the reader as a statement of the obvious. But the fact is that, although the tide is beginning to turn now, for most of the twentieth century linguistics has almost wholly ignored writing. It is not necessary to accept all the theories of the French critic Jacques Derrida in order to agree with him when he describes writing as 'the wandering outcast of linguistics' (1967, p. 44).† Derrida is describing chiefly the European tradition of linguistics founded by Ferdinand de Saussure, but the situation in North America was no different. F. W. Householder (1969, p. 886) lists eight propositions accepted as axiomatic by followers of the American linguist Leonard Bloomfield, of which the first is 'Language is basically speech, and writing is of no theoretical interest'; according to Harvey Minkoff (1975, p. 194), 'Writing systems as such are virtually ignored by modern American linguistics'. Until recently the only group of linguists to take writing seriously were the Prague School (e.g. Vachek 1973), but their ideas were little discussed outside Continental Europe.

Within scientific linguistics it has been a cardinal principle since the beginning of the twentieth century that all languages are on an equal footing with respect to their suitability for study. This does not, obviously, mean that a book about linguistics is expected to mention each of the several thousand languages that exist. It means, rather, that we must avoid the tempting fallacy of assigning a special status to the structural principles that happen to be displayed by our own language (or by any other one particular language) and of turning that language into the measure of all others, so that alien languages come to seem like perverse distortions of 'normal' language. Our own mother-tongues are so much a part of us that this ethnocentric attitude to linguistic differences is a very natural one, but scientific linguistics is supposed to enable us to rise above it.

Furthermore, a second principle of scientific linguistics is that languages

†Full biographical details of references quoted in the text appear in the References section beginning on p. 215.

are *structures* of symbols defined by their interconnections. What gives any particular element of a language its role in the language is not its superficial physical properties but, rather, the relationships it enters into with the other elements of the language. The fact that the French word *il*, for example, is pronounced as it is is a relatively trivial matter – French would still be to all intents and purposes the same language if the masculine pronoun happened to be pronounced in some other way. But the fact that the element *il* contrasts in French only with the element *elle* rather than belonging to a three-way choice analogous to English *he, she, it*, or the fact that *il* has a special relationship with a form *lui* to which English has no equivalent – facts such as these about the relations between elements are part of the essence of the language.

Writing is an aspect of language which has taken much longer than others to be affected by these revolutions in intellectual assumptions; the passage quoted from Harvey Minkoff above continues, 'most studies of writing ignore linguistic theory and methodology'. Books on writing still tend to concentrate more on the physical appearance of scripts than on analysis of the formal relationships between graphic elements; and they are ethnocentric, in that they place our own writing system and those related to it firmly in the focus of their view, allotting to relatively 'alien' systems a treatment which is at best cursory and, in some cases, full of factual errors.

The first question worth our consideration, then, is why written language has been largely ignored by linguistics. There are several factors which make the long-standing preoccupation with exclusively spoken language understandable – though, of course, to understand a prejudice is not to condone it.

One reason why twentieth-century linguists have emphasized spoken language to the exclusion of written language is as a simple reaction against an older tradition of language-study which was equally partial in the opposite direction. Before the twentieth century – and, much more so, before the nineteenth – scholars concerned with questions of language tended to approach the subject in an evaluative spirit, they were concerned to identify 'good', approved usage and to weed out what were regarded as popular linguistic errors. Anyone who thinks about language in this way is likely to concentrate mainly on written language, because it is in writing that we put on our linguistic Sunday best, as it were, pondering over and editing our expressions in order to produce a polished end-product. Furthermore, before the shift of focus towards synchronic linguistic analysis which occurred in the opening years of our century, scholars studied contemporary linguistic forms mainly with a view to their historical etymology; this also tends to direct attention towards writing as opposed to speech, since in very many languages the written form is relatively conservative by comparison with the spoken. Indeed, until late in the nineteenth century linguists simply had no vocabulary in which to make precise statements about the *sounds* of language; the science of phonetics did not yet exist, and philologists perforce discussed the historical development of words in terms of changes of 'letters' even with respect to early stages when the language in question had no written form.

The new science of synchronic linguistics which grew up in the present century had to wage a long-drawn-out and sometimes arduous battle to establish its validity as a subject which studied language 'descriptively rather than prescriptively' – which concentrated on how people do use language, irrespective of whether their usage coincides with the rules of purists governing how people should use language. For many linguists, particularly in the middle part of the century and particularly in North America, it became a matter of missionary zeal to insist in season and out that if a given group of English-speakers commonly utter the word *ain't*, for example, then the linguist should incorporate that form into his description of their language, and should ignore the horrified objection by laymen that to do this is to sanctify a usage which is socially condemned. Quite naturally, scholars who insisted that it was their job to investigate proscribed forms of language were bound to concentrate on speech rather than writing: even the speaker who utters *ain't* unselfconsciously in speech will invariably try to conform to the precepts of the purists when he puts pen to paper. To quote Ruth Weir (1967, p. 170), 'It was a difficult enough task to free ourselves from looking at language only through its written representation. . . . The victory of accepting the primacy of spoken language has in fact been won so hard that any concession to writing savored of retreat.'

But, while this reaction from one extreme to its opposite is understandable enough, it cannot be accepted permanently as an appropriate stance for linguistics to adopt. If we are to approach language descriptively, then we should describe all aspects of language, including writing. In any case, it was always a little romantic of linguists to think of spoken language, or at least casual, rapid speech, as 'natural' language undefiled by artificial prescriptive rules; nowadays it is well understood that all kinds of language are influenced in various ways by social pressures – and modifying one's language for purposes of social prestige is a kind of linguistic behaviour, after all, and as such a proper subject for linguistic study.

But spoken language has been perceived as 'natural' by contrast to written language also in a deeper sense. A principal reason why the study of linguistics has been attractive to many people is that language seems to be the feature *par excellence* which distinguishes man from beast; it appears to be the most distinctively human of human characteristics. From this biological viewpoint, it is certain that speech is central and writing peripheral. Spoken language is primary both phylogenetically and ontogenetically: that is, there were spoken languages long before there were written languages (and some human communities still have no writing system, while all have spoken languages), and each individual child brought up in a literate community learns to speak and to understand spoken language before learning to read and write (and some individuals never do become literate, whereas speech is always mastered except by children with special physiological handicaps of deafness and/or dumbness).

There is even some evidence that the anatomy of the human mouth and throat, and possibly also of our hearing apparatus, may have evolved biologically to make the production and perception of speech-sounds more efficient for us than it would be for our nearest evolutionary kin-species. (Nobody, by contrast, has suggested that our hands or eyes have undergone special biological developments to adapt them to the tasks of writing and reading, and such an idea would be extremely implausible given the short time-scale relevant for written language.) During the 1960s and 1970s, very many linguists were influenced by a point of view according to which biological adaptation to language was much more than just a matter of being able to utter and hear a relatively wide range of sounds; theoreticians argued that our ability to learn and use the complex, abstract syntactic, semantic, and phonological rules which constitute a language depends crucially on biologi-cally-inherited structures in the brain which fix most aspects of linguistic rules in advance, leaving the child only a small amount to be learned by experience of his elders' language.

Again it would have been out of the question to extend this notion to the written medium; writing was isolated from other aspects of language as an exclusively cultural rather than largely biological phenomenon, and accord-ingly seemed irrelevant to scholars who were attracted to linguistics by the idea that it offered a window on to biological machinery of the human intellect. (Some scholars went so far as to suggest that literacy contaminated linguistic data, so that even such languages as standard French ought to be studied exclusively through the highly atypical minority of their adult speakers who are illiterate; see Love 1980, pp. 205–7.)

If this 'nativist' view of language were correct, it might well suggest a discontinuity between the study of writing and the study of other aspects of language – one might not expect much 'carry-over' of analytic principles and techniques from the latter to the former domains. Even so, this would hardly be a reason for bypassing the study of writing entirely. Investigation of biologically-inherited neural machinery is only one reason for being interested in language, though it happens to have been a particularly fashionable motive in the recent past. Cultural phenomena are interesting too, and if linguists do not study the cultural phenomenon called writing it is not clear who else is competent to do so. And in any case the nativist view of language now looks considerably less plausible than it once did. I have argued elsewhere (Sampson 1980b) that, so far as the evidence goes, it suggests that the complex structures of spoken languages are as much 'cultural' products as any other, not biologi-cally predetermined (even though the emergence of spoken languages no doubt antedated – and may have been a precondition for – the emergence of most or all other cultural phenomena).

This general point of view seems less controversial now than it was a few years ago. If it is accepted, the neglect of writing by linguistics comes to seem quite irrational; why should one overlook a particular cultural phenomenon just because it is relatively new (that is, only a few thousand years old)? Even in contemporary Western societies the written medium plays a subsidiary role in the sense that it is inaccessible to a minority of members of society, and the literate majority undoubtedly exchange far more words via the spoken than via the written medium. On the other hand, the messages for which writing is used are often rather important ones. People have frequently made large claims for the crucial role of literacy in individual intellectual activity and in the life of complex societies. J. H. Breasted believed that the invention of writing 'had a greater influence in uplifting the human race than any other intellectual achievement. . . . It was more important than all the battles ever fought and all the constitutions ever devised' (1926, pp. 53–4). For specific analyses of this influence, see e.g. Goody and Watt (1963); Havelock (1978); Stratton (1980).

Admittedly, the intellectual and social consequences of literacy may have been exaggerated in a number of respects. Elizabeth Eisenstein (1979) has argued that many of the phenomena commonly associated with the invention of writing in fact only appeared with the much more recent invention of printing. Sylvia Scribner and Michael Cole (1981) suspected that intellectual habits often attributed to literacy might rather be caused by the disciplines of schooling; they tested this by investigating the use of a script (that of the Vai of the Liberia/Sierra-Leone border) which is learned exclusively in informal, non-school settings, and they conclude that the intellectual implications of literacy as such may be fairly limited. Arguably, the reasons why States strive to eliminate illiteracy have to do less with the benefits of literacy to the individual than with the fact that literacy enables people to fulfil their duties as citizens (cf. Stubbs 1980, p. 14). But writing is, at any rate, much more than an inessential frill on the margin of linguistic behaviour. It therefore seems high time for the discipline of linguistics to recognize that written language falls squarely within its domain.

From now on, then, I shall take it for granted that linguistic study of writing is a worthwhile enterprise. Let us now consider the question of what general headings such a study might divide into. What chief aspects of the subject can be distinguished? Different answers could no doubt be offered to this question, but I propose three categories as covering most of the ground between them. These may be labelled *typology*, *history*, and *psychology*.

Under the heading 'typology' we ask: what different kinds of writing-system are there? Presumably there can be only a limited number of alternative principles available for the reduction of spoken language to visible form: what are they? Once we have the range of theoretically-possible principles, they will serve as a scheme of classification for the hundreds of individual scripts that are, or have been, actually used; but we may expect that actual systems will differ in the extent to which they are 'pure' representatives of one particular principle of writing, and many scripts will have to be characterized as mixtures of different principles.

One particularly interesting question, under the 'typology' heading, is whether particular types of script tend to be associated with particular types of spoken language. Are certain kinds of spoken language intrinsically more compatible with one rather than another of the various alternative methods for reducing speech to visible marks, or do the choices of writing-system made by various speech-communities depend wholly on external historical factors?

Clearly, factors external to linguistic structure do play a major role in the adoption of particular scripts by different communities. Thus it has been pointed out that, in many cases, 'script follows religion': because religions, often, are founded on holy books, and because the propagation of literacy has often been a function of religious authorities, territorial boundaries between different scripts frequently coincide with, and are explained by, boundaries between religions. One obvious case is the use of Roman versus Cyrillic alphabets by speakers of different Eastern European languages: Russians, Bulgarians, Serbs use Cyrillic, while Poles, Czechs, Croats use Roman, and the division coincides with that between the Eastern Orthodox and the Western Catholic churches. It has nothing to do with differences between the languages; the nations listed all speak fairly closely-related Slavonic languages, and indeed Serbs and Croats speak the same language although they write it with different letters.

Nevertheless, the importance of such correlations between script and external factors such as religion does not rule out the possibility that there may also be correlations between internal, structural characteristics of spoken languages and types of script used to write them. As this book progresses we shall notice that there do seem to be influences from type of spoken language on script-type, and surely it would be a little strange if that were not so.

Under the heading 'history', obviously, we examine the developments that various scripts have undergone through time. Just as traditional historical linguistics studies the various changes by which, for instance, (spoken) Anglo-Saxon has gradually evolved into modern (spoken) English, or (spoken) Latin has developed into Spanish, French, and the other contemporary spoken Romance languages, so we may investigate the processes by which one writing-system changes into another over the years and centuries.

Here it is worth remarking that there is one major difference between the historical linguistics of spoken language and the historical linguistics of writing, which makes the latter possibly a more rewarding branch of the general study of writing than the former is of general spoken-language linguistics.

Spoken language is a phenomenon that had a beginning. There must have been a time when early Man, or the species out of which Man evolved, lacked any pattern of behaviour that we would want to equate with language as we know it today. At some point, perhaps just once or perhaps many times independently among separate communities, language appeared. Unless full-scale languages of the kind we know suddenly emerged, as it were overnight, through some massive biological mutation – a notion which is surely grossly implausible (even though it might be congenial to some of the wilder spirits who have worked in the field of theoretical linguistics in the recent past), the earliest spoken languages must have been very different in kind, far simpler and cruder, than their contemporary descendants. (It is often suggested that language may well have gradually developed by a process of cultural evolution from the – by comparison – extremely crude signalling-systems used by other species, so that there would be in principle no one stage at which one could specify that a transition had occurred from no-language to language.) However, when we investigate the history of particular spoken languages, the time-span for which we can get any detailed knowledge – a few millennia in the most favourable cases – is very short in comparison with the probable length of time over which spoken languages have been developing, the lowest serious estimate of which known to me is 30,000 years but which may easily have been a million years or more. Although much of the impetus for the original growth of linguistic science in the early nineteenth century stemmed from the hope that examination of the history of languages would reveal the laws by which sophisticated modern communication-systems had evolved out of more primitive antecedents, nowadays it seems more plausible to think that even the oldest languages for which data are available represent essentially the same high level of development as our contemporary languages, so that significantly less-evolved stages are lost to us for ever (unless, possibly, present-day pidgins and creoles may offer us a contemporary analogue of the earliest origins of our own languages).

In the case of the evolution of writing systems, the situation is very different. The total history of writing, as already mentioned, is much shorter than that of spoken language; and much of the point of writing is that it is permanent, in contrast to the air-waves that carry spoken utterances, which dissipate as fast as they are produced. For these reasons, we have access to a portion of the history of various scripts which is large relative to their total history. Indeed, we may be able to trace right back to the birth of some systems, possibly including the oldest of all.

Clearly the study of the typology of writing and the study of its history will not be unrelated enterprises. One obvious question that arises in the historical linguistics of written language is whether there are any regularities in the succession of types; do, say, scripts of type *A* regularly or commonly develop eventually into scripts of type *B*, or does one type mutate into another type in an essentially random, unpredictable fashion? Within the framework of this book it will not be possible to present sufficient evidence to justify a definitive answer to this question, but we shall encounter hints suggesting that there are indeed regularities of written-language evolution.

The third general heading proposed for the study of writing systems was 'psychology'. By this I refer to questions about how various types of writing work in practice for those who learn and use them. What are the mental processes by which a fluent reader, confronted with a page of written English, extracts the messages which author and printer between them have buried in it? Do these processes differ significantly for users of scripts of other types, for instance the Chinese script?

One subset of questions under the 'psychology' heading which are of specially obvious interest are questions about the relative goodness or efficiency of different types of writing, and of individual scripts within single typological categories. What makes a writing system 'good' or 'bad' is doubtless an issue to which very diverse considerations are relevant, but it falls into two main sub-issues: how efficiently does the system function for those who have already mastered it? and, how easy is it to learn? We shall see that these two desiderata are to some extent in conflict with each other.

Questions of this evaluative kind do not normally arise in the linguistics of spoken language. We have already seen that linguists avoid judging alternative forms within a given language as 'better' or 'worse', and still less do they discuss which languages are 'better' than which other languages. To the contrary, there is a widespread assumption among linguists that such questions would be fruitless because all languages are equally 'good', equally structurally subtle, equally efficient.[1] † This axiom of equal goodness of spoken languages is held partly for ideological reasons. A person's mother tongue is so much a part of his personality that, in an equalitarian age, scholars have wanted to repress any idea that there might be 'better' or 'worse' among languages. But there are also more respectable justifications for the axiom.

In particular, the very long period of historical development, already referred to, from which all normal spoken languages (excluding pidgins and creoles) seem to descend might well suggest that cultural evolution will have had plenty of time to eliminate inefficient traits and create all the features that languages need (at least with respect to phonological and grammatical structure, if perhaps not with respect to vocabulary, where technological or environmental change may outstrip the ability of a language to provide useful coinages). Also, the concept of 'efficiency' in any domain implies that the task to be achieved can be measured independently of the tool whose efficiency is being assessed, but spoken language is in a sense functionally self-defining: its function is often said to be to express ideas or thoughts, yet these can scarcely be identified other than through the language which expresses them. If spoken languages are 'tools' at all, they are clearly not tools in the sense of having been consciously fashioned in order to carry out a predetermined job. Both the age of spoken languages and this 'self-employed status' they possess might well suggest that it is pointless to try to rank them on evaluative scales.

None of these considerations apply to writing systems. These clearly are tools forged to carry out a task, which they may do more or less well – in the case of early writing systems the task was often much more narrowly circumscribed than it is in the case of writing in a modern Western community. Writing is felt quite generally to be an aspect of technology, something that people use, rather than part of personality, of what people are. If a foreigner tells me that English spelling is very inefficient, I may demur on factual grounds and argue (as I shall argue later in this book) that our spelling has hidden virtues which go some way to compensate for its obvious vices; but I

†Superior figures refer to the Notes beginning on p. 214.

am less likely to raise my hackles in an emotional response than I might be inclined to do if told that, say, the English tense system, or our range of consonant-sounds, was cumbersome and undesirable. Furthermore, we have seen that writing has a relatively short history, most of which is open to inspection; it would be absurd to deny that many of the developments observable in the historical record were cases of evolution from inferior to superior systems. (That is not to suggest that *all* changes in writing systems have been improvements; many changes have had external causes, and some may have led to less rather than more efficiency.) For all these reasons, it is very easy to include in the linguistics of written languages an evaluative dimension which scarcely exists in the traditional linguistics of spoken language.

The strategy of this book will be to use the first of the three headings proposed for the study of writing, namely typology, as its organizing principle. The following chapter will outline a classification of the various logically-possible kinds of writing, illustrating the theoretical discussion by reference to small-scale examples drawn from material likely to be more or less familiar to the English-speaking reader. Later chapters will discuss the various types of writing identified in Chapter 2, via detailed examination of one script chosen as a relatively pure representative for each type. No attempt is made to include scripts merely because they are internationally-important; e.g. the Cyrillic alphabet is ignored because, at the level of detail with which we are concerned, it is not significantly different from the Greek alphabet, which is covered. In several cases the scripts discussed, and the spoken languages that they are used to record, will be quite unfamiliar to most readers; I hope that one of the incidental benefits of this book to the student of linguistics may be to introduce him to spoken-language data that are more exotic (and hence educative) than he has encountered elsewhere. Considerations relating to the other branches of the subject, history and psychology, will be introduced as they become relevant in the discussion of particular scripts; these topics are not assigned chapters of their own.

However, this scheme is executed with some departures from perfect rigour. Thus the discussion of Sumerian writing in Chapter 3 is justified in terms of its special relevance for the historical, rather than the typological, branch of the subject; and in Chapter 6 I take advantage of the fact that the Greek alphabet is discussed in order to include a fairly detailed account of the derivation of the modern Roman alphabet from the Greek – this passage is motivated more in terms of satisfying the reader's curiosity about the symbols of our own script than in terms of introducing novel theoretical principles. The English version of alphabetic orthography is treated in detail in the last chapter.

Let me conclude this introductory chapter with some considerations relating to terminology and notational conventions to be used in the rest of the book.

I shall use the terms *script, writing-system*, or *orthography*, to refer to *a given set of written marks together with a particular set of conventions for their use*. English and German are written with more or less the same set of symbols (more or less, because German but not English writing uses ⟨ä ö ü⟩ and sometimes ⟨ß⟩ – it is surprisingly difficult to find pairs of European languages written with *precisely* the same letters); but the 'English script', or 'English writing-system', or 'English orthography', is rather different from the 'German script/writing-system/orthography', because the conventions for using the symbols are rather different. (The conventions differ with respect both to specific matters, such as that ⟨ch⟩ stands for /tʃ/ in the English system, for /x/ and /ç/ in the German, and to general matters such as that each individual symbol or digraph normally corresponds to an actually pronounced sound in the German system while English script is full of 'silent letters' such as the ⟨e⟩ of *lake* or the ⟨b⟩ of *doubt*.) Likewise, Latin printed according to modern conventions exemplifies a different script from Latin as classically written with no distinction between upper and lower case letters: both scripts are normally identified imprecisely as 'the Roman alphabet', since one is lineally descended from the other, but the modern version is really a different script with twice as many symbols (actually rather more than twice as many) as its ancestor, and correspondingly new conventions for using the symbols, concerning capitalization of sentence-initial letters and proper names.

In everyday speech the term 'script' is commonly associated with superficial properties of the visual appearance of writing. Thus the traditional German type-face exemplified in the line

Kennſt Du das Land, wo die Zitronen blühen?

is commonly described in English as 'gothic script' (the usual German term is *Fraktur*). As linguists, however, we are interested in the *structure* of writing-systems more than in their physical appearance; from the structural point of view we are hardly justified in treating German written in *Fraktur* as exemplifying a different script from German written in Roman letters:

Kennst Du das Land, wo die Zitronen blühen?

There is a simple one-to-one correspondence between almost all the symbols used in these two type-faces. The only differences between the two *systems* are that *Fraktur* distinguishes two symbols ⟨ ſ s ⟩ corresponding to the single roman symbol ⟨ s ⟩ (compare the first and third words in the two examples), and that *Fraktur* uses a single symbol ⟨J⟩ corresponding to both of the distinct roman symbols ⟨I J⟩.

In the main, 'writing-system', 'script', and 'orthography' will be used interchangeably, though I shall tend to use 'writing-system' when a script is cited as exemplifying a particular *type* of writing, and 'orthography' in connection with alternative conventions for using a given set of written marks. I do not suggest that there is any precise answer to the question whether two examples of writing represent the same or different scripts. For instance, should the writing system current in the USA be counted as a different script from that current in the British Isles on the ground that, while using the same set of symbols, the American system uses slightly different conventions (as exemplified by spellings such as ⟨harbor, defense⟩)? Or are the two systems merely variants of a single script? The conventions of German orthography are much more different from those of (American or British) English ortho-graphy than the alternative conventions for English are from each other, but even German and English conventions are strongly related – one could imagine a hypothetical orthography in which the conventions for using the Roman alphabet were far more exotic (by English standards) than the current German conventions are. So should German- and English-speakers all be said to use varieties of a single script? Ultimately, such questions are as unanswerable as are questions whether two related varieties of spoken language are 'different languages' or 'dialects of one language': where we draw the boundaries between related languages, or between related scripts, is for us to choose, there is no 'right' or 'wrong' in these domains.

One of the difficulties in talking about scripts is that individual scripts are commonly associated with particular languages, and in common parlance a single name is made to do duty for both the script and the spoken language which it represents. For instance, the Hebrew script is strongly associated with the Hebrew language, and many laymen no doubt suppose that the two invariably go together. In fact they do not. The Hebrew script (the same alphabet of symbols, with roughly the same conventions of usage) is also regularly used to write Yiddish, which is a language quite different from Hebrew, though used by members of the same religious group – Yiddish is a dialect of German. Conversely, the Hebrew language can be, and sometimes is, written in scripts other than the Hebrew script. Both Hebrew script and Hebrew language may be colloquially referred to as just 'Hebrew', inviting the hearer to forget that there is a distinction. For our purposes this is very unfortunate, since it is crucial in the study of writing systems always to keep in the forefront of one's mind the idea that *a script is only a device for making examples of a language visible*; the script is not itself the language. One language may be written in different scripts, and the same script may be used to write different languages.

The point must be stressed, because beginners often find it difficult to grasp. Again and again one hears students of writing making remarks such as 'Hebrew originally had no vowels, but acquired them in the Middle Ages'. Of course the Hebrew language, like all others, has always had vowels. What happened in (probably) the early Middle Ages was the invention of an extended version of the script used to write Hebrew; the new script for the first time provided a complete indication of the vowels as well as the consonants of the Hebrew language (but the language itself did not change).

In order to keep languages and scripts separate, it will be important to bear in mind that a language-name, such as 'Hebrew', 'English', 'Korean', when used as a noun always refers to a language rather than a script. When a script is intended, phrases such as 'Hebrew script' or 'the English writing system' must be used. Some scripts have their own names, which are not also names of languages: thus Korean is written in a script called 'Han'gŭl', and there is no language called 'Han'gŭl' – the (sole) language written in this script is called 'Korean'. Therefore it is permissible to use 'Han'gŭl' as a noun, rather than resorting to paraphrases such as 'Han'gŭl script'; but the reader must remember which proper names are names of scripts and which are names of languages.

Another topic requiring a decision about terminology is that of the elements used in writing systems. Here ordinary English usage is rather unhelpful. Units of our own script are called 'letters'; but this term is not suitable as a general name for the elements of various writing systems, for two main reasons.

In the first place, what we want is a term meaning simply 'distinctive written symbol', and even with respect to our own script the term 'letter' means something much more than that. Thus, the punctuation marks and (for other languages written with the Roman alphabet) the diacritic marks, or 'accents', are not called 'letters', yet they are as much part of the writing system as the letters themselves. Furthermore, a pair of symbols such as ⟨g⟩ and ⟨G⟩ are regarded as 'the same letter', yet the distinction between them is highly significant in our script: it is just wrong to begin a sentence or a proper name with a small letter, for instance.

Second, the term 'letter' is used colloquially in a way that ties it to scripts that are typologically fairly similar to our own. An Englishman will be happy to talk of 'Russian letters' (or 'Cyrillic letters'), for instance, and may be willing to refer to 'Arabic letters' (though the fact that Arabic words are printed continuously makes this phrase less comfortable); almost certainly he would reject 'Chinese letters', at least if he knows anything about how the Chinese language is written. A unit of the Chinese script is in English colloquially called a 'character'; this term traditionally referred to *any* script or its elements, but has somehow become specialized recently in connection with Chinese writing. The word 'character' is surely too cumbersome and ugly to revive as a general name for 'unit of writing' (even though this usage does live on in one specialized domain, that of computer technology); indeed it is not clear just how the word is used in modern colloquial English. (For instance, Japanese, as we shall see, is written in a mixed script, including elements identical to those of Chinese script together with other elements which differ from these both in appearance and in function; would an English-speaker call all units of Japanese script 'characters', or only the former class? Presumably in practice most English-speakers are saved by ignorance of Japanese writing from having to make the decision.)

The obvious (and usual) choice is to use the word 'graph' as the general term for any unit of any script. Standardly, the citation of a graph, or sequence of graphs, is enclosed in angle brackets. Thus we may write that 'German script uses ⟨ü⟩ to represent the vowel /y/' (phonemic transcriptions are enclosed in solidi), or that '/mɛin/ "my" is spelled ⟨mijn⟩ in Netherlands Dutch and ⟨myn⟩ in Afrikaans'.

When we discuss scripts that do not use the Roman alphabet, the symbols appearing between angle brackets will often be, not the exotic symbols actually used in the scripts in question, but Roman letters transcribing those symbols. Thus, referring to the Hebrew script, we may write that 'the form ⟨ḥwh⟩ represents the word /ḥawwā/, "Eve" ' – meaning that the sequence of three Hebrew graphs conventionally transcribed:

ḥwh

and which actually looks like this:

חוה

is used to write the Hebrew proper name pronounced /ḥawwā/ and for which the English equivalent is 'Eve'.

Choice of transcription-system for representing the forms of an exotic language in terms of our alphabet is itself a very knotty problem. For some languages written in non-Roman scripts there exist more than one – sometimes very many – alternative systems of romanization; and, even for languages where a single system is widely accepted, the conventions used in connection with one language often have little in common with those used in connection with another language. When words from such languages are used as part of my text, for instance as proper names of institutions or people that are relevant to the discussion, I write them in whatever is the most widely used scheme of romanization for the language in question. When words are quoted as examples, however, small details of transliteration are often important and it is necessary to take a more scientific approach. I therefore adopt a practice which may offend readers versed in the traditions of scholarship of some of the individual languages discussed, but which has the advantage of keeping things as simple as possible for readers unfamiliar with the languages in question. In transcribing examples, I ignore all the standard conventions of transcription for particular languages, in favour of systems based on the alphabet of the International Phonetic Association (IPA). Since many of the languages in question have variant pronunciations in different dialect-areas or at different historical periods, this means that one often has to make an arbitrary choice of one particular pronunciation to base the transcription on (and sometimes this choice will involve guesswork, when the pronunciation of a dead language is not fully known). But, this way, the reader need only be familiar with the IPA alphabet in order to be able to attach some reasonable approximate pronunciation to all the forms quoted from a wide diversity of languages in this book. (Naturally my transcriptions will be only as 'narrow' as is required by the phonological structure of the respective languages, which means that the transcriptions will often ignore details of pronunciation even where these are known with certainty and are invariant across different varieties of the language in question.)

There will be cases where it is inconvenient to use the symbol offered by the IPA alphabet, or where the pronunciation of a vanished phoneme is wholly conjectural; in such cases, if the symbol traditionally used by those who study the language in question is convenient, I shall use it. But the fact that a transcription may conflict with the normal practice of a particular philological tradition will never be treated as a bar to using it, if usage within general linguistics makes it appropriate. (Likewise, I have been ruthless in discarding terminology or other scholarly conventions that are standard in particular specialist fields whenever it seemed to me that deviating from such conventions would make things clearer to the non-specialist reader without distorting the facts involved.)

Unfortunately the IPA alphabet itself has serious defects, and I shall regularly depart from it in the following ways. The IPA alphabet uses a colon to mark long vowels and has no special sign of shortness; this is frequently awkward, particularly in languages where short vowels are the 'marked' variety, so I shall indicate long and short by macron and breve: [ē ĕ]. The IPA alphabet lacks convenient symbols for affricate consonants, although these often function structurally as single phonemes, so where necessary I shall define symbols representing affricates in an *ad hoc* fashion. The use of handwritten [ɑ] and printed [a] as contrasting symbols leads in practice to frequent confusion, so I shall write back and front open vowels as [a æ] respectively, using the former symbol in the many cases where no contrast occurs. (It is an ethnocentrism for the IPA to use a special symbol for the vowel of English *bat* merely because, like many vowel phonemes in other languages, it is not at a 'cardinal' position.) I use the variants [ɪ ɷ] of the signs for lax close vowels. In other respects my transcriptions of English conform to the conventions of Wells and Colson (1971).

In some cases, for instance when discussing scripts that are not based on phonological units, it will be necessary to quote non-Roman graphs directly, rather than transliterating them. It would be unnecessarily pedantic to surround all such cases with angle brackets, and I shall not do so.

When writing this book I was struck by a difficulty that must have occurred to other authors of works which range over many millennia, namely the inadequacy of the expressions 'AD' and 'BC'. A phrase such as 'the fifth century AD' makes no sense, and it is odd to call the thousand years preceding Christ's birth the 'first millennium before Christ' when it was the last such millennium. Furthermore the constant referring of events to the birth of Christ is often provincial, for instance in the context of ancient China, and may even offend some readers' religious sensibilities when Hebrew is under discussion. Those of us who acknowledge Jesus as the Saviour have more substantial ways of demonstrating our allegiance. I therefore follow the lead of Joseph Needham and use plus and minus signs in the normal mathematical way, omitting the plus sign where no confusion is possible: thus Sumerian civilization arose in the -5th millennium and lasted until the early -2nd millennium, the Olympian Games began in -776 and were abolished in $+393$. I also write, for example, '-6c', '17c' for '-6th century', '$+17$th century'.

Having introduced the technical term 'graph', let me close this chapter by drawing attention to a parallel with the linguistics of spoken language.

The analogue, in speech, of a 'graph', or elementary unit of written language, is a 'phone' or unit of sound. One of the basic principles of linguistics is the notion that, within any given spoken language, not all differences between phones are significant or 'distinctive'; in some cases two or more physically-distinct phones group into families called 'phonemes', in which case the members of a phoneme are called its 'allophones'. Thus, in English, although the velarized lateral [lʷ] heard in the word *hill* is physically different from the plain lateral [l] heard in *hilly* the two phones are not significantly distinct; in English the difference between them is never used to keep different utterances apart (though in other languages, Russian for instance, a similar distinction is). In English the choice between [lʷ] and [l] is always determined by context: before a vowel only the variant [l] occurs, in other positions only [lʷ]. The two phones [lʷ] and [l] are allophones of a single phoneme, /l/. (Conventionally, solidi are used for phonemes, square brackets for narrower phonetic transcription.)

An analogous phenomenon is found in writing, and it is convenient to use the terms *grapheme* and *allograph* accordingly. An example very similar to that of the two lateral sounds of spoken English is offered by the alternative versions of lower case *s* which were found in the Roman alphabet until the 19c (as we saw on p. 20, a parallel alternation occurred in German *Fraktur* until its recent obsolescence, and Greek sigma displays such an alternation to this day).[2] The two graphs ⟨ſ s⟩ were allographs of a single grapheme. They did not stand for distinct sounds, rather the choice between them was determined by position in the word. At the end of a word (speaking graphically rather than phonetically), ⟨s⟩ was used; elsewhere, ⟨ſ⟩. Thus:

ſea   ſhell   meaſure   miſt   kiſs   circus   loſe   news

More generally, the different appearances of letters in different fonts, or in handwriting as opposed to print, can be regarded as allographic. Such differences are analogous to the slightly-differing pronunciations that will be given to the same phoneme by different speakers of a single language, or even by a single speaker on different occasions. Thus, the graphs ⟨g g ɤ⟩ would all be allographs of a single grapheme ⟨g⟩. On the other hand ⟨g⟩ and ⟨G⟩ would *not* belong to a single grapheme; as already noted, the upper v. lower case distinction is significant in our script.[3]

We shall not go to the length of adopting separate bracketing conventions for graphemic and allographic transcriptions, parallel to the solidus/square-bracket distinction used in spoken-language linguistics. Angle brackets will enclose graphemes and allographs, since confusion is unlikely to arise in practice. In examining non-Roman scripts we shall ignore minor differences comparable to font-differences in print, and we will illustrate the scripts via single standardized varieties. Where allographic differences comparable to the ⟨ſ s⟩ distinction are important enough to consider, attention will be drawn to them explicitly.

2 Theoretical preliminaries

What is writing? To 'write' might be defined, at a first approximation, as: to communicate relatively specific ideas by means of permanent, visible marks.

The term 'permanent' is included in this definition because we would not normally count, for instance, the sign language used by the deaf and dumb as an example of 'writing'. More problematic is the term 'specific'. This word is included in order to eliminate cases where ideas are conveyed through a durable visible medium which no-one would want to call writing: most obviously, artistic drawing or painting. Picasso's painting 'Guernica', for instance, succeeds very well in communicating ideas of horror, carnage, cruelty, without being an example of writing. The definition of 'writing' given above excludes 'Guernica' on the ground that the ideas it communicates, though powerful, are vague rather than explicit. For instance, a 'translation' of the message of 'Guernica' into English would hardly be open to correction in the same sense as a translation into English of a passage of Spanish or German.

Just what makes a visible medium of communication explicit enough to describe as writing is admittedly very hard to say. Perhaps it was a mistake to include this in our first attempt at a definition of writing; one might suggest that the characteristic property of writing is not that it communicates *specific* ideas but that it communicates ideas in a *conventional* manner. Clearly, a script can be understood by its readers only because they have learned the conventions for interpreting it, and it might seem that graphic art, by contrast, is independent of convention – you just look at it and see what it expresses. But the truth is that the arts are full of convention: consider how differently Breughel, Cézanne, or a Chinese painter would render the same landscape on canvas or paper. It is difficult to use the concept of convention in order to distinguish writing from art.

The reader may object here that neither specificness of ideas communicated nor conventionality of the means of communication is the crucial factor, and that I am missing the point of my own statement, in the previous chapter, that a script is a device for representing a language (rather than a language itself). The proper definition of 'writing' is that it is a system for representing utterances of a spoken language by means of permanent, visible marks. However, this definition too is problematic.

In the first place, it is well known that written language is not straightforwardly a transcription of spoken language. Our own script is capable of being used to represent spoken English directly, but it is fairly unusual for people to use it that way. By this I mean not merely that written messages are commonly composed on paper, rather than being taken down from oral dictation, but that the language in which written messages are couched is somewhat different from the language which Englishmen and Englishwomen speak. For instance, the contracted forms *don't*, *I've*, *he's* and the like are for written English merely optional variants of the full forms *do not*, *I have*, *he is*, etc., and on the whole it is more usual to write the full forms (many people would regard use of the contracted forms in writing as a downright mistake). In spoken English, on the other hand, it is compulsory to use the contracted forms except in certain special environments – to *say* 'I have got your book' rather than 'I've got your book' (unless the *have* is given special 'contrastive' stress) would sound absurdly stilted. And there are many other small differences between the rules of spoken and written English.

Furthermore, in many other language-communities the analogous differences are very much greater than they are in ours. In the Arabic-speaking world, for instance, there are considerable differences in vocabulary, grammar, and phonology between written and spoken varieties of Arabic. It is possible to transcribe Arabic speech directly into Arabic script, but such writing strikes Arabs as bizarre – the forms of spoken Arabic are perceived as simply inappropriate for writing down. Written Arabic can be spoken, but this will be done only in unusually formal speech-situations such as public lectures. In China the situation as it existed until the early decades of this century was yet more extreme: the language used for written communication not only was not normally spoken, but (for reasons having to do with special characteristics of the Chinese language, to be discussed in Chapter 8), if it was spoken – for instance, if a document was read aloud – it could not possibly be understood by even an educated man without consultation of the written text.

If written and spoken languages can diverge as far as this, are we justified in defining writing in general as a system for representing spoken language? In fact I believe we are, but only provided we understand the phrase 'spoken language', paradoxically, as something that is not necessarily spoken. The kind of English that we use in writing and the kind we use in speech are, in the linguist's technical sense, closely-related dialects – that is, they both descend from a single ancestor-language, which was a spoken language. But, just as some dialects, once they have diverged sufficiently for their separate identity to be recognized, are used in one restricted area of territory, so the dialect which we may call 'literary English' is used in one restricted area of behaviour, namely writing. Literary English inherits all the apparatus of a spoken language, including phonology, from its spoken ancestor, but it happens that this particular dialect is not normally spoken (except when written documents are read aloud). Similar remarks apply in cases where literary and colloquial languages exhibit greater divergence. The reader will have noticed, for instance, that I included phonology as one of the respects in which Literary

Arabic differs from the various regional varieties of Colloquial Arabic; Literary Arabic has its own phonology, including one or two phonemes that do not appear in some versions of Colloquial Arabic, despite the fact that Literary Arabic is not normally spoken (an Arabic speaker has to use the special Literary phonemes if he reads a written document aloud). Even Literary Chinese can be spoken, in the sense that a text written in it has a definite pronunciation,[1] though it happens in this case that there is very little point indeed in speaking the language since it cannot be understood by a hearer. If we think of a 'language' (as linguists often do) as a system of relationships between meaning and speech-sound, then a script will be a device for representing a language in this sense, even though it often happens that languages or language-varieties which are commonly written down are not spoken (except in artificial circumstances such as reading aloud), and that languages or language-varieties which are spoken are not written down (except, for example, when tape-recordings are transcribed verbatim).

But there is another difficulty in the way of defining writing as a phenomenon essentially parasitic on spoken language. There are forms of communication which one might want to describe as 'writing' but which are not in any sense dependent on spoken language.

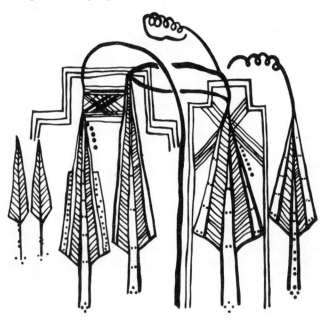

Figure 1

Consider, for instance, Figure 1, which is a copy of a letter sent by a girl of the Yukaghir tribe of north-eastern Siberia to a young man. Before going on to read the explanation given below, the reader might find it instructive to see whether he can guess independently something of the message it contains. I imagine that he will have little success.

The conifer-shaped objects in Figure 1 are people. The second from the right is the writer (the row of dots represents plaited hair and thus shows that she is a woman); the next one leftwards, the recipient of the letter, was previously her lover, but has now gone off to live with a Russian woman (plaited hair, together with a skirt with panniers distinguishing Russian from Yukaghir costume). The Russian woman, naturally, has broken up the relationship between writer and addressee (line from the head of the Russian woman cutting through the lines joining the two Yukaghir); nevertheless, the new *ménage* is stormy (criss-cross lines linking the two). The writer is unhappy (crossed lines) alone in her house (the rectangular enclosing structure), and she is still thinking of the addressee (curly tendril reaching towards him). On the other hand the addressee should bear in mind that there is another young man at home (far right) sending a tendril towards her. If the addressee wants to act on this message, he had better hurry before his new household has children (two small conifers on the left).

This message is rather specific and detailed: it goes far beyond a mere generalized expression of longing, such as might for instance be expressed by a representational painting of a pensive girl staring into the distance. And the ideas are expressed in a highly conventional fashion – one has to learn the symbolism before being able to decode the message. Yet the symbols do not represent particular elements of a spoken language. There are many ways of verbalizing the contents of the letter, each of which would be equally valid. One of these might begin, 'I know you aren't getting on with that Russian girl of yours, and I miss you . . .'; another might begin, 'Even though the Russian you are living with now made you break off with me I'm still thinking about you . . .'; and many other forms of words would be possible (in English, or in the language of the Yukaghir). The 'translations' just suggested are quite distinct utterances, and would look different in any script which communicates ideas indirectly by providing representations of spoken utterances that express those ideas directly. Instead, the Yukaghir system represents ideas directly – it is, as it were, on the same logical level as spoken languages, rather than being parasitic on them, as 'scripts' in the ordinary sense are. Many relatively primitive cultures have used such communication-systems, although Figure 1 is a particularly elaborate example. (Gelb 1952, ch. 2 discusses many comparable examples from different areas of the world.)

We shall use the term *semasiographic systems* for systems of visible communication akin to that of the Yukaghir example, which indicate ideas directly, in contrast to *glottographic systems* which provide visible representations of spoken-language utterances. (These terms, and others to be introduced in this chapter, are adapted from Haas 1976a.) Writing systems as the term is ordinarily understood are all glottographic. Indeed, by the definition given at the bottom of p. 26 a system must be glottographic to count as 'writing'. Whether we wish to insist on this definition and, accordingly, categorize semasiography as something other than writing (as some linguists would – see e.g. Chao 1968, p. 101), or whether we feel that semasiographic systems are sufficiently like 'core' examples of writing to count also as 'writing' of a marginal kind (so that the definition of writing at the top of p. 26 must be preferred to the proposed alternative), is ultimately a personal choice about how to use words. It is not necessary to impose a decision one way or the other here.

There would appear in principle to be no reason why a society could not have expanded a semasiographic system, by adding further graphic conventions, until it was fully as complex and rich in expressive potential as their spoken language. At that point they would possess two fully-fledged 'languages' having no relationship with one another – one of them a spoken language without a script, and the other a 'language' tied intrinsically to the visual medium. Messages in the semasiographic system could be *translated* more or less faithfully into the spoken language, but it would make no sense to talk of *reading* them aloud word by word. However, in practice no semasiographic system is anywhere near this comprehensive. And that is perhaps not surprising. One can see that it would involve a great deal of redundant effort for members of a society to have to master two unrelated 'languages', one for spoken and the other for written use, when the alternative option is available of developing a system for encoding their spoken language into the graphic medium. That may be a reason why, when we transfer attention from primitive to more highly civilized societies, we invariably find that semasiographic systems are replaced by glottographic writing of one type or another (though whether glottographic writing, historically, has always *grown out of* earlier semasiographic systems is an open question).

However, one must be wary of pressing the 'redundant effort' argument too hard. There are many societies whose members do indeed regularly master two or more *spoken* languages, often unrelated ones; the near-monolingualism of English society is not very common on a world scale. Possibly, therefore, the explanation for why we do not find semasiographic systems that are comparable in expressive power to spoken languages is that, for some reason that remains unclear, speech is simply a more suitable medium than visible marks in which to develop a comprehensive system for the articulation of thought – so that a general-purpose written communication-system can function only by encoding the elements of an existing spoken language.

Although semasiographic systems are usually quite limited in scope by comparison with spoken languages, one should not make the mistake of dismissing them as invariably associated with a primitive state of civilization. The written 'language' of mathematics, for instance, is one highly sophisticated example of semasiography. The way in which a mathematical statement is formulated in written symbols does not depend on the way that the equivalent statement is formulated in any particular spoken language, as it would if the system of symbolization were glottographic. Thus the formula $\langle 10^9 = 1\ 000\ 000\ 000 \rangle$ translates into English as *Ten to the ninth equals one thousand million* and into German as *Zehn hoch neun gleicht eine Milliarde.* The English and German expressions have rather different structures, but the structure of the mathematical formula is quite different from either. Thus, the material after 'equals' is three words in English, two words in German, but ten graphemes in mathematical symbols; what precedes 'equals' is four words in English (one of which, *nin-th*, consists of two morphemes), three words in German, and three mathematical symbols, but despite the latter coincidence the individual symbols cannot be equated with the individual German words (*Zehn* corresponds not to the first symbol, ⟨1⟩, but rather to the pair of symbols ⟨10⟩; the symbol ⟨1⟩ appears in two places and the symbol ⟨0⟩ in a total of ten places in the formula, but no repetitions are found in either of the spoken-language utterances; and so forth. Mathematical symbolism is a 'language' which articulates thought directly and independently rather than merely standing for its spoken articulation, and clearly it is in no sense 'primitive' even though its scope is strictly limited (it allows the writer to make statements about mathematical abstractions but not about, say, cabbages or kings).

Indeed, far from being merely an uncivilized precursor of writing which modern cultures have long since abandoned, semasiography is at present widening its field of application very considerably. Road signs for messages such as 'no left turn' or 'stop at major road ahead', cleaning instructions on garments such as 'do not bleach', information about how long frozen food can safely be stored, are all expressed semasiographically, by symbols unrelated to the words of English or any other language. To someone of my generation it is very striking how semasiography has been taking over domains of public communication in which, thirty years ago, ordinary English script was the norm. The reason, of course, is the gradual political and commercial unification of Western Europe which is occurring in our time, and which makes officials and entrepreneurs alike unwilling to favour one European language at the expense of others.

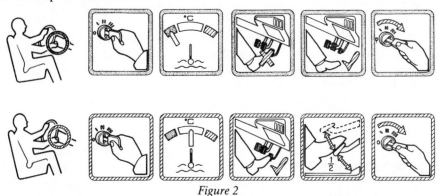

Figure 2

As semasiography becomes more widespread, it is coming to be used for increasingly sophisticated messages. For instance, when I recently bought a new Ford car with an automatic choke, the sun-visor sported a paper sleeve bearing the inscription shown in Figure 2 (the speckled and hatched areas were respectively blue and red in the original).

The translation of Figure 2 into English is quite complex; it would run, roughly, 'When starting from cold, turn on the ignition without touching the gas-pedal; if the engine is warm, press the gas-pedal halfway down as you turn the ignition key.' It is interesting to speculate how far this trend may ultimately proceed. Doubtless it is hardly likely to lead to the evolution of a fully-fledged semasiographic language rivalling English, French, or German in expressive potential; but, as already suggested, logically speaking such an outcome seems not absolutely excluded.

Let us now examine the various glottographic systems of writing – 'writing proper', if semasiography is deemed not to be true writing. Figure 3 displays a classification scheme.

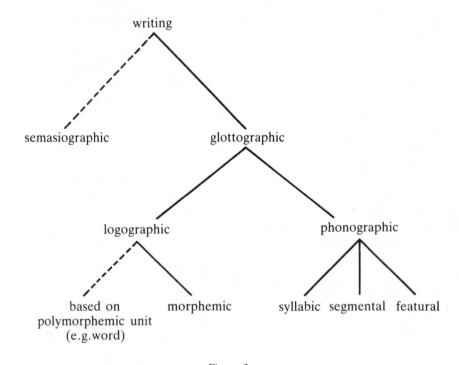

Figure 3

At the top of Figure 3, writing as a whole is divided into semasiographic and glottographic systems, the former dominated by a dotted line to show that their inclusion under 'writing' is open to question. Among glottographic systems, the major division is between *logographic* and *phonographic* writing.

The basis of this distinction is a phenomenon which has been called by the French linguist André Martinet the 'double articulation' of language. Any language is a system which articulates thought into a large range of units and provides vocal symbols for those units – words, or meaningful components of words known as 'morphemes', such as the *un-* and *-ing* of a word like *uncaring*. In principle things would be simple if a language could provide a separate unit of sound to symbolize each unit of thought that the language isolates. But the range of possibilities provided by the human vocal organs, though quite large, comes nowhere near offering enough separate sounds for the several thousands of meaningful units contained in a typical language – or at least, if so many different sounds were used, the distinctions between them would have to be so minute as to defeat any possibility of people learning to pronounce and perceive them. Instead, therefore, a language imposes a quite independent articulation on the sound-medium, analysing it into a relatively small and manageable set of phonological units having no relationship with the first articulation either with respect to number of units or with respect to the principles on which units combine into larger phonological wholes. Then the various meaningful units of the first articulation are associated with *groups* of phonological units in a way that is usually quite arbitrary (in the sense that the internal composition of the sound-group used for a given meaningful unit will not correlate with any facts about the meaning of the unit); although there are relatively few individual sound-units, enough combinations are available to provide pronunciation for all the many meaning-units.

Given that languages are 'doubly articulated' in this sense, the possibility exists for a writing system to represent either units of the first articulation or units of the second articulation; logographic systems are those based on meaningful units, phonographic systems are those based on phonological units. Thus, if one were to invent a logographic writing-system for English, it might represent the sentence *The cat walked over the mat* as, say:

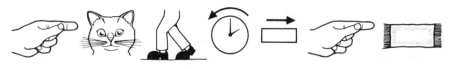

Figure 4

– in which the pointing hands in first and sixth place are being used to represent the word *the,* the walking legs in third place represent the root *walk* and the clock with anticlockwise arrow in fourth place represents the past-tense morpheme *-ed*, the horizontal arrow over a block in fifth place represents *over,* and the symbols for *cat* and *mat* are self-explanatory. On the other hand, one particular phonographic system (that of the International Phonetic Association) represents the same English sentence as:

ðə kæt wɔkt əovə ðə mæt

– in which individual symbols represent 'segments' of sound.

Here and there on the periphery of our own writing-system are some clearly logographic elements. A standard typewriter keyboard, for instance, includes the graphs ⟨& %⟩ which represent respectively the word *and* and the phrase *per cent.* (We might add ⟨@⟩ for *at*, though this is a less straightforward example because the cases of *at* which can be written ⟨@⟩ are strictly confined to certain positions in particular commercial documents – one would not encounter ⟨@⟩ in a novel; and the logographic nature of ⟨£⟩ for *pound* is still more questionable, because of the difference in order between, for example, *one pound* and ⟨£1⟩, and because the same graph ⟨£⟩ is used whether the spoken name for a sum of money includes *pound* or *pounds* – it might be preferable to regard ⟨£⟩ as belonging to the semasiographic notation of mathematics.) Notice in particular that it would be quite wrong to think of, say, ⟨&⟩ as a *phonographic* symbol which happens to stand for a sequence of three sounds /ænd/ (as ⟨x⟩ stands for a sequence of two phonemes /ks/); this is clear from, for example, the fact that in ordinary English writing (leaving aside children's puzzle-page rebuses or the like) words such as *land, Andrew* would never be written ⟨l&⟩, ⟨&rew⟩, whereas this ought to be possible if the symbol were phonographic.

(In everyday usage, people commonly describe some exotic writing-systems as 'ideographic' – and I introduce this term here in order to stress that we shall not be using it at all. The reason for avoiding this term is that the meaning people attach to it is quite unclear, and in fact it seems to be used in a way that blurs the crucial distinction between semasiographic and logographic systems.)

Before moving on to consider the lower branches of the classification-scheme in Figure 3, it will be convenient to introduce two further principles of classification which cut across the distinction phonographic/logographic/ (semasiographic), as well as across each other. These are the contrasts of *motivated* (sometimes called *iconic*) v. *arbitrary* systems and of *complete* v. *incomplete* (or *defective*) systems.

The terms 'motivated' and 'arbitrary' refer to the relationship between the graphs of a writing-system and the spoken-language units they represent. If there is some natural relationship, the system is motivated; if not, it is arbitrary. For instance, the graphs of the hypothetical logographic system of Figure 4 above are clearly motivated: the graphs for *cat* and *mat* look like a cat (or at least a cat's head) and a mat respectively, and the graphs for morphemes not referring to physical objects display some logical connection with the respective ideas (a fairly tenuous connection in the case of *the*, admittedly). On the other hand the IPA transcription is entirely arbitrary – there is no natural connection whatever between the shape of the graph ⟨k⟩ and the consonant which begins *cat*, or between the shape of ⟨æ⟩ and the vowel of *cat:* one just has to learn which shapes go with which sounds.

From the examples given so far, one might suppose that logographic scripts are always motivated and phonographic scripts always arbitrary. But this is by no means necessarily so. For instance, the shape of the logograph ⟨&⟩

betrays no resemblance to the idea of addition or conjunction; and although the hypothetical logographic system of Figure 4 used motivated graphs, another system might be invented which would assign entirely arbitrary symbols to the same words *The cat walked over the mat*. Indeed, Chinese script is such a system. The Chinese for *The cat walked over the mat* would be written 猫走過席子. Can the English reader correlate any of these graphs with the ideas in the sentence on the basis of their visual appearance? I hardly think so. Conversely, it would be quite possible to design a phonographic script in such a way that the shape of the graphs was related to the positions of the vocal organs when making the corresponding sounds. Indeed, 'motivated' phonographic scripts exist, both as technical systems of transcription within scientific phonetics (cf. Abercrombie 1967, pp. 116–20) and, in one case, as an ordinary national system of orthography (see Chapter 7 below).

The properties 'motivated' v. 'arbitrary' are primarily properties of individual graphs in a writing-system; a system might include some graphs which are motivated and others which are arbitrary (as, for instance, in the Arabic numeral system the graphs ⟨0 1⟩, portraying respectively an empty hole and a single stroke, are motivated while, say, ⟨6 7⟩ are arbitrary). Furthermore, 'motivatedness' of an individual graph is a matter of degree rather than a simple yes-or-no matter. A logographic symbol ⟨ 🐖 ⟩ for *pig* would highly motivated; but the symbol ⟨ ߃ ⟩, alluding to the curly tail, would be a possible alternative that could still be regarded as somewhat motivated, though less so than the former. No doubt, within any single writing-system, there is a tendency for the various individual graphs to be roughly similar in their degree of motivatedness, so that often it will be appropriate to describe a script as a whole as 'highly motivated', or as 'almost wholly arbitrary'.

(Another term from everyday language which is worth mentioning here in order to reject it as confusing is 'picture-writing' or 'pictography'. When people describe something as 'picture-writing' it is not clear whether they mean that it is a relatively clearly motivated script of some kind, or that it is a semasiographic rather than glottographic system. It may well be that to some extent the two tend to go together, but this tendency is very far from absolute. The semasiographic Yukaghir system of Figure 1 (p. 28) contains considerable elements of arbitrariness – what natural connection exists between criss-cross lines and unhappiness, for example?; and many aspects of modern semasiographic systems are likewise thoroughly arbitrary – consider for instance the 'give way' sign, consisting of a downward-pointing triangle, or the symbolism of mathematics which contains scarcely any motivation. Conversely, while the more familiar glottographic systems, such as our own script, are highly arbitrary, we shall in later chapters encounter other glottographic scripts which display a great deal of motivation. Like the term 'ideographic', the terms 'pictographic' or 'picture-writing' should be shunned because they blur distinctions which the student of writing needs to keep carefully apart.)

The dimension 'complete' v. 'incomplete/defective' – again a gradient rather than all-or-nothing dimension, in the sense that different scripts may show different degrees of incompleteness – refers to the extent to which a script (whether logographic or phonographic) provides representations for the whole range of units of the relevant level in the language concerned. To what extent does the script leave out material that exists in the spoken language? It is improbable that any script in everyday use attains total completeness, but scripts certainly differ considerably in degree of defectiveness.

Scripts that are historically early are often quite incomplete. To explain why this should be so, we need first to take into consideration the fact that relatively early scripts tend to be logographic rather than phonographic, a fact for which two reasons can be given. In the first place, the units of the 'first articulation' of a language tend to be relatively apparent to native speakers of the language without special study – a child does not need to have learned to read and write in order to be able to split up a spoken sentence into separate words – while the units of the phonological 'second articulation', particularly phonological units smaller than syllables, are not obvious. A child has to be taught to hear the word *cat* as 'ker-a-ter', and such learning is far from easy for many; there is nothing self-evident or natural in the splitting of a speech-chain into separate vowels and consonants. (See e.g. Downing and Leong 1982, pp. 99–100, 111; Bradley and Bryant 1983.) Also, many units of the 'first articulation' of a language have meanings for which it is easy to invent motivated symbols (whereas to become aware of the activities of the vocal organs in order to invent motivated phonographic symbols is a highly sophisticated intellectual achievement), and, clearly, when a script is being created from scratch, the iconicity principle is a particularly obvious way to facilitate the task of inventors and first learners. If a script is invented by providing motivated symbols for the meaningful units of a language, however, a problem arises in that some of these units are much easier to represent pictorially than others. Sticking to our example *The cat walked over the mat*, the words *cat* and *mat* lend themselves far more readily to graphic representation than *the* or the inflection *-ed*. However, it is also true that the less 'picturable' units are also often less crucial to the message than the more easily picturable parts; so a script may simply leave them out – an incomplete logographic script for English might write our sentence as just:

Figure 5

Figure 5 fails to distinguish *The cat walked over the mat* from *A cat walked over the mat*, *The cat is walking over the mat*, and so forth, but it might be unnecessary to make these distinctions explicit for the purposes for which the script is used. An incomplete script is a great deal better than no script at all.

A script can be 'incomplete' not only by failing to provide any representation for some linguistic units but also, or alternatively, by providing representations that are ambiguous. Thus, a more complete version of the logographic system of Figure 5 might include the graph 🖐️ , but use it not merely for *the* but also for *this* and *that* – so that the inscription:

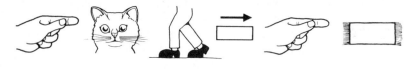

Figure 6

would, unlike Figure 5, succeed in eliminating e.g. the interpretation *A cat walked over the mat* but still fail to distinguish e.g. *The cat walked . . .* from *This cat walked . . . .*

Very early scripts, as already said, are often quite incomplete; but this should not be taken to imply that up-to-date writing-systems are fully complete. Thus, there is one notable respect in which modern English orthography is highly incomplete, namely intonation. To some extent punctuation gives clues to intonation; but it is easy to show that the indications provided by punctuation (which in modern English orthography has more to do with the logical structure of a text than with any aspect of its pronunciation) fall far short of a complete representation of English intonation-distinctions. Consider a group of sentences which consist of the same sequence of words spoken on different intonation-patterns (indicated here in the transcription system of M. A. K. Halliday (1967), which is one attempt to fill the gap in completeness that we are discussing; in this system, // and / represent the boundaries of 'tone-groups' and 'feet' respectively, underlining marks the 'tonic syllable' of the tone-group, and numerals represent various English 'tones' or patterns of pitch):

//2 is he / sure of it//   – rising to high pitch: a neutral question
//−3 is he / sure of it//   – low level pitch rising to mid: 'I'm asking "Is he sure of it?", not that it really matters . . .'
//5 is he / sure of it//   – rising to high, then falling: 'Is he sure of it, because if he *isn't*, . . .'
//4 is he / sure of it//   – falling to low, then rising: 'You ask whether he's sure of it? Of course he is!'

These four sentences are in spoken English quite distinct in pronunciation and in meaning. Yet in English orthography they cannot be distinguished. At a pinch the third sentence might be differentiated from the others by italicizing *sure*; however, this would normally imply not merely that the sentence was pronounced on tone 5 but also that the word *sure* bore contrastive stress – in reality it is perfectly possible to have the intonation contour without special stress on *sure*. Apart from this, all the sentences must be written alike as ⟨Is he sure of it?⟩.

The reader may feel that I am in some sense cheating by offering this example in support of the claim that English orthography is 'incomplete', and may be inclined to object that intonation-patterns are not 'really' part of sentences in the way that the words they contain are – so that the question of completeness scarcely arises with respect to intonation. But this would be circular. The reason why we instinctively feel that intonation-patterns are not 'of the essence' of sentences, while words are, is that our instinctive ideas about our language are heavily coloured by the orthographic system we have learned for reading and writing it, and this happens to neglect intonation. True, intonation-patterns are usually not the most significant elements of sentences, but often they are far from the least significant. The intonation-differences between my four example sentences carry far more significance than the choice of *it*, rather than *this* or *that*, as the last word in the respective sentences; the fact that the latter distinctions are consistently recorded by our orthography, while the former distinctions are consistently overlooked, is surely merely a fact about the arbitrary limits to the completeness of our particular script, rather than something that one would naturally expect to be the case for any practical script for English.

All this is not to suggest, however, that the best script for a language will necessarily be the most complete script. Halliday's intonation-notation was invented for very specialized technical linguistic purposes – Halliday certainly does not propose that his notation, or one like it, ought to be used in everyday writing. Completeness is one desideratum in a script, since it permits the largest possible number of thought-distinctions to be transferred from speech to paper; but there are other desiderata which will often conflict with this one – notably economy, in the sense both of fewness of different symbols to be learned and of fewness of symbols used to represent any given utterance. It may perhaps be that the kind of incompleteness found in English script represents a good compromise between these conflicting desiderata; although in the cases quoted above intonation patterns are crucial, there will be many cases where, in context, intonation could be predicted from word-sequence – sufficiently many, perhaps, that it is just not worthwhile for our script to include detailed representation of intonation. Likewise, the relatively extreme incompleteness of some early scripts may not always be merely a flaw of immaturity; if a script is used only for highly specific purposes, so that much of any utterance is predictable from context, a highly incomplete script might actually be the *best* script since the balance of advantage would tip away from completeness towards economy.

Let us return to the classification scheme of Figure 3 (p. 32). We have yet to deal with the subclassification of logographic and of phonographic systems.

At each of Martinet's two levels of articulation, a language has units of different sizes. The smallest elements of the 'first articulation' are morphemes, but in most languages, including our own, there are also 'words '– some words will consist of a single morpheme but many will be polymorphemic. In all languages morphemes (and/or words) will be grouped into larger syntactic units: phrases, clauses. Likewise, at the level of the second articulation the smallest units are phonetic features – elements such as 'consonantal', 'labio-dental contact', 'fricative', 'voiced'; but phonetic features combine into 'seg-ments' or 'phones' (e.g. the set of features just listed add up to the segment [v]), and into the larger units called 'syllables'.

At the level of the 'first articulation', the size of unit which can be used as the basis of a logographic system is constrained by the obvious requirement that a script must contain only a finite number of elementary graphs. It is a commonplace of modern linguistics that the number of potential well-formed sentences in any human language is infinitely large; clearly, then, it would be out of the question to invent a script which represented whole sentences by single graphs. The same consideration rules out the possibility of basing a logographic script on the clause or the phrase. In principle, at least, it would be possible to use the word as the unit of graphic representation: the number of words in the vocabulary of a language is larger than the number of its morphemes, but it is only finitely large. Thus, one might imagine a logographic script for English in which, say, the words *walk*, *walked*, *walking* were represented by three distinct and unrelated graphs, rather than being split into their constituent morphemes as in Figure 4 (p. 33). In reality, though, I know of no logographic systems based on units larger than single morphemes (which is why the left-hand line descending from 'logographic' in Figure 3 is dotted – it is a hypothetical rather than an actual possibility). This absence is not surprising: a chief drawback of logographic systems in general is that they are relatively uneconomical in terms of the number of graphic units which must be invented and committed to the users' memories – to use separate graphs for various words derived from the same roots would greatly increase this burden, for little gain in terms of reducing the amount of linguistic analysis required in order to be able to grasp the system.

At the level of the second, phonological articulation, on the other hand, everything is finite. In any language there is only a finite range of phonologi-cally-admissible syllables (and in many languages this range will be consider-ably smaller than in English, whose complex consonant-clusters, diphthongs, and triphthongs make for an unusually large inventory of syllables). The syllables of any language can be analysed as sequences of elements drawn from a much smaller set of consonant and vowel segments, which in turn can be treated as bundles of simultaneously-occurring phonetic features: the inventory of features used by a language will usually be at least somewhat smaller than its inventory of segments.[2] Thus it is possible to base a phono-graphic system on any of these units, and there are real examples of all three categories of script.

The notion of a script based on segments scarcely needs illustration, since European orthographies are (at least approximately) segmental. The notion of a syllabic script perhaps deserves a word or two of clarification here (before actual examples are discussed in detail in Chapters 4 and 9). Looking back to the hypothetical script of Figure 4 (p. 33), one might well ask whether this is clearly distinct from syllabic writing: it was offered as an example of logographic as opposed to phonographic script, but in fact most of the graphs of Figure 4 represent syllable-sized elements of English: *the, cat,* etc. However, in the first place there are two exceptions to this statement: the fifth graph stands for a disyllable, *over,* and the fourth graph for the past-tense morpheme which is pronounced as part of a syllable. In a syllabic script the number of graphs in an inscription depends on the phonology of the utterance transcribed – words which are long in terms of pronunciation will be represented by more graphs than are needed to write short words. In a morphemic script, on the other hand, the number of graphs in an inscription is independent of pronunciation: even a long word like *catamaran,* being only one morpheme, will be written with just one graph. Furthermore, in a morphemic script elements will not be written alike merely because they sound alike, provided they are in fact distinct meaning-units: the last graph in Figure 4 represents the word *mat,* and if the script is logographic a different graph would be used for the semantically-unrelated word *matte,* even though it too is pronounced /mæt/. In a syllabic script, on the other hand, *mat* and *matte* would be written alike, and the graph which writes *cat* would also appear as the first graph in the writing of *catamaran.*

Turning to 'featural' script (I regret the neologism, but no standard term is available): again we shall be examining in detail (in Chapter 7) a standard national orthography which works on this principle, but meanwhile the reader might be interested in examples which are drawn from closer to home and may be more familiar. A pure, scientific featural script is the notation used by 'generative phonologists' (e.g. Chomsky and Halle 1968), in one version of which the English word *cat,* for instance, would be transcribed as in Figure 7. The rows of a table such as that of Figure 7 stand for various phonetic features which may take plus or minus values (e.g. '+voiced' means voiced, '−voiced' means voiceless); the columns stand for successive segments of the utterance transcribed.

consonantal	+	−	+
vocalic	−	+	−
sonorant	−	+	−
anterior	−	−	+
coronal	−	−	+
close	−	−	−
open	−	+	−
back	−	−	−
round	−	−	−
voiced	−	+	−

Figure 7

This notation was designed for specialized scientific purposes and would clearly be too cumbersome for everyday use. As an example of a more practical featural script for English, consider Pitman's Shorthand. Figure 8 shows the basic elements of this system. (Pitman's system as a whole contains

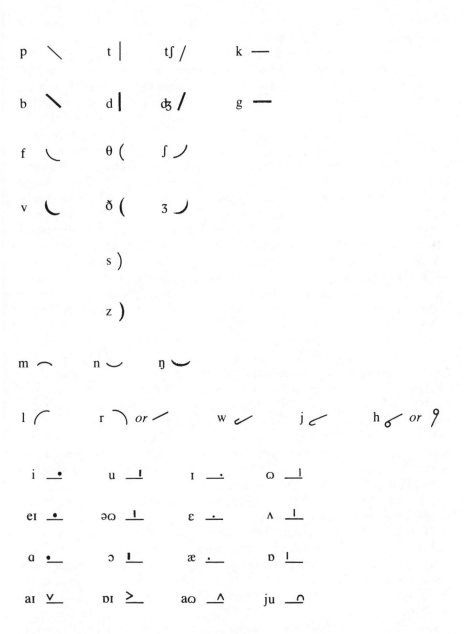

Figure 8

many complexities, most of which relate to conventions for reducing the written shapes of words to the simplest possible outlines for speed of writing; we shall examine only the fundamentals of the system.) The script does not represent phonetic features by assigning them individual graphs which are written separately; rather, a graph represents a whole segment, but the various visual properties of the graph correlate with the different phonetic features making up the segment. The major contrast between consonants and vowels is represented as a contrast between extended lines versus small dots and dashes in different positions adjacent to consonant-lines. (Figure 8 uses the line for /k/ to illustrate positioning of the vowel signs; thus the grouping of marks shown for /i/ stands for /ik/ *eke*.) Among the graphs for obstruent consonants, the contrast between thick and thin represents the voiced/voiceless contrast; place of articulation is shown by orientation (left-leaning = labial, vertical = apical, right-leaning = palato-alveolar, horizontal = velar); curved lines stand for fricatives, straight lines for stops (including affricates). Among the vowel signs, the heavy/light contrast distinguishes 'tense' vowels (those that do not require a following consonant in the same syllable) from 'lax' or 'checked' vowels. Dot v. dash stand for front spread v. back rounded; position in relation to the adjacent consonant sign represents the close v. mid v. open contrast. (The system slightly distorts the phonetics of English by treating /eɪ əʊ/ as if they were pure vowels /e o/ – as, in some regional dialects, they are.) The alternative signs for /r/ and /h/ are allographs, choice between which is determined by convenience in joining the signs to those that precede and follow.

A few of Pitman's basic graphs, notably that for /h/ (which is difficult to analyse into features from the phonetic point of view) must be treated as unitary segmental signs; in the main, though, his system is clearly featural.

These, then, are the principal categories of glottographic script in terms of the type of unit represented. But it must be stressed that the actual orthographies used in real life are not usually pure, textbook examples of one or another of these categories. When a speech-notation system is invented and used for scientific purposes it may be all of a piece and pure, but we shall see as the book proceeds that scripts which have evolved over long periods as the everyday writing systems of whole speech-communities or nations are almost always something of a mixture. In some cases the different types of writing are mixed in such proportions within a given script that one cannot say which predominates; thus in Chapter 9 we shall see that Japanese writing cannot be called 'essentially logographic' or 'essentially phonographic', it is partly one and partly the other. Perhaps more commonly, one of the various principles will control the majority of components within an orthographic system, but there will almost always be an admixture of elements inconsistent with that principle.

Apart from the distinctions between different kinds of linguistic unit represented, between complete v. incomplete systems, and between motivated v. arbitrary graphs, there remains one further classification principle for glottographic scripts which must be introduced before we close this chapter. This last distinction, between *deep* and *shallow* orthographies, is rather more technical than those discussed earlier, but it is quite important to an understanding of the linguistics of writing.

Students of linguistics are familiar with the idea that analysis of a linguistic structure frequently leads one to set up 'underlying' levels of description at which a given utterance is treated as being composed of a rather different sequence of units from those it contains at the 'surface'. The point is most easily exemplified from phonology. In the first place, we know that various families of two or more sounds in a given language will often function as replacements for one another in different phonological environments, so that, although the sounds are physically – 'superficially' – distinct, they are conveniently regarded as different manifestations of a single phoneme at a 'deeper' level. Familiar examples in English are the plain and velarized laterals [l lʷ], of which the former occurs before a vowel and the latter elsewhere, and the pairs of plain and aspirated voiceless stops, such as [p pʰ], [t tʰ], of which the former occur in clusters following /s/ and the latter elsewhere. In each of these cases English orthography is 'phonemic rather than phonetic': it uses an invariant graph, ⟨l⟩, ⟨p⟩, etc., for the phoneme as a family of sounds, rather than using different graphs for the different allophones. We could easily imagine a variant orthography for English which resembled the standard system except that it used different graphemes, say ⟨l λ⟩, for the plain and velarized laterals. In such an orthography, words such as *lip, lily, Lil, hill, hillock* would be written ⟨lip lily Liλ hiλλ hillock⟩ respectively (I assume that other orthographic rules, e.g. those governing the use of single v. double consonant-letters, are unchanged). An orthography which used ⟨l λ⟩ in this way would, in that respect, be slightly 'shallower' than ordinary English orthography. As we shall see in later chapters, scripts actually used in practice sometimes do provide separate graphs for distinct allophones in this way.

Notice that, in a hypothetical orthography as just described, it would be incorrect to call ⟨l λ⟩ 'allographs' of a single 'grapheme', like the graphs ⟨ſ s⟩ discussed on p. 25 above. The signs ⟨l λ⟩ would be distinct graphemes, used to represent distinct elements of the spoken English language, although elements at a particularly shallow level within the structure of spoken English. The signs ⟨ſ s⟩, on the other hand, were not used to represent separate allophones of the /s/ phoneme; there was no systematic difference in spoken English between the sounds written ⟨ſ⟩ and those written ⟨s⟩, and the choice between the two allographs was determined by a purely graphic consideration (word-final v. non-word-final position), so that both allographs would appear for a single instance of the /s/ phoneme in words such as ⟨miſs loſs⟩, and a term which could be written as one word or two would appear now with one allograph, now the other: ⟨bees wax⟩, ⟨beeſwax⟩.

The phonemic level of English phonology is deeper than the surface phonetic level, but it is not very deep. Linguists argue that we must recognize levels of 'morphophonemic' representation which are yet more abstract, further removed from the physical facts of pronunciation, than the phonemic level. Consider, for instance, the formation of noun-plurals in English. Regular plurals take one of three suffixes, phonemically speaking: /ɪz/ if the noun stem ends in a sibilant /s z ʃ ʒ tʃ dʒ/ , /s/ if the stem ends in a voiceless sound other than a sibilant, and /z/ otherwise. Thus we have:

pɪtʃ pɪtʃɪz	pitch pitches
lɒs lɒsɪz	loss losses
kæt kæts	cat cats
mɪθ mɪθs	myth myths
fɒg fɒgz	fog fogs
həʊ həʊz	hoe hoes

Clearly there is considerable phonetic logic in the distribution of the three allomorphs of the plural morpheme; the variation between the three is not just a matter of arbitrary irregularity (like the use of the allomorph /ən/ after *ox* and the zero allomorph after *sheep*). A linguist would analyse this situation by saying that, 'underlyingly' (or 'morphophonemically'), there is just one regular plural suffix, and this has the form /z/. Thus the underlying forms of the words *pitches, cats, fogs* are |pɪtʃz kætz fɒgz|. ('Underlying' forms are standardly written between vertical bars.) The phonemic forms are derived by the application of two rules:

1 an epenthetic /ɪ/ is inserted between two sibilants (thus |pɪtʃz| becomes /pɪtʃɪz/);
2 a voiced consonant is devoiced following a voiceless consonant (thus |kætz| becomes /kæts/).

These rules must apply in the order given; if rule 2 applied before rule 1, |pɪtʃz| would be changed by rule 2 to /pɪtʃs/ which by rule 1 would then become */pɪtʃɪs/, which is not the correct pronunciation of *pitches*.

How does ordinary English orthography treat this situation? Interestingly, it represents a level intermediate in depth between the phonemic and the morphophonemic level – namely, the level at which rule 1 has already applied but rule 2 has not. The epenthetic /ɪ/ produced by rule 1 is written, as ⟨e⟩ (which is the standard spelling of this phoneme in grammatical suffixes, cf. Albrow 1972, pp. 29–30); on the other hand, the distinction between /s/ and /z/ produced by rule 2 is ignored, so that the suffixes of *cats* and *fogs* are both written ⟨s⟩, which standardly represents the sound /z/ in this position (Albrow 1972, p. 25). If English orthography were maximally 'deep', it would write ⟨pitchs cats fogs⟩; if it were maximally 'shallow' it would write ⟨pitches catss fogs⟩ (since ⟨ss⟩ is the standard spelling of /s/ in non-initial position).

The analysis of 'underlying' levels in phonology is a controversial aspect of linguistics; many linguists believe that any phonological analysis which departs significantly from the brute facts of pronunciation is an artificial linguists' invention and irrelevant to the processing of utterances by ordinary speakers.

3 The earliest writing

As already mentioned, one distinction between the linguistics of writing and the linguistics of speech is that in the case of the former we can delve far enough back into the past to come close to the beginnings of the phenomenon. In this chapter we shall examine the development of one early writing system, the Sumerian system whose later stages were known as 'Cuneiform'. This is a specially important script for two reasons. First, the Sumerian script appears to be the oldest known writing system in the world. Second, and more importantly, in the case of this script we have evidence showing not only how its later, relatively sophisticated stage evolved out of simpler beginnings, but also how the simple early version of the script itself evolved from an antecedent cultural institution that was not 'writing' at all: in other words, in this case we may be able to inspect the very birth of writing. As we shall see, there is considerable controversy surrounding the proper interpretation of the evidence in question. But nothing like it is available at all elsewhere. For other old scripts, the earliest versions known to us are already quite clearly systems of writing, and their ultimate beginnings are lost from the archaeological record.

Indeed, these two facts – the fact that Sumerian is older than the oldest other scripts, and that it is the only script for which we have evidence about its origins – have led various scholars including I. J. Gelb (1952, pp. 218–20) and M. A. Powell (1981, p. 431) to suggest that all writing systems in the world may ultimately be related to one another, with the earliest version of Sumerian writing being the ancestor of all other scripts. (Gelb notes, as strengthening this case, that 'all Oriental systems outside of Sumerian came into existence in periods of strong cultural influences from abroad'.) The principal script for which Gelb's suggestion seems implausible on geographical grounds is the Chinese; yet an eminent sinologist too has been willing to suggest that Chinese script may share a common origin with Western Asiatic writing, though he has subsequently judged that the balance of the evidence is against this (Pulleyblank 1979).

I am sceptical about the monogenetic hypothesis. Gelb seems to me to exaggerate the similarities between different early scripts, and he is too ready to dismiss systems which do not fit his case as not being fully-fledged glottographic writing. (For instance, although the inscriptions of the Mayas of Central America are not yet deciphered, I believe it is far from clear that

Gelb is justified in denying (1952, p. 61) that they constitute writing in the full sense.) But for our purposes the issue is not important. Even if other scripts originated independently, an examination of the origins of the Sumerian script may well give us clues about how those other systems first came into being – we have little enough independent evidence. It is certainly true that the later evolution of Sumerian script reveals strong parallels with developments that occurred independently in other writing systems, and this is another reason for beginning our series of case-studies with a sketch of the Sumerian system: it serves as a convenient introduction to ideas that will be examined in more detail in later chapters.

The culture called 'Sumer' flourished from perhaps −4500 to about −1750 (when it was absorbed by the Babylonians), in lower Mesopotamia – southern Iraq, in 20c terms. Sumer was probably the first civilization in world history, in the sense that it produced the earliest cities (the ideas of 'city' and 'civilization' are commonly taken to be related by more than etymology). It is not surprising, then, if the Sumerians were the world's first scribes; it has often been claimed that writing is the essential distinguishing feature of urban life (Wheatley 1971, p. 401). The Sumerians spoke an agglutinating language comparable in type to Turkish or Hungarian, but apparently unrelated to any living language. Their alluvial terrain had no wood or stone, so the Sumerians wrote on what they had: clay, which they formed into tablets (frequently squarish in shape, and convex rather than flat), and on which they made marks with a stylus cut from a reed. The earliest Sumerian writing, as such, is believed to date from the latter half of the −4th millennium, possibly as late as −3000; most extant examples are from the Sumerian capital Uruk (the Biblical Erech, modern Warka). This 'archaic' stage of Sumerian script is not wholly understood by modern scholarship; and Sumerology is a tightly-knit, somewhat secretive academic discipline, which does not make it easy for the outsider to form a clear view of the current state of knowledge in the field. Nevertheless, it is possible to speak with some confidence about the general nature of archaic Sumerian script. In the following paragraphs we shall examine this system and its subsequent developments. Later in the chapter we shall look at the system out of which writing is thought to have evolved.

Archaic Sumerian writing was used for administrative purposes, in particular for keeping brief records of such matters as tax payments or distribution of rations. A typical archaic tablet is quoted by Driver (1954, p. 40) as reading in translation: 'Ḥegiulendu (the priest of) the god Ensarnun: 600 *bur* of (?) land'. Driver's question-mark alludes to the fact that one graph is not now understood.[1] The relationship between Ḥegiulendu and Ensarnun, which Driver gives in brackets, is not spelled out on the tablet since the writer took it for granted. Records were tied to a particular administrative context; it would have been as pointless for the Sumerian scribe to write out 'the priest of' explicitly (assuming that the script allowed him to do so) as it would be for me to expand the jotting in my diary, 'Noon – Vice-Chancellor', into 'At noon I go to see the Vice-Chancellor'.

A first point to make is that archaic Sumerian writing was quite typical of early scripts in being primarily or exclusively used for somewhat humdrum (though, to those affected, important) administrative purposes. The modern European education system almost invariably links the study of languages with that of belles-lettres, and this often leads people to imagine that poetry, or other writing of high aesthetic value, is in some sense the primary or most central use of writing, so that they expect early scripts to have been used for literary production. This is misleading. Even in 20c Europe, where literary writing is widespread, it is surely swamped in quantity and importance in people's lives by the mass of documents we deal with of a more practical nature – job advertisements, tax returns, newspapers, hobby magazines, etc. etc. Writing in Sumer was an advanced technology developed, as new technologies commonly are, to solve pressing material problems; we might not too fancifully draw an analogy between writing in Sumer and computing in our own culture, and liken the Sumerian scribe, who was a respected 'white-collar worker', to the systems analyst or data-processing engineer. It is true that computers have come to be used for 'humanistic' purposes such as investigating the authorship of the Pauline epistles or enabling composers to use new techniques to generate music, but their original applications were in more technical or practical fields such as science, business, and defence, and these are still their primary functions. According to Marcel Cohen (1958, pp. 7–8):

Practically everywhere, the first use of writing must have been for more or less official messages. The next uses would have been commercial and legal: accounting and the drawing up of contracts. [Various magical or religious uses] often occur at an early stage. Then one finds increasing numbers of governmental proclamations and edicts, or texts of treaties. . . . Chronicles or ritual texts only appear later. Writing designed for instruction or entertainment, later still.

(Stratton (1980, p.100) notes that even the outstandingly intellectual Greeks appear to have made very limited use of alphabetic writing for up to 400 years after they acquired it in the first half of the −8c, although according to Marrou (1965, p. 83) the institution of ostracism which operated in Athens throughout the −5c implies that the average Athenian citizen must have been *able* to write by the beginning of that century.)

Because archaic Sumerian writing consisted of brief, context-bound administrative inscriptions, it used only a restricted graphic vocabulary. Many inscriptions mentioned only quantities of goods of various sorts together with the people concerned in transactions, so that we find mostly graphs for numerals, units of measurement, personal names, and material objects such as 'sheep', 'cow', 'cloth', 'land', and so forth. The numeral graphs were unmotivated, geometrical shapes; the graphs for material objects were in many cases stylized but recognizable pictures of the things in question. There were quite a large number of different graphemes – M. W. Green (1981, p. 356) counts nearly 1200 at the early period – but the system represented only a limited range of the elements that spoken Sumerian must have contained: we find little in the way of grammatical elements akin to English *the*, *was*, for instance.

It might be misleading to describe the script at this stage as incomplete or defective, since there is no reason to believe that scribes at this early period ever wanted to write those forms in their spoken language which are not represented in the inscriptions. (Analogously, it would be odd to call a computer-programming language such as Basic or APL 'defective' on the ground that it provides no way of encoding the statement *I wandered lonely as a cloud.*) Nevertheless, the extreme austerity of the early inscriptions has made some scholars reluctant to categorize archaic Sumerian writing as a logographic system. Thus Powell (1981, p. 421) prefers to call the writing 'mnemonic' rather than 'logographic'. This strikes me as a false opposition. My diary jotting, *Noon – Vice-Chancellor*, is mnemonic, in the sense that it suggests a thought whose full expression requires a complete sentence by recording only its most salient elements. But those elements are written in a specific script of a particular type (in this case, approximately phonographic). Likewise, archaic Sumerian writing appears to be a genuine writing system, of the logographic type: graphs of the script stand for morphemes of spoken Sumerian.

It may be that, by calling the script 'mnemonic', Powell means to suggest that it should be seen as semasiography, in our terms, rather than as true glottographic writing. Several factors make this suggestion reasonable. One is that Powell emphasizes the continuity with the earlier system out of which the script under discussion appears to have emerged; as we shall see below, this certainly was not 'writing' in the sense of glottography. Indeed, given that pre-writing seems to have developed into writing by a slow process of gradual evolution, it may be a rather artificial exercise to decide that the transition to writing has definitely occurred by any particular stage. This point is reinforced by the fact that, when inscriptions are limited to abbreviated jottings rather than full sentences, the distinction between semasiography and logographic writing tends to dissolve. If I write ⟨Noon⟩ in my diary in a phonographic script like ours, there is no doubt that I am writing English – despite the lack of grammatical material – because only in English does the sequence of sounds /nun/ stand for a time of day. If, on the other hand, we used a logographic script in which *noon* was written, say, ⟨☉⟩, then it would be difficult for an outsider to know whether an inscription involving just this sign and a sign for *Vice-Chancellor* was to be interpreted with ⟨☉⟩ standing specially for *noon* rather than for *Mittag* or *midi*, or rather whether it directly represented the idea common to all these words. (On the other hand, if the whole sentence *At noon I go to see the Vice-Chancellor* were written out logographically, the grammar would make it clear that the graphs were to be read as English rather than German or French words.) In the oldest Sumerian tablets, furthermore, even when phrases more complex than a single word were written, the corresponding graphs were not arranged in a systematic order (thus, in the tablet translated on p. 47 above, the numeral '600' interrupts the name 'Hegiulendu'). However, linear ordering and other formatting conventions were soon adopted (Driver 1954, pp. 39ff.; Green 1981, pp. 348ff.).

Once a script uses linear ordering consistently its glottographic status seems indisputable. It would presumably not have affected the intelligibility of the Yukaghir love-letter of Figure 1 (p. 28) if the figures representing the errant young man and his Russian lover had been placed to the right of, or below, the figure representing the writer, rather than to its left. The only reason for consistent linear (horizontal or vertical) placement of graphemes is to mirror the sequential utterance of spoken forms.

Another characteristic of early Sumerian writing which might seem to establish decisively that it was glottographic rather than semasiographic (Gelb 1952, p. 279 n. 11, takes it as doing so) was the separation of numeral graphs from graphs indicating the objects enumerated. In a semasiographic system, one would expect to find an idea such as 'four sheep' expressed by a set of four 'sheep' graphs. But no spoken language would express the idea by four repetitions of a word for 'sheep', and thus in a glottographic script we expect to find the idea written with a single sheep graph associated with a separate graph or group of graphs, standing for the number 'four'. This is what we find from the time of the earliest Sumerian inscriptions. Likewise, one would expect to find an adjective-noun combination, say 'black cow', expressed by one graph in semasiography – a 'cow' sign with some modification such as cross-hatching to indicate blackness – but by two graphs in a glottographic system: an unmodified 'cow' graph together with a separate graph standing for the word 'black'. Unfortunately, it is not clear whether archaic Sumerian script included any phrases of this kind. And the force of the argument from numeral expressions, which did occur, is somewhat undermined by the finding (to be discussed below) that the use of separate numeral signs appears to be inherited from an antecedent system that was not in any sense glottographic writing.

Perhaps one should conclude, then, that the oldest stage of Sumerian script occupies an ambiguous middle ground between clear semasiography, as represented by the Yukaghir love-letter, and the clear glottography into which Sumerian script eventually developed. Later Sumerian writing is well understood, and it is unquestionably glottographic. From about −2400 onwards it was used for extended texts: myths and other literary genres, legal judgments, letters, and so on. The script was written in a linear sequence with word-order reflecting consistent rules of syntax, and it was complete, in the sense that it included a range of devices that were capable of recording all lexical and grammatical elements of the spoken Sumerian language. It is true that elements which would have appeared in a given spoken Sumerian utterance often failed to occur in practice in the written version of the utterance: Civil and Biggs (1966, p. 13) assert that Sumerian orthographic conventions encouraged scribes to omit grammatical items whenever they were predictable from context, rather as telegraphic style in English leaves out many instances of words like *the*. But, as Civil and Biggs rightly say, this practice does not affect the status of the system as a full-scale glottographic script. Whenever a scribe chose to write out a phrase in full, the system offered him the means to do so.

The development of archaic Sumerian script into this later version can be described from two points of view: the outward shape of the graphs, and the inner logic of their structure and values. In this book we are chiefly concerned with the inner structure of writing systems. However, the history of the shapes of Sumerian graphs is also worth spending a little time on, since it is quite characteristic of developments which have happened in the history of many other writing systems.

A few examples of Sumerian graphs are shown in Figure 9 (after Kramer 1963). Column I gives their original form, in which most of them are recognizable pictures. Graph 1 stood for /sag/ 'head'; graph 2, in which the mouth area was picked out by hatching, for both /ka/ 'mouth' and /dug/ 'speak'. Graph 3 stood for /a/ 'water', and graph 4, combining 'head' and 'water', for /nag/ 'drink'. The foot depicted by graph 5 stood for all of the following words: /du/, /ra/, /gin/, which are approximate synonyms for 'go', /gub/ 'stand', /tum/ 'bring'. Graph 6, a picture of a star, stood by association of ideas for /an/ 'heaven' and hence also for /dingir/ 'god'. (The word /mul/ 'star' itself was written with a slightly different graph having more rays.) Graph 7 is known to have stood for /ki/ 'earth/land': in this case, as in many others, the motivation of the graph is not clear – after so many millennia it would be surprising if there were no signs whose logic is obscure to a modern reader, though it may have been obvious enough to a participant in Sumerian culture. Graph 8, a picture of the female pudendum, stands for /sal/ 'pudendum' and for /munus/ 'woman'. Graph 9 is /kur/ 'mountain'. Graph 10, combining 'woman' and 'mountain', stands for /geme/ 'slave-girl'; the reason for this is that the Sumerians took female slaves from the tribes inhabiting the mountainous area to the east.

Soon after the script was first used, all the signs were rotated 90° anticlockwise, as in column II. A development of this kind may well look gratuitous and bizarre. The fact is, though, that comparable changes have happened over and over again in the history of scripts: individual graphs, or (as here) whole inventories of graphs, have been turned on one side or the other, inverted, or replaced by their mirror-images. The reasons for such developments are no doubt various. The systematic 90° rotation of the Sumerian script is claimed by Powell (1981, p. 425) to be linked with the way that scribes found it convenient to hold tablet and stylus when writing (though his explanation is not very clear to me); see also Green (1981, p. 370 n. 19).

Another development during the first half of the −3rd millennium involved the change from a pointed stylus, which was used to draw lines in the clay rather as one draws with pencil on paper, to a blunt stylus with which the scribe pressed lines into the clay with minimal lateral movement. There was a practical reason for this change: moving a point through clay causes it to

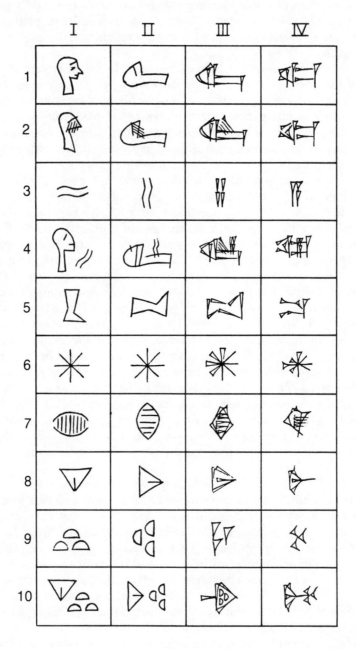

Figure 9

heap up and clog the lines already written, so that graphs were easier to form legibly with the new technique. But it naturally led to modification of the shapes of the individual graphs, as continuous curved lines were as far as possible replaced with straight segments. Each single impression made by the new stylus was shaped like a wedge or nail, hence the name 'Cuneiform' (from the Latin for 'wedge-shaped') for the script as a whole. Again it is entirely characteristic of the history of writing for a change in the materials employed to lead to a large change in the form of the script.

Once the cuneiform technique had been adopted, there was a tendency to use wedges only in those orientations which could be made without excessive bending of the wrist; in practice this meant that the head of the wedge must point in some direction on the arc running from southwest clockwise to north – that is, the set of wedges used to form graph 6 in columns III and IV was the favoured inventory. Column III displays the early cuneiform version of the script, from about −2500: some graphs still involve dragging the stylus through the clay (e.g. to form the line representing the back of the head in graph 1) or placing the stylus in an awkward orientation (e.g. the line representing the forehead in graph 1). By the period about −1800 when most of the Sumerian literary documents were written (represented by column IV) these elements had been eliminated.

These changes in form of the graphs entailed a change in their status from motivated to arbitrary. Even at the stage represented by column I, the graphs were highly conventional; Green (1981, pp. 356–7) points out that graph 1, for instance, 'may be realistically drawn with clearly delineated eye, nose, and chin, but it has to be a right side-view and include both head and neck but not hair, mouth, or ears'. Still a user of the script might at this stage perceive the graphs as pictures, even if heavily stylized pictures. Once the graphs were rotated, as in column II, one would suppose that literate Sumerians must have thought of them most of the time simply as conventional shapes: no doubt they would have been well aware intellectually that they were pictures laid on their sides, but presumably it would have taken an effort of will to perceive them as pictures during fluent reading or writing. After the move to cuneiform writing in column III, it would have been difficult for a new learner who had no access to historically earlier versions of the script to detect any motivation at all in most of the graphs. At this stage, graph 1 for instance must surely have appeared to be an entirely arbitrary collection of wedges. And once that was true, there would have been nothing restraining scribes from following their natural tendency to simplify their labour by replacing difficult stylus-strokes by easy ones and reducing the total number of wedges in a graph (as in the column IV versions of graphs 3 and 5).

I have examined the reasons for these developments in the form of Sumerian writing in some detail, in order to make clear, to readers used to the high degree of standardization and long-term stability in letter-shapes that comes with printing, just how natural and normal it was for the forms of graphs to change drastically before this technology was invented; there were few mechanisms making for stability of graph-shapes before printing, so that it would be surprising if graphs did *not* change shape. When we come to examine the many other scripts that will be discussed in this book, it will be too time-consuming to investigate all the changes that their graph-shapes have undergone (and in any case to do so would rapidly become tedious). But the reader will frequently notice such outward changes in other scripts, and he should not be surprised either that they occur or that they are often passed over in these pages in silence.

At the same time as it was evolving in terms of its outward appearance, the Sumerian script was undergoing equally radical changes in its internal logic. In its initial state, many words of the Sumerian language had no written form, and many of the graphs which did exist were ambiguous between quite different words (as graph 2 in Figure 9 stood for both /ka/ 'mouth' and /dug/ 'speak', and indeed also for /zu/ 'tooth' and /inim/ 'speech'); according to Cohen (1958, p. 83) some graphs had as many as twenty distinct values. These deficiencies were met by the introduction of the phonographic principle into the script (Driver 1954, pp. 56ff.).

One of the first ways in which phonological relationships were exploited lay in the extended use of certain graphs to stand for words homophonous with their original values. Thus graph 3 was invented to stand for /a/ 'water', but was then also used for /a/ 'in', a word whose abstract meaning made it difficult to picture; and a graph for /ti/ 'arrow' was extended to stand also for the near-homophone /til/ 'life', again a less-picturable concept. Cases of this kind, which occurred within the earliest centuries of the existence of the script, were not yet true phonography; the 'arrow' graph did not stand for *any* occurrence of the syllable /ti/, but only for certain specific morphemes which had those sounds in common. But, a short while later, graphs began to be used to indicate grammatical affixes. For instance, the graph for the word /me/ 'oracle' (the original shape of the graph was a simple T, the motivation of which is now obscure) was adapted to stand for the plural suffix /-me/ or /-meʃ/, and other graphs were similarly used to represent case and conjugation affixes.

When graphs stand for relatively 'meaningless' grammatical elements it is difficult not to perceive them as having purely phonological value. Later in the −3rd millennium phonographic use of the symbols of Sumerian script became more widespread. Most Sumerian roots are monosyllables, of CV (consonant + vowel) or CVC shape, so individual graphs represented syllables (rather than, for instance, separate segmental sounds or phonemes).

What led to the adoption of the phonographic principle, according to Gelb (1952, pp. 66–7), was less the problem of writing grammatical elements than the problem of writing proper names. In the early period when the script was used only for accountancy, grammatical niceties were unimportant, but names, obviously, were vital; and Sumerian personal names were typically composed of morphemes from outside the set of numerals and names of goods which sufficed for the rest of the work of recording accounts. As for place-names, these were often quite meaningless sequences of sounds for the Sumerians, as *London, Glasgow* are for us – the reason being that the original inhabitants of what became the land of Sumer had spoken a language other than Sumerian, and the Sumerians took over their predecessors' names for places as we have taken over many Celtic place-names. If a proper name is a meaningless sound-sequence, it can be written only phonographically, unless one invents a special logographic sign just for the name (and this becomes very cumbersome if a large number of different names have to be written). Very early Sumerian writing does contain graphs which appear to represent proper names, but names were soon regularly written phonographically, at a stage well before it became normal to give a full written indication of the grammatical elements of a sentence.

The phonographic use of Sumerian writing, however, fell far short of amounting to a 'complete' syllabic script. Many phonologically-possible syllables had no graphs; and devices were adopted to indicate them, either by graphs for words of similar sound, or by combinations of existing graphs (for instance the syllable /raʃ/ was spelled with graphs for /ra aʃ/). On the other hand, individual graphs did not have unique phonological values; as we have seen, many graphs originally stood for a range of different words all of whose meanings were connected with the object depicted, and these different words would often give rise to very varied phonographic values for the graph in question. Thus graph 5 might be used not only for the syllable /gub/ and possibly for phonetically-similar syllables, but also for /du/, /gin/, etc., and for syllables phonetically similar to those.

Words which had logographic writings continued to be written logographically (and far more words were eventually provided with logographic signs than the few which had sufficed for keeping accounts in the dawn of writing). The Sumerians tended to use signs phonographically only when the limitations of their logographic system forced them to. Another way in which the phonographic principle was exploited, though, was in disambiguating logographic signs which stood for different words. Thus, in order to establish that graph 6 stood on a given occasion for /dingir/ 'god' rather than /an/ 'sky', the scribe would write a graph with the phonetic value /ra/ after it to indicate the last consonant of the required reading; a suffixed /na/ would indicate that the reading should be /an/. Graphs functioning in this way are called 'phonetic complements'.

Conversely, a few key graphs were used as so-called 'determinatives' in order to disambiguate other graphs by reference to the *logographic* values of the former. For instance a graph showing blades of a marsh plant had the logographic vaues /naga/ and /te/, which were names of two such plants, and also /nidaba/ and /ereʃ/, the latter being names of respectively a goddess and a town both of which were associated with marshes. When the graph was used for /te/ it had the graph for /u/ 'plant' written before it; when it stood for /nidaba/, graph 6 ('god') was prefixed as determinative; when it stood for /ereʃ/, graph 7 ('land') was written after it.

The fact that, in the earliest period, one Sumerian graph could stand for a range of semantically-related words is another reason why some writers have felt that the system was semasiographic rather than logographic. But Gelb (1952, p. 107) makes the point that, as soon as the Sumerians invented devices for distinguishing between the various readings possible for a graph, they applied these rather consistently; and he suggests that this gives us good reason to interpret the system, even as it was before these devices were invented, as an – admittedly very defective – logographic rather than semasiographic system (cf. Civil 1973, p. 21).

When graph 6 was used as a determinative, the potential confusion between 'god' and 'sky' was not troublesome: 'god' is used as a determinative, 'sky' is not. However, it should be pointed out that when one reads a Sumerian inscription nothing indicates explicitly which graphs are to be treated as determinatives, which as phonetic complements, and which stand directly for Sumerian words either logographically or phonographically.

Perhaps halfway through the −3rd millennium, the Akkadians, a neighbouring people to the north who spoke a Semitic language unrelated to Sumerian, adapted the Cuneiform script to their own language, developing it greatly in the process. Since the culture of the Akkadians (or, as the relevant sub-group was later called, Babylonians) came to dominate Mesopotamia, eventually extinguishing Sumer as a political entity and Sumerian as a language, the great majority of Cuneiform writing that has come down to us is in Akkadian rather than Sumerian.

The Akkadians greatly extended the use of the phonographic principle in writing. Akkadian was an inflecting language, in which the chain of spoken sounds could not be neatly divided up into morphemic meaning-units (compare the way that English *men* collapses the ideas of 'man' and 'plurality' into a single sound-shape). Pure logography was less practical for such a language than it was for an agglutinating language like Sumerian, in which each spoken syllable could be identified unambiguously with some one particular unit of lexical or grammatical meaning. Having been forced by the nature of their language to develop the phonographic aspect of Cuneiform script, the Akkadians extended the principle to aspects of writing where they could have managed without it. Sumerian Cuneiform, to the end, was an essentially logographic script with a limited admixture of phonography.[2] In Akkadian, virtually any linguistic form might be written either phonographically or logographically, and which writing was chosen for a given word on a given occasion would depend on the stylistic effect aimed at, or the whim of the scribe.

Furthermore the relationship between sounds and graphs used phonographically became much more complicated in Akkadian script than it had been in Sumerian. We have hinted that the Sumerians would on occasion use a graph invented for a word with one particular pronunciation to represent a slightly different syllable: this happened much more extensively in Akkadian writing, partly because Akkadian contained sounds which did not occur in Sumerian. Moreover, the Akkadians derived phonographic values for a given graph not only from the pronunciations of the various Sumerian words for which the graph stood, but sometimes also from their own Akkadian names for the same things, which were naturally quite different.

When one adds that Akkadian scribes sometimes deliberately cultivated archaism and gratuitous obscurity in their orthography, it will be seen that the study of Akkadian Cuneiform is a highly complex discipline. (A good brief introduction is in Labat 1963.)

We shall pursue it no further. Our main purpose in examining Cuneiform was a historical one. To examine in detail the workings of various phenomena of writing in scripts considered as synchronic systems it will be more fruitful to look at modern scripts (or at least at scripts dating from nearer to the present), for which the facts are more accessible; this we shall do in subsequent chapters. The reader may be interested to note how many of the themes which will become relevant with respect to the other scripts from diverse parts of the world to be discussed in later chapters are prefigured in the development of this one earliest of all writing-systems.

We shall conclude this chapter by considering a theory worked out in recent years about how the Sumerian script may originally have been created. It should be said at the outset that this theory is very much more controversial than almost any other material in the present work. Quite possibly, when the scholarly world has had longer to digest these ideas, the consensus will be that they are wholly mistaken. However, a number (though certainly not all) of those qualified to judge are currently favourable to the theory, and its intrinsic interest is such that it would be a pity to ignore it here out of excessive scholarly caution.

The theory was originally put forward by Pierre Amiet of the Louvre Museum (Amiet 1966) and has since been elaborated by Denise Schmandt-Besserat of the University of Texas (e.g. Schmandt-Besserat 1978, 1979a, 1979b). Their point of departure is the fact that excavations in Mesopotamia have yielded large numbers of small clay objects of various simple geometrical shapes: spheres, discs, cones, tetrahedra, etc., some of which have lines incised on them in set patterns (for instance there are discs with a cross on one face), or have small pellets or coils of clay added to them. For want of a more neutral term I shall call these objects 'tokens'. They are commonly found in the storage areas of dwellings. Archaeologists have usually paid them little attention, dismissing them briefly as 'gaming pieces', 'amulets', or the like.

Late in the −4th millennium, as urban life was beginning, the inventory of token-shapes increased; some of the new shapes were relatively naturalistic, for instance they included highly stylized models of animal heads and jars. At this same period we find examples of sets of tokens being enclosed in clay envelopes or 'bullae', balls of clay which were hollowed out and sealed after the tokens were inserted. In many cases the bullae carry rows of marks on the outside corresponding to the tokens within, made either (rarely) by pressing the tokens themselves into the outside of the bulla before sealing them inside or (more usually) by simulating the shapes of the tokens.

Pierre Amiet argues that the clay tokens must have been used to stand for goods in a system of accountancy. Amiet treats this system as having been invented in the −4th millennium by the inhabitants of Elam (a civilization neighbouring Sumer to the east, based on Susa, modern Shūsh). However, Schmandt-Besserat casts her net wider: she notes that comparable tokens are found not just in Mesopotamia but at many sites over a wide area of the Near East, and that at some sites they go as far back as the −9th millennium, when the hunting-and-gathering way of life was first giving way to farming. The tokens appear to represent the earliest use of fired clay for any purpose. Tokens of the same set shapes continue to appear in the archaeological record up to the −3rd millennium, the peak of production seemingly being about −3500.

Schmandt-Besserat argues that the coincidence of the earliest tokens with the beginnings of farming is readily understandable: whereas hunter-gatherers live literally from hand to mouth, agriculturalists need to make long-term plans of things such as the division of the harvest into grain for current consumption versus seed-corn. Before the invention of writing, it might have been very useful to have a system in which crops and livestock were represented by small tokens which would perhaps be shifted from one tray to another in order to model activities on the farm. With the growth of towns the range of goods available would have increased, and this may be reflected by the increase in number of token-types.

Urban life also implies the beginning of large-scale trade, and this may explain the appearance of the bullae. The farmer now needs not only to keep at home a model of the disposition of his working capital; he must also exchange documentation with others. A bulla may have been a bill of lading, recording consignments of stock or goods sent to market in the charge of a servant. The envelope would function not merely to keep the tokens together but to protect them from fraudulent alteration; since they could be inspected only by breaking the bulla, it would have been convenient to keep a record of the contents on the outside for casual checking. (A proportion of the tokens are perforated, suggesting that they were kept together on strings. Schmandt-Besserat at one point suggests that this method might have been used in order to enable the tokens to stand for a linear sequence of spoken words, but this somewhat daring idea is not pursued.)

Amiet argues that, once people were accustomed to mark the outside of bullae as a record of their contents, the inevitable next step was to simplify matters by dispensing with the contents of the envelope and exchanging just marked clay surfaces: in which case one has writing, or something very like it. Schmandt-Besserat supports this by observing that the archaeological record shows a short period when tablets, similar to those later used for writing, bore only the kind of markings made by pressing tokens into the clay rather than by drawing on it with a point. And the fact is that *numerals*, up to the end of the Sumerian period, were normally recorded not by cuneiform graphs but by pressing cylindrical shapes into the clay at different angles – it seems that later Sumerian scribes used the 'wrong end' of their reed stylus for writing numbers.

Schmandt-Besserat has argued for this theory of the origin of writing in a rather more radical form than was proposed by Amiet (and has publicized it remarkably widely in a short time). She believes that the token system represents the origin not merely of the general principle of communicating by marks on clay but of the details of Sumerian script. Schmandt-Besserat notes that a number of the earliest logographs of the Sumerian system (whose values are established by their continuity with later, better-documented forms of the script) seem to be thoroughly unmotivated – contrary to the common assumption that any script will naturally begin pictorially and gradually evolve into a less-motivated form. For instance, 'sheep' was written with a cross in a circle: ⊕ In fact the most motivated early Sumerian graphs tend to be either names of *wild* animals, e.g. 'wolf', or items of advanced technology such as 'chariot'.

Others have explained this by supposing that the oldest known examples of Sumerian writing themselves constitute the result of an earlier period of development now lost to us, at the beginning of which the graphs would have been more motivated. But Schmandt-Besserat finds it strange that all trace of the postulated earlier periods of the script should have vanished from the archaeological record; and (following a suggestion of Amiet's) she suggests that the arbitrary shapes of the written graphs are quite understandable, on the other hand, if they were created as imitations in two dimensions of antecedent three-dimensional tokens (since small clay tokens would, as a matter of practicality, have had perforce to be made in simple shapes). Wild animals would have been irrelevant to the purposes of the token system, and technological advances such as chariots may have postdated it, so that words for these things would have been written two-dimensionally from the start and hence were naturally given motivated graphs. Schmandt-Besserat compares the inventory of early Sumerian graphs and that of token-types, and claims that the correspondences between them are striking. (She even argues that this theory explains why the Sumerians wrote on clay, which she regards as a relatively inconvenient medium, and why their tablets were usually somewhat convex – this could have been a hangover from the convexity of the hollow bullae. But it is not clear that the Sumerians had any alternative to clay; and Driver (1954, p. 9) suggests that convexity protected the tablets from the risk of cracking.)

Schmandt-Besserat's theory has encountered serious criticism, which is perhaps not surprising in view of its sweeping nature and the uncompromising manner of her advocacy. An obvious problem is that – particularly when the shapes involved are simple geometrical ones – it is a very dangerous assumption to equate the signs of two separate systems merely on the basis of similarity of appearance, as Schmandt-Besserat does with the token system and the Sumerian logographs. There are, after all, only so many simple shapes possible, so coincidences can be expected to happen by chance. Furthermore, if we do accept Schmandt-Besserat's identifications we must assign meanings to some of the tokens which are difficult to reconcile with her notion of how the token-system was used: what use would there have been for clay tokens meaning 'good', 'legal decision', 'heart'? In any case, Schmandt-Besserat's chief public opponent, Stephen Lieberman, claims (1980) that Schmandt-Besserat greatly exaggerates the degree of coincidence between token-system and early Sumerian script, both by equating two or more distinct Sumerian graphs with a single token-type and vice versa, and by casting her net unreasonably wide in investigating the tokens, ignoring the fact that many of the token-types which look most like Sumerian graphs are never found at Mesopotamian sites – cf. also Le Brun and Vallat (1979). (Lieberman claims also that Schmandt-Besserat's articles are frequently inconsistent in their statements about the archaeological evidence. In fairness it should be pointed out that Powell (1981, pp. 423–4) defends Schmandt-Besserat's findings against Lieberman's objections.)

Finally, Schmandt-Besserat seems somewhat unimaginative in her belief that the shapes of the tokens, and the early Sumerian logographs equated with them, 'were totally symbolic and completely unrelated to the shape of the objects they stood for' (1979b, p. 27). The two examples she gives are the token she interprets as 'oil', which looks to me like a passable model of the kind of jar Ali Baba might have hidden in, and the token for 'sheep' already mentioned: in the latter case I note that Jacob's sheep, one of the earliest surviving breeds, have four horns in a rough cross shape, and if this was true of the breeds familiar to the Sumerians the token and logograph in question could have been highly motivated.

Lieberman, together with Le Brun and Vallat, suggest that, if any aspect of Sumerian writing descended from the use of tokens and the habit of making corresponding marks on the surface of bullae, it is likely to have been exclusively the numeral system – which, as we have seen, remained graphically quite distinct from the rest of the Sumerian script throughout its history (as indeed our own notation for numbers is distinct from our alphabetic orthography). Amiet had originally proposed that all the tokens represented classes of goods, or set quantities of specific goods, but he had not attempted to equate particular token-shapes with particular elements of Sumerian writing. Schmandt-Besserat's version of the theory depends crucially on making such equations; and Lieberman (1980, p. 341 n. 9) quotes an admission by her that, of the whole range of extant token-types, only the limited subset which can be equated with Sumerian numeral graphs appear to be associated with the bullae. Schmandt-Besserat's critics see no good grounds for tracing any other aspects of Sumerian script back to the use of tokens.

Another difficulty arises here, though: within the kind of communication-system supposedly represented by the bullae, it is not clear what role there could be for numeral signs in particular. In true writing it is more convenient to record, say, ten sheep and twenty cows as ⟨10 SHEEP 20 COW⟩ rather than as ten 'sheep' graphs and twenty 'cow' graphs. But if one's 'graphs' were pieces of clay rattling round inside a hollow ball, there would be no way of preserving the proper grouping of tokens standing for 'ten', 'sheep', 'twenty', and 'cow'. The bullae often contained dozens of tokens, so this is surely a real problem for the proposed interpretation of their function.

In one of her most recent articles (1981) Schmandt-Besserat goes some way to meet this difficulty by adopting a proposal by A. A. Vaiman that the words which eventually became number-terms stood originally not for pure numbers but for numbers of specific goods. Such expressions are not unknown in modern languages (cf. the Engish *brace* meaning 'two game-birds'), and they may possibly have been commoner in the languages of primitive cultures which had not evolved abstract mathematical concepts. Schmandt-Besserat points out (p. 327) that the 'impressed tablets' which briefly preceded the first written tablets carried a wider range of marks than the ones which can be identified with the numerals used when the Sumerians developed true writing. However, the suggestion seems too speculative to be assessed at this stage.

Perhaps the most judicious conclusion at present would be that the marks made on the bullae may well have been purely numerical (and Lieberman may be correct in supposing that a large proportion of the 'token'-types discussed by Schmandt-Besserat were in reality objects serving quite other purposes), but that a simple accounting system using only a few kinds of token could nevertheless, as Amiet suggests, have led via the use of the bullae to the creation of writing. When bullae were used to protect numerical communications from fraud it would have been a natural step to reproduce them on the surface of their clay envelope; once this practice had come in, it would have been equally natural to make similar marks on clay not formed into envelopes; and, when a simple accounting system using number-graphs impressed on clay tablets had been created, it would again have been natural to begin supplementing the indications of number with pictures of the items numbered. Pending further archaeological investigations, it is reasonable to suppose that Amiet may indeed have shown us the route by which, through a series of small steps none of which, probably, seemed momentous at the time, one portion of the human race for the first time in history made the transition from a stage at which they clearly lacked the institution of writing to a stage at which they clearly possessed it.

4 A syllabic system: Linear B

Cuneiform script was a complex system which rather untidily combined various orthographic principles in differing proportions at different stages of its history. In this chapter we shall examine an orthography which was much more neatly logical: the 'Linear B' script used to write an early form of the Greek language during part of the −2nd millennium, well before the Greeks first encountered alphabetic writing. Linear B is an interesting script for two reasons: first, because it is a relatively pure example of syllabic writing, and secondly because it is a highly 'incomplete' script (in the sense defined on p. 36), while at the same time being quite systematic and consistent within its own limitations.

Linear B was used, probably from about the −16c to the −13c, for record-keeping purposes by the civil service of the 'Mycenaean' civilization which then flourished in southern Greece. Early in the −2nd millennium a civilization now called 'Minoan', speaking an unknown, possibly non-Indo-European language, had grown up in Crete, and used a script known as 'Linear A' (which remains largely unintelligible). The Mycenaeans derived much of their culture from the Minoans (until they conquered Crete in about −1450), and the Linear B script seems to have been created as an adaptation of Linear A to the Greek language. Linear B ceased to be used when the Mycenaean cities were destroyed in about −1250, possibly by invaders from the sea. (However, a syllabic script distantly related to Linear B was used to write Greek in Cyprus in the Classical period.)

Linear B was written on unbaked clay tablets – the examples we have are those that were baked when the palaces burned down around them. From the subtle, curvilinear shapes of the symbols (contrast Cuneiform) it seems possible that Linear B may also have been written with pen and ink or the like, though no direct evidence of this survives. It appears that the tablets which have come down to us are temporary files dating to the last year before the destruction of each archive, and the information would perhaps have been transferred annually to more permanent records which have not survived. It is fascinating to observe that some of the tablets appear to record troop movements and civilian evacuation measures in anticipation of an invasion.

Linear B was deciphered in 1952 by an English architect, Michael Ventris. It had previously been thought unlikely that the language of Linear B was Greek; Ventris discovered that it was, although (naturally) an archaic form of Greek. (For comparison, the oldest Greek literature, the Homeric *Odyssey* and *Iliad*, is thought to have been fixed in the form we know towards −700, and the classical Attic Greek that modern schoolchildren are taught represents a period eight to ten centuries later than that of the Linear B tablets.) The basic reference on Linear B is Ventris and Chadwick (1956, 2nd ed. 1973); and the shorter and more popular account in Chadwick (1958) can be thoroughly recommended as a book which combines instruction with much of the excitement of a detective story. For a general account of Mycenaean civilization see Chadwick (1976).

Figure 10 offers a reconstruction of the phonological inventory of Mycenaean Greek (about which much was known independently of the Linear B evidence). 'Suprasegmental' matters such as stress and tone are necessarily ignored; and various details of the segmental phonology are open to question − for instance Mycenaean Greek may already have had the distinction between half-open and half-close long vowels which developed in Attic, and it probably also had a long/short contrast in some but not all diphthongs. (For that matter, it is quite likely that the Linear B tablets do not represent a single totally-homogeneous dialect.) The symbols /k^{wh} k^w g^w/ stand for 'labio-velars' − probably realized as velar stops co-articulated with lip-rounding. In

Vowels

pure						diphthongs				
ĭ ī		ŭ ū								
ĕ ē		ŏ ō			ei	eu			oi	ou
ă ā						ai	au			

Consonants

p^h	t^h	k^h	k^{wh}	h
p	t	k	k^w	∅
b	d	g	g^w	
m	n			
	(j)	w		
	s			
	l			
	r			
	z			

Figure 10

later Greek these changed into other consonants (labials or dentals, depending on environment), and /w/ disappeared; thus we have Mycenaean /$hik^w k^w os$/ 'horse' (cf. Latin *equus*) corresponding to Classical Greek *hippos*, Mycenaean /wanaks/ 'king' corresponding to Classical *anax*, etc.[1] The symbol /z/ is used conventionally for the phoneme symbolized in the Greek alphabet as ⟨ζ⟩. This is pronounced [z] in Modern Greek, but was probably [zd] in Classical Greek, and in Mycenaean Greek its pronunciation is uncertain − it may have been an affricate such as [dʒ], and indeed it may be that 'z' covers a pair of Mycenaean phonemes contrasting in terms of voice. The symbol Ø is inserted in the consonant table in order to make the point that a word can begin with no consonant at all, as in English. (The /h/ symbol in the same column also relates only to word-initial position; because [h] occurred nowhere else in Greek, it is not regarded as a separate phoneme but rather the h/Ø contrast is treated as a distinction between 2 ways of pronouncing words beginning with vowels.)

Except possibly for the distinction between [j] and Ø, all the distinctions in Figure 10 were contrastive; no pairs of the sounds listed were mere allophonic variants of one another. (When [j] occurred, it was commonly just a glide produced automatically by the transition from an /i/ to a following vowel – e.g. /hiereus/ 'priest' was heard as [hijereus]. There are a few cases in which [j] seems to have occurred other than following /i/, in which case it would have had phonemic status – e.g. /jō/ 'thus', /mewjōn/ 'lesser'; but the uncertainties of the transcription are such that it might be rash to claim a phoneme /j/ on the basis of these few examples.) In English, unaspirated voiceless stops are allophonic alternants of aspirated stops (see p. 43); but in Mycenaean Greek (as in Classical Greek) /pʰ/ and /p/, and the other aspirated/unaspirated pairs, were entirely separate phonemes – e.g. a minimal pair from Classical Greek is /ponos/ 'toil' v. /pʰonos/ 'murder'.

However, the Linear B script ignored very many of the distinctions that were contrastive in the language for which it was used. That is what I mean by calling it an 'incomplete' system. The phonographic components of Sumerian or Akkadian Cuneiform, for that matter, were 'incomplete' in the sense that many syllables had no graph and were written with combinations of graphs for other syllables, and that various groups of phonologically-similar syllables were written with the same graph. But in Cuneiform script there was no particular logic that decided which syllables had graphs and which did not, and the methods used to spell syllables lacking their own graphs were fairly *ad hoc* and diverse. Linear B was not like that. The range of phonological contrasts encoded in the script was a relatively neat, logical subset of the range of contrasts found in the spoken language, and the orthographic rules were likewise rather simple and straightforward.

The 73 Linear B syllable-signs with known values are displayed in Figure 11 (there are sixteen further rare graphs which appear to belong to the same system but whose values have not been established). Most of the graphs look purely arbitrary; where a pictorial motif is recognizable, it does not link in any obvious way to a Greek word for the thing pictured, which is unsurprising if the values of the graphs derive from an earlier script (Linear A) used for another language.

The first point to make about Figure 11 is that the script is genuinely syllabic. The point needs making, because scripts are often called 'syllabic' which in terms of Chapter 2 are nothing of the kind. Thus, compare Figure 12, which shows a sample of the 182 graphs of the Ethiopic script. The Ethiopic

Figure 11

graphs are 'syllabic' rather than segmental in the sense that each physically-continuous written mark stands for a syllable; but the shape of the graphs is determined by the segmental composition of the syllables, so that syllables beginning with a given consonant share the same basic outline and each vowel is indicated by a consistent method of modifying the consonantal outline

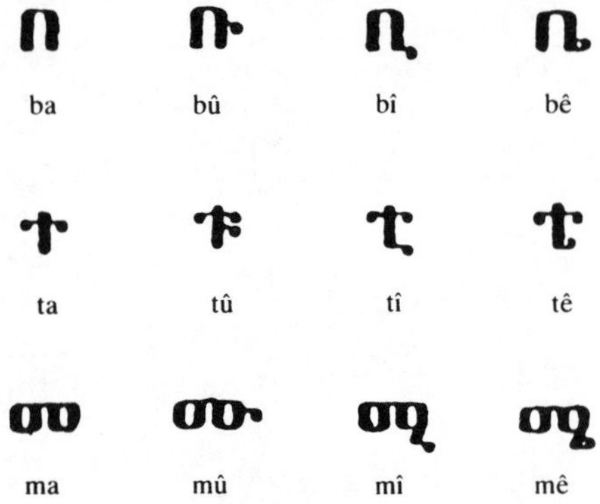

ba	bû	bî	bê
ta	tû	tî	tê
ma	mû	mî	mê

Figure 12

(/a/ is indicated by absence of modification). In the full inventory of Ethiopic graphs there are a few exceptions to this system, but in essence the Ethiopic writing system is a segmental script in which segments are encoded as features of graphs rather than as independent, spatially-disconnected marks. In Linear B, by contrast, there is nothing in common among the graphs for e.g. the various syllables beginning with /m-/ or the various syllables ending in /-a/.

The graphs of Figure 11 were mapped on to the sound-system of Mycenaean Greek in accordance with the following conventions.

Normally, the aspirated/unaspirated distinction was not recorded, and similarly the sound [h] was ignored. (This rule had minor exceptions: there is a special graph that could optionally be used instead of ⟨a⟩ to represent /ha/, and a graph optionally used instead of ⟨pu⟩ to represent /pʰu/.) Also, the voiced/voiceless distinction was unrecorded except among the dentals – /d/ syllables were distinguished from /tʰ, t/ syllables, but /b, g, gʷ/ were equated with /pʰ p/, /kʰ k/, and /kʷʰ kʷ/ respectively. (The two phonemes /s/ and /z/ were kept separate; but, as we have seen, /z/ – even if it was a single phoneme – was not a voiced counterpart of /s/.) The distinction between the liquids /l r/ was ignored. Length was ignored both in vowels (e.g. /ē/ and /ĕ/ were treated as identical) and in consonants (e.g. the geminate /ss/ was not distinguished from /s/).

Thus when, in Figure 11, three of the graphs are shown with the conventional transcriptions ⟨o, po, ro⟩, this really means that the first stands for a mid back vowel of unspecified length with or without a preceding /h/; that the second stands for an unspecified bilabial stop followed by a mid back vowel; and that the last stands for an unspecified liquid followed by a mid back vowel. It would be equally appropriate to transcribe the signs in question as ⟨ho, bo, lo⟩; but it happens to have become conventional in Mycenaean scholarship to transcribe graphs for syllables beginning with stop consonants using the symbols for voiceless unaspirated stops, to transcribe graphs for syllables beginning with liquids with *r* rather than *l*, and so forth. Likewise, *q* is conventionally used to transcribe graphs for syllables beginning with labio-velars.

Furthermore, as can be seen from Figure 11, almost all Linear B graphs stand for simple CV syllables. Since Mycenaean (like Classical) Greek had a variety of more complex syllables, the Linear B scribes had to use a moderately complex set of rules for converting spoken words into written form.

As one might expect, there was a certain amount of variation between alternative scribal conventions; and the extant texts also include cases of what seem to have been downright errors on the writer's part. But the following set of rules comes fairly close to being a complete and general statement of the Linear B orthographic rules.

In the first place, the treatment of diphthongs depends on the identity of the final vowel. Diphthongs in /-u/ are treated as sequences of two vowels, e.g. /g^{w}asileus/ 'chief' (Classical Greek *basileus*) is written ⟨qa-si-re-u⟩. But with diphthongs in /-i/ the /i/ is ignored, e.g. /poimēn/ 'shepherd' is ⟨po-me⟩. This does not imply that diphthongs in /-i/ are never distinguished in writing from pure vowels, however; whenever such a diphthong is followed by another vowel, this will be written with the graph for the corresponding /j-/ syllable, e.g. /palaios/ 'old' is ⟨pa-ra-jo⟩. (One might imagine that it is the frequency with which an /-i/ diphthong is revealed in this way that made the rule about omitting the /-i/ appropriate; but in that case /-u/ diphthongs should be treated similarly, since [w] glides are perceived in sequences of /u + vowel/ just as [j] is perceived in /i + vowel/ – /kuanos/ 'lapis lazuli' is ⟨ku-wa-no⟩.) There are special graphs that can be used to indicate the two diphthongs /ai au/ in word-initial position only, so that /aiwolos/ 'nimble' could be written either ⟨ai-wo-ro⟩ or ⟨a-wo-ro⟩.

The transcription of a consonant which immediately precedes a vowel is straightforward. However, when a consonant phoneme occurs in speech preceding another consonant or word-finally, so that it is not part of a CV sequence, its treatment depends on whether it is a continuant (/s, m, n, r, l, w/) or a stop.

If it is a stop it is written by 'borrowing' the next vowel to make up a CV syllable: e.g. /ktoinā/ 'plot of land' is ⟨ko-to-na⟩, /ptelewās/ 'of elm-wood' = ⟨pe-te-re-wa⟩, /aksones/ 'axles' = ⟨a-ko-so-ne⟩, /tripos/ 'tripod' = ⟨ti-ri-po⟩, /alektruōn/ 'cock' = ⟨a-re-ku-tu-ru-wo⟩. If there is no follow-ing vowel, it seems (though the examples are too few to be sure that this is a general rule) that the preceding vowel is used: /wanaks/ 'king' = ⟨wa-na-ka⟩, /ait^{h}iok^{w}s/ 'sunburnt' = ⟨ai-ti-jo-qo⟩.

On the other hand, when a continuant consonant has no vowel immediately following, it is written with a 'borrowed' vowel only if the next sound is a sonorant (/m, n, r, l, w/). If a continuant consonant is word-final or is followed by an obstruent (i.e. a stop or /s/), it is simply omitted. All the consonants that can occur word-finally in Greek, namely /n r s/, are continuants, so no consonant that is word-final in speech is noted in Linear B writing: /tripos/ 'tripod' is ⟨ti-ri-po⟩, /poimēn/ 'shepherd' = ⟨po-me⟩, /patēr/ 'father' = ⟨pa-te⟩. Examples of continuants omitted before obstruents are: /pʰasgana/ 'swords' = ⟨pa-ka-na⟩, /worzōn/ 'performing' = ⟨wo-zo⟩, /kʰalkos/ 'bronze' = ⟨ka-ko⟩, /aiksmans/ 'points' = ⟨ai-ka-sa-ma⟩. (In the last example /n/ is omitted as preceding the obstruent /s/, which is itself omitted as word-final.) Examples of continuants written with borrowed vowel before sonorants are: /amnīsos/ (a place-name) = ⟨a-mi-ni-so⟩, /dosmos/ 'contribution' = ⟨do-so-mo⟩, /wrīnos/ 'leather' = ⟨wi-ri-no⟩, /ksenwios/ 'intended for guests' = ⟨ke-se-ni-wi-jo⟩.

One would obviously like to know whether there is any general linguistic rationale for the rules about when a consonant is omitted and when it is written with a borrowed vowel.

Ruijgh (1967, pp. 24–5) gives the rules essentially as they are given above, and suggests that the explanation may be that sonorants are more like vowels than obstruents are, so that the sequence 'consonant + sonorant' is closer to the sequence 'consonant + vowel' (the consonant of which will always be written) than is the sequence 'consonant + obstruent'. But there are two objections to this. First, it does nothing to explain why it is only continuant consonants which are omitted before obstruents. Secondly, it may be true that in some sense a sequence such as /sm/ is closer, phonetically, than a sequence such as /sp/ to the pattern CV, but if that fact were relevant to the way Mycenaean speakers perceived the phonology of their language it should have led them to provide their writing system with a special graph for /sm/ – since they did not, why did they feel the need to write /s/ in this combination?

An explanation which looks more likely than Ruijgh's is offered by Ventris and Chadwick (1956, p. 45), who suggest that the rule is that continuant consonants are omitted when final in their syllable. Sounds at the ends of syllables are inherently less prominent than sounds at the beginnings of syllables, so this is a plausible rule. Compare /kʰalkos/ = ⟨ka-ko⟩ with /amnīsos/ = ⟨a-mi-ni-so⟩. The consonant-cluster /lk-/ is not a possible beginning for a Greek word, so we know that /kʰalkos/ must divide into syllables as /kʰal$kos/ rather than as /kʰa$lkos/ (the symbol $ represents phonetic syllable-boundary): the /l/ in this word is final, so it is ignored in Linear B writing. (The third conceivable syllabification, /kʰalk$os/, would be eliminated by a general rule that syllable-boundaries in Greek are placed as far to the left as possible.) On the other hand, /mn-/ *is* a possible initial cluster in Greek (it occurs for instance in /mnēmē/ 'memory', the root from which we derive English *mnemonic*). Therefore *Amnisos* is syllabified /a$mnī$sos/, and the /m/ is written with a borrowed /i/.

Indeed, there are a number of cases where the Ventris and Chadwick explanation makes better predictions than Ruijgh's. Consider the words /sperma/ 'seed', /korwos/ 'boy': /r/ precedes sonorants /m, w/, yet these words are consistently spelled ⟨pe-ma⟩, ⟨ko-wo⟩. Since /rm-, rw-/ are not possible initial clusters in Greek, the words must be divided as /sper$ma/, /kor$wos/, and the syllable-final rule predicts omission of the /r/.

In fact one might go further than Ventris and Chadwick, and reformulate their principle in a way that makes it more general and allows us to specify which consonants are written and which omitted without making any reference to consonant-classes such as 'obstruent', 'continuant', or the like. The general rule (which, as we shall see, is not entirely satisfactory but comes close to being correct) would be: consonants are written (if necessary, with borrowed vowels) whenever they precede the vowel of their syllable, and are omitted whenever they follow the vowel of their syllable. The constraints on possible consonant-clusters in spoken Greek are such that this rule would automatically give results very much as Ruijgh describes. Greek permits stops to cluster relatively freely with other following consonants, so in a sequence 'vowel + stop + consonant + vowel' the syllable-boundary will normally precede the stop, hence this will be included in the Linear B spelling. (For instance, /aksones/ 'axles' is syllabified /aksones/ because in Greek /ks-/ is a permitted, indeed common initial cluster – hence the many Greek-derived words in English that begin with *x,* e.g. *xylophone* from /ksulon/ 'wood'.) One might query the spelling ⟨a-re-ku-tu-ru-wo⟩ for /alektruōn/: it is true that /ktr-/ is not a possible Greek word-initial cluster, but on the other hand /kt-/ is possible (e.g. /ktenos/, genitive of 'comb'), whereas /-k, -kt, -ktr/ are all quite impossible in word-*final* position, so on the whole /alektru$ōn/ seems the most appropriate syllabification, and this predicts the Linear B spelling ⟨-ku-tu-ru-⟩.

There are two imperfections in the rule as stated. In the first place it predicts that none of the consonants in word-final consonant-clusters should be written, but we have seen that e.g. /wanaks/ 'king' is ⟨wa-na-ka⟩ not *⟨wa-na⟩. The explanation here may be that, since the general rule led to the overwhelming majority of stops being written, the rule was expanded so as to require all stops to be written – the only stops that would have been omitted under the simpler rule are those of the word-final clusters /-ks -kʷs -ps/. Second, neither Ventris and Chadwick's suggestion nor my more general reformulation does anything to explain why /s-/ is ignored when it precedes an obstruent, as it consistently is: e.g. /sperma/ 'seed' = ⟨pe-ma⟩, /statʰmos/ 'farmstead' = ⟨ta-to-mo⟩, and likewise /ksunstrokʷʰā/ 'aggregate' = ⟨ku-su-to-ro-qa⟩ where the syllabification must surely be /ksun$stro$kʷʰā/ (the word is a compound of the prefix written in Classical Greek σύν 'together' with the root στροφή 'rolling'). These two points must be accepted as departures from the rule in its most general form. Thus, the rule that I would actually defend is: a consonant which is not a stop is omitted if it occurs after the vowel of its syllable, and (in the case of /s/) if it immediately precedes a stop; otherwise all consonants are written, with borrowed vowels where necessary.

Even this relatively complicated version of my rule fails in some cases. For instance, the word /ararmotmenā/ 'fitted together' is written ⟨a-ra-ro-mo-te-me-na⟩; yet the syllabification is /ararmotmenā/, so the graph ⟨ro⟩

should not appear. (The cluster /tm-/ occurs in initial position in Greek, but /rm-/ does not.) This spelling is predicted by Ruijgh's principle, on the other hand. However, for Ruijgh ⟨pe-ma⟩ for /sperma/ is unexpected: he would predict *⟨pe-ra-ma⟩. It seems implausible that these alternative treatments of /-rm-/ are to be explained in terms of any general properties of their respective phonological environments. Rather, we must surely choose one of the following views of the matter:

1 scribes varied freely as between writing and omitting the first element of /-rm-/ and comparable clusters (or perhaps some scribes regularly wrote them and others regularly omitted them);
2 the rule required the first element in such clusters to be written, and spellings such as ⟨pe-ma⟩ for /sperma/ are irregular (or mistakes);
3 the rule required the first element in such clusters to be omitted, and spellings such as ⟨a-ra-ro-mo-te-me-na⟩ for /ararmotmenā/ are exceptions.

I am supposing that 3 is correct, because this assumption enables me to state the rule governing the writing of consonants in a relatively elegant way. Ruijgh notes that spellings omitting the first element of consonant clusters of the relevant type are commoner than spellings which include them; this implies that 3 is at least a better account of the data than 2, and if the difference in frequency is quite large 3 might be judged to have more explanatory force than 1.

A more serious problem for the rule I suggest is that it depends on a set of principles for syllabification which are themselves open to question. W. S. Allen (1968, pp. 98–9) acknowledges that the principle I have given, according to which a syllable-boundary is placed as far to the left as is compatible with the limitations on permissible initial clusters, was traditionally accepted by Greek grammarians, but he argues that considerations having do with poetic metre show that it must be wrong; Allen states a different principle. As it happens, the particular examples Allen quotes of syllable-division according to his principle would yield the same Linear B spellings as the traditional principle if my spelling-rule is correct; but there are other examples where this is not so. For instance /dosmos/ 'contribution', which by the traditional principle is divided /do$smos/ and hence correctly spelled by my rule ⟨do-so-mo⟩, would by Allen's principle be divided /dos$mos//, for which my spelling-rule wrongly predicts the spelling *⟨do-mo⟩. If Allen is right in saying that the traditional principle of syllable-division must be rejected, then it seems that the relatively simple spelling-rule I have given could be defended only if there were evidence in Greek for differences between shallow and deep syllabification (see e.g. Kiparsky 1979, Lowenstamm 1981).

Figure 11 contains various gaps – combinations of sounds for which no Linear B graph is shown – but it is likely that only two or three of these represent gaps in our knowledge of the system: the syllables /ju zu/ probably occurred in Mycenaean Greek, but happen to crop up so rarely in the corpus of tablets we have that their written forms have not been firmly identified. (In fact there are graphs which have been tentatively identified as ⟨ju⟩, ⟨zu⟩, but the evidence is weak.) The other gaps are likely to represent phonological impossibilities in Mycenaean Greek: /ji/ and /wu/ would not have been distinguished from /i/ and /u/, likewise /kʷu/ (and its counterparts with aspirated and voiced stops) were probably not distinguished from /ku/. There are reasons for believing that /zi/ was not a possible syllable, though this may alternatively be an accidental gap in our knowledge comparable to /zu/.

The existence of a few graphs which disturb the general logic of the Linear B script, such as the optional graphs for /ha/, /pʰu/, /ai/, or graphs for combinations such as /nwa/, /pte/, is not in itself particularly surprising: compare the way that our own script contains a letter X for a consonant-cluster /ks/ which has no special importance in the phonology of English or other modern European languages, while possessing no single graph for such a common phoneme as /ʃ/. However, the Linear B syllabary does seem to be oddly ill-adapted to the Greek language. It is not merely that there are isolated cases of redundant graphs, but also that what is systematically provided seems to have little to do with the structure of Greek. The distinction between voiced, voiceless plain, and aspirate stops was as crucial in Greek phonology as the distinctions between voiced and voiceless, stop and fricative are in English phonology – yet the Greek distinctions are almost entirely ignored by the script. (The one case where the voiced/voiceless distinction is indicated, namely among the dentals – /d/ versus /t tʰ/ – cannot be explained by suggesting that dental stops may have been more frequent in Greek so that fine distinctions in writing were more useful for that consonant-class, since dentals were not in fact commoner than consonants made at the other places of articulation.) On the other hand, the script provides a whole series of graphs for recording [j] when this was normally a mere automatic glide between vowels which probably had only marginal phonemic status. It is no great surprise that there should have been a handful of graphs for complex syllables of the CCV type as well as the basic series of graphs for simple CV syllables, but it does seem surprising that so many of the complex syllables for which special graphs were provided should have involved clusters with /w/: even in the pre-Classical Greek which still included this consonant, it was a relatively rare one.

The likelihood is that these unexpected characteristics are a consequence of the fact that Linear B was not created from scratch as a script for Greek, but was developed from an already-existing system (Linear A, or a lost common ancestor-script) which had been developed to write the sounds of a quite different 'Minoan' language. L. R. Palmer (1963, pp. 36ff.) suggests that we may be able to infer something of the phonology of 'Minoan' from the nature of Linear B. He notices that almost all the complex syllables that have their own graphs are either of the form CwV or of the form CjV. (Graphs conventionally transcribed in the latter way, e.g. ⟨tja⟩, may have been used to write pairs of syllables, so that the single graph ⟨tja⟩, for instance, would have been an alternative to the sequence ⟨ti-ja⟩ for /tia/; it is not clear whether Mycenaean Greek phonology contained clusters of consonant + /j/.) The exception to this generalization is ⟨pte⟩; but it is known that Greek /pt/ often developed from an earlier /pj/, so it is possible that ⟨pte⟩ might originally have had the value /pje/. Palmer also argues that a good guess for the pronunciation of the Mycenaean phoneme conventionally transcribed /z/ would have been a palatalized velar, say [kʲ]. He then suggests that much of what seems puzzling in the Linear B system would fall into place if we suppose that the unknown Minoan language was one in which the important manner-distinctions among consonants involved secondary articulations of palatalization and lip-rounding, rather than voice and aspiration. That is, Minoan would have been a language in which each plain consonant, for instance /t/, contrasted with a palatalized counterpart /tʲ/ and with a labialized counterpart /tʷ/ – whereas voicing and aspiration either did not occur at all, or were mere subphonemic 'noise' playing no role in the language and therefore naturally ignored by its script.

Such a phonological system seems plausible in the abstract (though, since we know nothing whatever about Minoan, Palmer's suggestion can be only speculative). Certainly it would explain quite neatly why Linear B was organized as it was; it is common for people who borrow a script from speakers of another language to avoid tampering with the values of its graphs even when these are relatively unsuitable for their own language. Someone designing a syllabic script for Greek from scratch would scarcely have provided a graph for /tia/, but if a ⟨tʲa⟩ graph existed ready-made it is understandable that scribes would have used it on occasion as an alternative to ⟨ti-ja⟩ in order to transcribe /tia/. The fact that Linear B script does distinguish between voiced and voiceless among the dentals need not imply that Minoan speech included a voiced/voiceless distinction at just that place of articulation and no others (which would be linguistically rather implausible – if a voicing contrast is used at all in a language it normally runs right across the various categories of consonants). It could equally well be that Minoan had stops at two places of articulation in the coronal area – perhaps dental [t] versus retroflex [ʈ], say – and that one of these was seized on by the Greeks as sounding a little like their own voiced [d]; it is very common when scripts are borrowed for the borrowers to alter the values of some of the elements inadvertently because they interpret alien sounds in terms of their own sound-system, though (as already suggested) it is less common for people deliberately to choose to use a sign in what they know to be a novel value which happens to be relatively useful for their own language.

Whether or not Palmer's is the correct explanation, the fact at any rate remains that Linear B was a particularly 'incomplete' script with respect to the contrasts that played a role in the phonology of Mycenaean Greek. As a result, there are usually many different ways of reading any short sequence of Linear B graphs. Consider e.g. the pair ⟨pa-te⟩. This occurs in the tablets with at least two readings: /pătēr/ 'father', /păntĕs/ 'all'. Many other readings are phonologically possible: /bătʰē, pʰăntĕs, pāstēn/, etc. etc.; and probably one or two at least of the further possibilities would correspond to actual words of Mycenaean Greek. How is it that such a very incomplete system could have been usable in practice?

It may be that a system incorporating the degree of ambiguity found in Linear B would not be usable as the general-purpose tool of communication which written language became in later ages. Certainly, as far as our knowledge of it extends, Linear B was used only for very specialized bureaucratic purposes: most of the tablets are brief records concerned with such matters as inventorying goods, listing tenancies, and the like. It is probable that inscriptions of these kinds would have been read in circumstances which supplied strong contextual clues to their meaning: the reader knows that a tablet will describe tenancies if he takes it from a basket full of tenancy records.

A typical Linear B tablet is shown in Figure 13, which is the first line of tablet PY Ta722, inventorying a series of four footstools decorated in various ways. (Figure 13 shows a normalized version of the graphs corresponding to the transliteration given in Ventris and Chadwick (1956, p. 345): it is not a reproduction of the original tablet.)

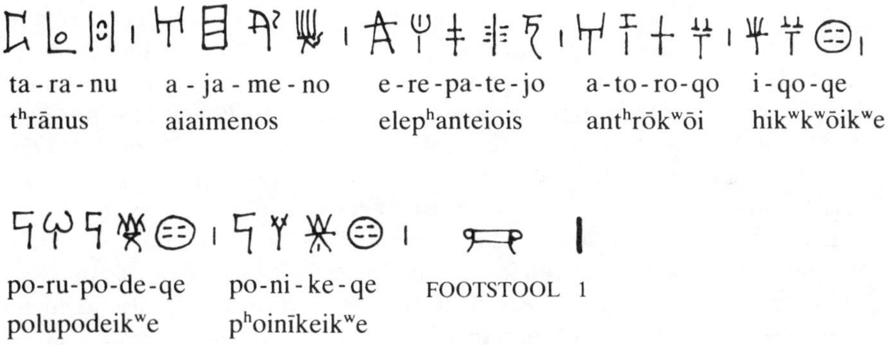

ta-ra-nu	a-ja-me-no	e-re-pa-te-jo	a-to-ro-qo	i-qo-qe
tʰrānus	aiaimenos	elepʰanteiois	antʰrōkʷōi	hikʷkʷōikʷe

po-ru-po-de-qe	po-ni-ke-qe	FOOTSTOOL 1
polupodeikʷe	pʰoinīkeikʷe	

Figure 13

In connection with Figure 13 I should explain that, as well as the graphs of the syllabary, Linear B inscriptions make a subsidiary use of symbols drawn from another class which Mycenologists call 'ideograms'; these are graphs (many of them motivated, unlike the graphs of the syllabary) standing individually for objects of the kinds inventoried by the tablets ('sheep', 'man', 'barley', 'gold', etc.) or for units of measurement comparable to our 'gallon', 'bushel', etc., and they are used, in conjunction with numeral-signs, to enable the reader to take in at a glance the general category of items described in detail in the syllabic text. Linear B 'ideograms' seem to serve the same function as the modern military habit of listing items with the head noun at the beginning of its phrase: where we write '6 cups, blue, china, tea, officers for the use of', a Mycenaean scribe would have written something like 'Blue china teacups for the use of officers: CUP 6'. It is conventional to transcribe Linear B 'ideograms' in capitals. Words are separated in Linear B script by a short vertical tick. (One word in the inscription of Figure 13, ⟨a-ja-me-no⟩, is not known independently although it is frequent in the Linear B corpus; the meaning 'inlaid' is deduced from context, but the exact pronunciation lying behind the spelling can only be conjecture.) The sentence runs in English: 'A footstool inlaid with a man and a horse and an octopus and a palm-tree in ivory: FOOTSTOOL 1'.

Given the 'ideogram' for FOOTSTOOL, it is evident that the reader of this inscription would have had little difficulty in reading ⟨ta-ra-nu⟩ as /tʰrānus/ 'footstool' rather than any of the other theoretical possibilities. Some of the other words may seem less predictable; but even here, if the function of such tablets was as a check on an inventory of objects meant to be kept in a certain place, presumably one would normally inspect the objects and then check them off against the tablets, which would greatly reduce the problems of interpreting the latter.

Nevertheless it is dangerous to assume, because Linear B provided a significantly less complete transcription of the language it was used for than do more familiar scripts, that it must have been impractical for fluent speakers of Mycenaean Greek to use it except in circumstances where context gave many clues to the contents of messages. After all, Ventris and Chadwick succeeded in reading the inscription of Figure 13, and they not only did not have the footstool to help them but were not even familiar with the language except via dialects of it that were many centuries younger. Chadwick (1958, p. 131) mentions that he and Ventris succeeded in writing postcards to one another in Linear B. A. J. B. Wace, who contributed a foreword to Ventris and Chadwick (1956), went so far as to say that 'so elaborate a system of writing cannot have been employed only for recording inventories of goods or payments of taxes . . . the Linear B script was probably also used for letters, treaties and even literary texts'.

It is not as clear to me as it seems to have been to Wace that the complexity of the system speaks for the view that Linear B actually was used for a wide range of communicative purposes. There are too many known examples of communities which possess quite sophisticated scripts while using them only for very limited purposes to make that conclusion a safe one. Where I am inclined to agree with him is in thinking that Linear B *could* potentially have been used more widely, despite its incompleteness.

Some people feel that such a highly defective script could only possibly have been used for very restricted purposes in which the physical context of written inscriptions could be relied on to resolve the ambiguities of the writing system. Indeed, there are a few scholars who do not believe that an orthography such as described by Ventris and Chadwick ever existed. I mentioned earlier that, before Ventris, it was not expected that the Linear B tablets would prove to be written in Greek, and there was considerable opposition to the Ventris–Chadwick decipherment when it was first propounded. Most of the critics were rapidly converted as fresh evidence came in, but Ernst Grumach, for instance, continued to argue against the decipherment until his death (cf. Grumach 1976).

There are two reasons why the 'incompleteness' of the system leads to doubt about the validity of the decipherment. One is that the ambiguity of each graph may appear to give Ventris too many jokers to play with. If, within his system, any short sequence of Linear B graphs has many alternative readings as phonologically-possible sequences of Greek sounds, then the fact that many Linear B sequences can be identified with actual Greek words, and even with words that are appropriate to their context, may seem to prove little – one might expect as much to happen purely by chance if values were assigned to the graphs at random.

The answer to this objection is that what could easily happen by chance in a few cases becomes overwhelmingly improbable as the number of cases increases: there is no great cause for surprise if the first two tosses of a dice are both sixes, but if six comes up fifty times in a series of a hundred tosses then it is almost sure that the dice is weighted. Experts in the field of Greek philology do not necessarily have a well-developed feeling for statistical issues such as this – normally, there is little reason why they should; and they are used to thinking of Greek as a language written in an alphabetic script which was not only the earliest but, in its eventual 'Byzantine' form, one of the subtlest of all alphabetic systems, so that the suggestion that Greek was once written in an exceptionally crude (as well as quite different) system perhaps seems almost scandalous. However, the strength of the objective evidence in favour of the Ventris–Chadwick decipherment has been sufficient to convince the great majority of the scholars concerned.

But it is clear that those who have refused to accept the Ventris–Chadwick decipherment have done so also because they find it implausible that any culture would use such a defective script. As an objection to the validity of the decipherment, this is adequately rebutted by pointing out that the known examples of the script are in fact restricted to just the genres of inscription with respect to which external context compensates for internal ambiguity. But the point raises an interesting general issue: how incomplete can a writing system be before it ceases to be conveniently usable as a general-purpose medium of communication?

Such questions are very difficult to answer; they can only be answered by empirical research which would need to be caried out on a rather large scale. In the case of Linear B, one might try training a community of speakers of some language phonologically comparable to Mycenaean Greek to read and write it using the graphs and conventions of Linear B; but there is little doubt that the subjects would find the system problematic at first simply because of its unfamiliarity – in order to be a fair test the experiment might need to be prolonged to the point at which it would seriously interfere with the subjects' normal lives.

Presumably, since completeness of a script is a gradient affair, the practical inconvenience that derives from incompleteness also varies smoothly, so that there will not be any threshold level of incompleteness below which a script suddenly becomes unusable. My guess, for what it is worth, is that we can manage with much *less* completeness than one might naïvely suppose; readers are skilled at resolving ambiguities in a written text by reference to the rest of the text, without needing to resort to features of the external physical world within which the text is located. We shall see in the next chapter that Semitic writing, which is in widespread use for general purposes in the 20c, is strikingly incomplete by comparison to modern European orthographies (although it is less so than Linear B). It would not surprise me to find that novels could be written and read in Linear B (though perhaps the reader of a Linear B text might need to expend rather more unconscious mental effort than the reader of an alphabetically-written equivalent, just as reading handwriting is presumably harder work than reading print – we shall return to this issue in Chapter 5). Unfortunately, for the reason already given, it seems unlikely that we will ever discover whether this surmise is correct (unless Linear B or some equally incomplete script turns out in fact to have been used for general purposes).

Should my guess be right, it suggests a sobering thought. Our own writing system is inherited from the Greeks. If Mycenaean civilization had not collapsed in the −13c, and if Greece had been spared the several-centuries-long Dark Age which then ensued, perhaps the Greeks would have had little use for the Semitic alphabet when they eventually encountered it. I might now be writing this book, and you reading it, in a syllabic script derived from Linear B. The idea of an alphabetic script of just a couple of dozen graphs could have been merely a curiosity confined to areas of the Middle East less influenced than Western Europe by Greek culture.

5 Consonantal writing

We saw in Chapter 3 that some scholars believe in a monogenetic theory of the history of writing, according to which all scripts used anywhere in the world derive from a single common ancestor. I suggested that this theory was unlikely to be true. However, if we restrict our vision to the segmental sub-type of phonographic writing, rather than considering writing as a general phenomenon, then a monogenetic theory becomes very probable. Most, and probably all, 'alphabetic' scripts derive from a single ancestor: the Semitic alphabet, created sometime in the −2nd millennium. (The possible exceptions are the Indian family of alphabets; see Diringer 1968, pp. 261–3.)

The term 'Semitic' refers to one of the branches of the larger 'Hamito-Semitic' or 'Afro-Asiatic' family of languages, whose representatives are found from the Levant westwards to the Atlas and southwards as far as Nigeria, Ethiopia, and Somalia. The Semitic branch itself includes a number of individual languages, two of the best-known being Arabic and Hebrew. The script from which most or all alphabetic writing systems descend is called 'Semitic' because the main thing we know about its creators is that they spoke one or other of the Semitic languages (possibly Phoenician), and because the structure of the script was strongly influenced by peculiarities of the Semitic spoken languages for which it was used.

The most important of these structural properties is that the original version, and some modern descendants, of the script have graphs for consonants but no vowel-letters. We shall see, below, why the nature of Semitic languages makes this appropriate. Obviously, many of the alphabets which ultimately descend from the original Semitic alphabet do now have vowel-letters: our own Roman alphabet is an example. It will be convenient to reserve the term 'Semitic script' for the original Semitic alphabet, together with those of its descendants which still lack letters for vowels (of which the main ones are the modern Hebrew and Arabic scripts). Modern Hebrew script remains identical, and Arabic script very close, to their common ancestor, except for the outward shapes of the graphs (in the latter respect Hebrew and Arabic scripts have diverged greatly from their ancestral form and from each other). In this chapter we shall be examining 'Semitic script' in this sense (while the next chapter deals with the more familiar kind of alphabetic writing that does incorporate vowel-letters). But it is important to bear in mind that, applied to a form of writing, the term 'Semitic' is no more than a handy label. There is no implication that Semitic languages are all written in 'Semitic' script, or that 'Semitic' script is used to write only Semitic languages. Akkadian was a Semitic language, but (as we saw in Chapter 3) it was written in Cuneiform, which was not an alphabetic script at all. Maltese is a Semitic language written in the Roman alphabet. Conversely, Arabic script is used to write many non-Semitic languages, such as Persian (which is an Indo-European language) and, until 1928, Turkish (an Altaic language); and Hebrew script is used to write Yiddish, a dialect of German.

Diringer (1968, p. 161) suggests that the Semitic alphabet may have orig-inated as early as the second quarter of the −2nd millennium (though others have suggested later dates, even as late as −1000), somewhere in the Pales-tine/Syria region. Culturally, this was a buffer zone in the 'Fertile Crescent' between the two major civilizations of Mesopotamia (where Cuneiform writing was used) and Egypt, which used Hieroglyphic script. Egyptian Hieroglyphic, which came into existence a little after Sumerian script and is thought probably to have been invented under the influence of the latter, developed as a mainly but not wholly phonographic system, rather similar in terms of structure (though not in the shape of its graphs) to the Akkadian version of Cuneiform.

Although many Hieroglyphic graphs stood for groups of sounds, some of them stood for single consonants, and in these cases the consonantal value of the graph was the first sound of the name of the thing pictured. (Many Hieroglyphic graphs remained clearly iconic throughout the history of Egyp-tian civilization, although cursive, non-iconic versions of the script – 'Hieratic' and 'Demotic' – were developed for less formal purposes.) It is thought likely that the inventors of the Semitic script took the idea of writing, and the 'acrophonic' principle of representing sounds by pictures of things whose names began with the sound in question, from the Egyptians (with whom there were many cultural contacts). However, the Semitic alphabet itself was clearly an independent creation: many of the graph-shapes are not similar to any Hieroglyphic graphs, and (more important) the relationships between object pictured and graph-value hold for Semitic languages but not for Egyp-tian. In some cases the inventors of the Semitic script seem to have taken over Hieroglyphic graphs but changed their values to make them appropriate for their own language. Thus the Hieroglyphic sign ∿∿∿, representing the rippled appearance of water, stood for /n/, the first sound of the Egyptian word for 'water'; the Semitic letter ⟨m⟩ (see Figure 14 below) appears to be an abbreviated version of that graph, used by the Semites for /m/ because their own word for 'water' began with that sound.

One might wonder how plausible it is to suppose that a community acquainted with an established form of phonographic writing should have created a wholly new set of graph/sound correspondences in this way – would it not have been simpler just to take those Hieroglyphic graphs which could be used to write Semitic speech and use them with their values unchanged? As we shall see, when the Greeks borrowed writing from the Semites this is just what happened. But it is rash to project our own sophisticated ideas about the conventionality of symbols into the minds of men at the dawn of civilization. It seems very possible that when the Semites first encountered writing they saw the acrophonic principle as part of its essence: writing might at first have *meant* drawing things to symbolize their initial sounds, so that a picture of water could represent no sound other than /m/ for people who called water /majim/.

Figure 14 shows, in the left-hand column, an early form of the 22 letters of the Semitic alphabet, and in the next column their forms in the modern Hebrew alphabet as a representative of contemporary Semitic script.[1] (The forms in the third column are word-final allographs of certain letters, to be discussed below.) The fourth column gives the Hebrew names of the letters, and the fifth column the phonetic value of the letters. The last column gives the Hebrew form of the Semitic word, with gloss, from which the letter-shape was derived. (In most cases the letter-name differs in details of vocalism from the word which gave rise to the letter; this is explained by Diringer (1968, p. 169) as due to borrowing of letter-names from one Semitic language to another in which the Proto-Semitic vowels had developed differently.) Sequences of letters were written right to left, and this continues to be the direction of writing in the modern Hebrew and Arabic scripts.

Certain points about the phonetic transcription need explanation. I use the symbols /ṭ ç q/ as convenient non-IPA symbols for what were probably pharyngalized stops properly transcribed /tˤ sˤ kˤ/, i.e. stops made with the root of the tongue retracted and lowered towards the [ɒ] position. The letter šīn represents two contrasting phonemes, for which one can quote minimal pairs such as Hebrew /śārā/ 'soak' v. /šārā/ 'struggle'. In modern Hebrew the contrast between /ś/ and /s/ (written with sāmek) has been lost, and in Arabic the contrast between /ś/ and /s/ has been lost. It is not possible to be sure how these three phonemes were pronounced when the alphabet was created, or why two of them were assigned the single letter šīn; the transcriptions /s š ś/ are therefore an arbitrary expedient. The symbols /ħ ʕ/ represent their IPA values of voiceless pharyngal fricative and pharyngal approximant respectively; other consonant-symbols are familiar.

It should be said that some of the experts are unwilling to admit that the Semitic letters began as pictures which derived their values acrophonically. At most, they suggest, the letters were invented as abstract shapes but then had names assigned by reference to vague similarities to real objects (cf. Diringer 1968, p. 168; Gelb 1952, pp. 140–1). According to these scholars, the Semites did not invent the letter ⟨ʔ⟩ by thinking of a picturable object (the ox) whose name began with /ʔ/ and drawing a stylized picture of it; rather, they designed the letter at random and assigned it the value /ʔ/ arbitrarily, but then called it 'ox' as a name beginning with the right sound which they found mnemonically satisfying because they noticed a loose similarity between their arbitrary letter-shape and the appearance of an ox. According to Gelb, 'None of the Semitic signs was drawn in a form which would immediately

			Name	Value	Word	
✗	א		ʔālep	ʔ	ʔelep	'ox'
⌐	ב		bēt	b	bajit	'house'
∧	ג		gīmel	g	gāmāl	'camel'
△	ד		dālet	d	delet	'door'
⅃	ה		hē	h	?	
Y	ו		wāw	w	wāw	'hook'
I	ז		zajin	z	zajin	'weapon'
⌶	ח		ḥēt	ḥ	?	
⊕	ט		ṭēt	ṭ	?	
⌐	י		jōd	j	jād	'hand'
⅄	כ	ך	kāp	k	kap	'cupped hand'
∟	ל		lāmed	l	lāmad	'to study'
⌐	מ	ם	mēm	m	majim	'water'
⅂	נ	ן	nūn	n	ʔnūn	'fish'
≢	ס		sāmek	s	ʔsāmak	'fulcrum'
o	ע		ʕajin	ʕ	ʕajin	'eye'
⊃	פ	ף	pē	p	pe	'mouth'
Γ	צ	ץ	çādē	ç	?	
Φ	ק		qōp	q	qōp	'ape'
⅂	ר		rēś	r	rōś	'head'
W	שׁ		šīn	ṡ,ś	śēn	'tooth'
＋	ת		tāw	t	tāw	'mark'

Figure 14

betray its pictorial character'. This theory presumably implies that the Egyptian contribution to the birth of Semitic script amounted to nothing more than the mere concept of recording speech graphically, and accordingly the theory may be attractive to people who would like for cultural reasons to magnify the originality of the Semitic achievement. I find it implausible.

Gelb's remark just quoted seems not to be to the point: the fact that a script has been *created* by drawing pictures of objects is not a reason for *maintaining* its motivated character, so the fact that the earliest known Semitic graphs are not obviously pictorial does not argue against their having originally been motivated. In Egypt the Hieroglyphic script retained a detailed pictorial quality for aesthetic, cultural reasons, but the Hieratic and Demotic alternatives losi all iconicity. The first Semitic scribes may well have valued speed and convenience over monumental appearance in their writing system, in which case they would rapidly have stripped down their graphs to the minimum needed for distinctiveness and distorted their shapes for ease of writing.

Perhaps more important, Gelb seems unimaginative in denying that some of the early Semitic letters have any iconic value. Thus he singles out gīmel and qōp as names which do not in any obvious way fit their graphs. Yet anyone asked to pick out the most distinctive visual feature of the camel would surely name the hump – the shape of gīmel is easily seen as a stylized camel's hump; and no-one familiar with the look of heavy simian eyebrows ought, surely, to find it difficult to see qōp as a full-face view of an ape?

It is true that not all the letter-names can easily be explained. Sometimes the problems are due to differences of culture; the triangle seems an odd shape for 'door' until it is appreciated that the creators of the script are likely to have lived in tents with triangular door-flaps. The shape of lāmed may represent that early audio-visual aid, the cane. The graph nūn does not look much like a fish, but Gelb (1952, p. 140) points out that in one Semitic language, Ethiopic, it is called /noħāś/ 'snake'. The letter-shape is quite similar to the conventional Hieroglyphic representation of a snake, **ᒡ** (which stood in Egyptian for a sibilant consonant); it is easy to imagine that the Semites borrowed the graph-shape and called it /noħāś/, using it for /n/, and later rechristened it nūn by analogy with the CVC shape of the preceding letter-name mēm, rather as the Americans have rechristened the Roman letter Z 'zee' by analogy with the names of B, C, etc. (In Arabic most of the letters have been rechristened in a similar fashion.) Other letter-shapes and names are more mysterious, though tentative explanations have been offered for all of them (Diringer 1968, p. 169). A high enough proportion of the letters are transparently iconic to make the explanation in terms of acrophony, to my mind, quite cogent.

(What has *not* been explained is the ordering of the letters of the Semitic alphabet. This has been fixed from the beginning, and – allowing for certain losses of letters and addition of new letters – is the order of our Roman alphabet today; but no phonetic logic is apparent in it, and there are no theories about how it was originally settled upon – see Jensen 1970, p. 282.)

Whether or not the creators of the Semitic alphabet were influenced by Egyptian writing, they were unquestionably innovators in producing a script in which individual graphs consistently stand for single phonemes, and in which – if we overlook the problem about /ś/ and /š/ – each phoneme of the category recorded by the script has one unambiguous graph. (Several scholars, including Antoine Meillet and, more recently, I. J. Gelb (1952,

1958), have argued that Semitic script should be called syllabic rather than segmental, on the ground that a single Semitic letter stood for syllables such as /ba be bi bo bu/.[2] But the vowel-less Semitic script is very different from a true syllabic script such as Linear B, in which the vowel of a syllable is as relevant as the consonant in determining which graph will be used to write the syllable. In early Semitic writing only the consonants of a spoken form were relevant to its orthography, so this script is not a syllabic script but a segmental script which ignores vowel segments.) The assumption that the Semites created their graphs by the acrophonic principle explains why the script provides graphs only for consonants (which Diringer (1968, p. 165), who does not make this assumption, treats as inexplicable). The fact is that all words in Semitic languages begin with consonants, so that if letters are invented acrophonically there is no possibility of getting letters for vowels.

Words which we might hear as beginning with a vowel are perceived by Semitic speakers as beginning with a glottal stop. In English a word like *ever* will often be pronounced with a marked initial glottal stop, [ʔɛvə]; but we do not normally treat this as a phoneme of Engish, partly because it will often be missing even at the beginning of a word (*for ever* is more likely to be pronounced [fərɛvə] than [fəʔɛvə], and partly because in standard English its distribution is extremely limited: it essentially occurs only at the beginning of words. In a Semitic language such as Hebrew, the glottal stop is as compulsory a feature of a word in which it occurs as any other consonant; a word beginning with a glottal stop will not lose it if a prefix is added (/w/ 'and' + /ʔādām/ 'a man' gives /wəʔādām/ 'and a man', not */wādām/), and the glottal stop resembles other consonants in occurring elsewhere in roots than initially (/jāʔab/ 'long for' contrasts for example with /jāhab/ 'give' or /jāçab/ 'stand').

While the acrophonic principle, together with the lack of initial vowels in Semitic words, may explain why the Semitic alphabet was not originally equipped with vowel-letters, in order to understand why such an alphabet functioned satisfactorily we need to examine the structure of the spoken languages for which the alphabet has been used. The truth is that vowel-letters are not as useful when writing a Semitic language as they are when writing Indo-European languages.

In order to investigate the detailed workings of Semitic script we must choose one particular Semitic language from which to draw our illustrations. I do not want to give the reader of this book the impression that the various types of script, other than the familiar Roman alphabet, which are discussed within its pages are of mainly antiquarian interest. Vowel-less Semitic writing is widely used in the 20c world, being the normal form of writing in many nations including some of the wealthiest. It is tempting, therefore, to choose modern Arabic or modern Hebrew to exemplify the system.

With some reluctance I have decided that neither of these languages provides ideal examples for our purpose. To choose modern Hebrew would require us to deal with many complexities that have nothing to do with the special characteristics of Semitic writing. Hebrew, having become extinct as a living spoken language early in the Christian Era, was artificially revived during the last hundred years. Modern Israeli Hebrew is phonetically simpler than Biblical Hebrew (it has fewer sounds), but phonologically it is arguably more complex, and it is certainly much more complex in terms of the relationship between spoken sounds and orthography (since it has retained Biblical orthography virtually unchanged despite major changes in the spoken language). It would be unfortunate to burden the reader with the task of unravelling the many complications in modern Hebrew orthography which can be explained only with respect to the Biblical language. To opt for Arabic, on the other hand, would introduce an unnecessary complication in that the Arabic alphabet is somewhat different in its structure from the original Semitic alphabet already discussed; and in another respect this choice would actually make the exposition too simple – the vowel system of Literary Arabic is so exceptionally restricted that a discussion of how it is represented in Arabic script would be rather brief. (On the other hand colloquial dialects of Arabic, which sometimes have more complex vowel systems, are not normally written.)

I have therefore chosen to discuss Biblical Hebrew, as a compromise between these countervailing considerations. By 'Biblical Hebrew' I refer to the pronunciation of written Hebrew as fixed about +900 by the 'Masoretic' editors of the Old Testament. Biblical Hebrew in this sense represents an attempt to analyse and record the pronunciation of spoken Hebrew as it was before it became extinct; however, since the Old Testament was composed over a period of about a thousand years during which time, like any living language, Hebrew undoubtedly changed greatly, Biblical Hebrew has the advantage for our purposes of being a more consistent system than its antecedent. (On the status of Biblical Hebrew as a language see Ullendorff 1971.)

Although Biblical Hebrew is in a sense a somewhat artificial language, let me stress that there is nothing artificial or unrealistic about the general kind of writing to be discussed below. As a written language this language is in daily use as the standard language of Israel, though Israeli pronunciation is different from the pronunciation we shall examine. (There are some differences of grammar and vocabulary also – cf. Rosén 1977, Rabin 1977; but these are irrelevant to a consideration of how the orthography works.) The orthographic principles of written Arabic are fundamentally the same as those of Hebrew, although different in detail. Biblical Hebrew – which from now on I shall call simply 'Hebrew' – happens to offer a pedagogically-convenient example of a type of writing which is one of the most significant types in use in the late-20c world.

The set of Hebrew consonant phonemes corresponds to the set of graphemes in the Semitic alphabet as shown in Figure 14, except for the phonemic distinction between /š/ and /ś/ which is neutralized in the grapheme ⟨š⟩. Five of the graphemes, ⟨k m n p ç⟩, have allographs (shown in column 3 of Figure 14), but there is no phonological significance in these: they are simply special written forms used at the end of a word. (These allographs might be compared to the swash letters found in some of our italic fonts, except that their use is compulsory.)

There are some important allophonic variations among certain of the consonant phonemes.

In the first place, the plain (i.e. non-pharyngalized) stop consonants /p t k b d g/ are represented by fricative allophones [f θ x v ð ɣ] when they occur after a vowel. This distinction between stop and fricative, typically contrastive in European languages, is for Biblical Hebrew purely allophonic, and I shall not mark it in my transcriptions. The fact that the script ignores this distinction does not imply subtle phonological analysis by its inventors: when the Semitic alphabet was created the fricative allophones had not yet developed in the spoken language. (In *modern* spoken Hebrew some of these fricative sounds have been lost, but those that remain are no longer mere allophones of stops; Rosén (1977, p. 65) argues that 'the spirant: stop opposition may well be one of the most heavily loaded in Israeli Hebrew'. This is one reason why, for simplicity of exposition, it is preferable to avoid discussing Israeli pronunciation.)

All consonants other than /ʔ h ħ ʕ r/ (and the fricative allophones just discussed) occur geminated as well as single. Again the geminated v. single contrast is probably allophonic; cutting through some complications, we may state as a rough approximation that if a consonant occurs between two vowels of which the former is short and unstressed, then it will be geminated, and otherwise it will be single: e.g. [kammón] 'cumin' v. [kāmús] 'hidden', [kéleb] 'dog'. Hebrew script writes geminated and single consonants alike with single letters. (However, my transcriptions will distinguish them.)

The vowels of Hebrew are as follows:

Reduced	Short	Long	Diphthongs
i u	ī ū	īa ūa
ĕ ə ŏ	e o	ē ō	ēa ōa
ă	a	ā	

By no means all of these sounds are independent phonemes.

Most easily disposed of are the diphthongs: these are allophones of the corresponding pure long vowels, and replace the latter automatically when the vowels occur stressed before the consonants /ħ h ʕ/. Thus [nóaħ] 'Noah' is phonemically /nōħ/. (Hebraists commonly analyse the language as containing also a series of diphthongs in -i, e.g. /ai ūi/; these are treated by Hebrew orthography as sequences of pure vowel + consonant /j/, and since this analysis seems linguistically reasonable we shall not discuss them further.)

The 'reduced' vowels (of which [ĕ ă ŏ] are found almost exclusively after the consonants /ʔ h ħ ʕ/, and [ə] after other consonants) occur in two circumstances: a reduced vowel is inserted epenthetically to break up consonant clusters which would otherwise be produced when a word is given a consonantal prefix such as /b/ 'in' or /l/ 'to' (e.g. [dīr] 'a stable', [bədīr] 'in a stable'); and reduced vowels replace other (long or short) vowels when these occur in certain positions in a word relative to the stressed syllable, which in Hebrew is usually the last syllable of the word. For instance, /dābár/ 'word' with the plural suffix /-īm/ becomes [dəbārím] 'words', because the first syllable of the root is now two syllables away from the stress; likewise /ḥākám/ 'a sage' v. [ḥākāmím] 'sages'. Within strict phoneme theory the Hebrew reduced vowels, like English shwa, might have to be treated as independent phonemes (for one thing because each of them neutralizes the oppositions between several of the full vowels and therefore cannot be identified with any one of them), but the phonetic distinction between reduced and full (short or long) vowels in Hebrew is never, or scarcely ever, contrastive. (Hebrew has many such stress-dependent alternations between vowels, and this is one reason why an orthography including vowels is relatively unattractive for Hebrew: few word-stems would retain a constant orthographic shape.)

This leaves the five short and five long vowels. Of these, the five long vowels and the short vowel /a/ all certainly contrast with one another, and it is easy to find examples to demonstrate contrast for any pair of them (e.g. /gāl/ 'rejoice' v. /gal/ 'a wave' v. /gōl/ 'a marble', etc.). The status of the other four short vowels is less clear. There are strong restrictions on their distribution and on that of the corresponding long vowels (for instance short vowels other than /a/ cannot occur in monosyllables), and it is almost possible to pair off the short vowels [i e o u] with the long vowels [ī ē ō ū] as allophones of four vowel phonemes. In fact minimal pairs can be found, e.g. [mīśōr] 'a plateau' v. [miśśōr] 'from an ox' (the possibility of locating the phonemic contrast in the consonant, by treating geminate and single consonants as distinct phonemes, seems to me less attractive than distinguishing long and short vowel phonemes, though it has been done by some linguists). However, such cases are somewhat rare and freakish, and there are many cases where V̆CC and V̄C are interchangeable (e.g. [giggīt], [gīgīt], alternative forms for 'tub'). It seems that we must recognize all ten short and long vowels as phonemes, but the 'functional yield' of the short/long opposition is very low except in the case of the pair /a ā/.[3]

The most important fact about the vowels of Hebrew and other Semitic languages, and the chief reason why it is less useful to mark them in writing than it is in Indo-European languages, is that to a large extent the linguistic contrasts realized by vowels are grammatical rather than lexical. This means that even if the contrasts are not recorded in writing they can to a very large extent be determined from context, and it also means that they tend to be less crucial for practical purposes of communication.

A high proportion of the vocabulary of a Semitic language such as Hebrew consists of words derived from a root (having a verbal or adjectival meaning) which is made up purely of consonants (usually three consonants), between which different patterns of vowels, representing different grammatical inflexions, are interdigitated; there may also be prefixes or suffixes.

Thus the root √ktb stands for the notion of writing, and the root √drś for preaching. A given pattern of vowels together with prefixes and/or suffixes will conjugate either root in the same way:

kātab 'he wrote'	dāraś 'he preached'
kātabtī 'I wrote'	dāraśtī 'I preached'
kātəbū 'they wrote'	dārəśu 'they preached'

etc.

jiktōb 'he will write'	jidrōś 'he will preach'
ʔektōb 'I shall write'	ʔedrōś 'I shall preach'

etc.

kətōb 'write!'	dərōś 'preach!'
kōtēb 'writing'	dōrēś 'preaching'
kātūb 'being written'	dārūś 'being preached'

etc. etc.

When we turn from inflexional to derivational morphology we find that, as in English, there are differences between roots with respect to which patterns of derivation they permit and how a given pattern of derivation affects their meaning. Thus we have e.g. /katbān/ 'a scribe' parallel in meaning to /darśān/ 'a preacher', but in other cases the parallel is inexact (e.g. the semantic relations of /kətāb/ 'a writing-system, script' and /dərāś/ 'a sermon' to their respective roots 'write' and 'preach' are not identical), and in other cases again the two roots take different derivations (we have /kətōbet/ 'an inscription', /kətubbā/ 'a marriage contract', etc., but no */dərōśet/, */dəruśśā/, and conversely there is /dərāśā/ 'homily', /midrāśī/ 'homiletical' but no */kətābā/, */miktābī/). Compare the fact that, in English, the semantic relationship between *poetry* and *poet* is different from that between *peasantry* and *peasant* or *infantry* and *infant*, and there are no words *smithry*, *parsonry*.

Given the limited role of vowels as distinctive elements in Semitic languages (and given that many inflected and derived forms include affixes containing consonants), a script which indicates only consonants is not unreasonably ambiguous in practice. If we were told in English that a verb with the consonants /l . . .k/ fits into the context *Did the dog ____ the bone?*, it would be hard to know whether *lick* or *like* was intended; but if we were told that the verb is *lick* and the only question is what form of the verb is appropriate, it is easy to choose *lick* rather than *licking* or *licked*. A better analogy might be with a more inflected language such as French. Given a French sentence with all the inflexions removed, say:

Ecouter, Israël, moi être l'Eternel ton Dieu, qui toi avoir tirer du pays d'Egypte

it is not hard to see that this must mean:

Ecoute, Israël, je suis l'Eternel ton Dieu, qui t'ai tiré du pays d'Egypte.

Accordingly, in the early days of Hebrew as a written language, no indication whatever was given of vowels; the orthographies of some Semitic languages, e.g. Phoenician, never throughout their history developed any method of giving information about vowels.

However, there are real disadvantages even for a Semitic language if vowels are completely ignored in writing. Distinctions such as those between 'he wrote' and 'they wrote', or 'he wrote' and 'he is writing', are admittedly less crucial for communication than the differences between one lexical item and another, but they are not wholly trivial. Furthermore, cases where distinct lexical items differ only in vocalism are by no means absent; many nouns, in particular, are formed independently of the system of three-consonant roots, and possess intrinsic vowels (and furthermore when one of the consonants in a triliteral root is /w/ or /j/ it frequently becomes a vowel in inflected forms). Thus we can find sets of Hebrew words such as /dīr/ 'a stable' v. /dar/ 'mother-of-pearl' v. /dōr/ 'generation' v. /dūr/ 'ruin' v. /dār/ 'to dwell'.

This problem was solved, for some Semitic languages, by making certain consonant-letters do double duty and serve also to indicate vowels. Letters functioning in this way are called *matres lectionis*, 'mothers of reading'.

The use of *matres* for Hebrew evolved gradually as Biblical texts were written down by many different scribes, so that it is possible to find exceptions to almost any statement one makes on the subject. Futhermore, because of the status of the written Old Testament in the life of contemporary Israel, many such individual exceptions have become entrenched in current orthographic usage. Nevertheless, it is possible to state rules which are valid for the great majority of words.

Rule 1: Short (and reduced) vowels are ignored, with one exception to be discussed below.

Rule 2: Among the long vowels, /ī ū/ are obligatorily written ⟨j w⟩ respectively.

Rule 3: The vowels /ē ō/ can optionally be written ⟨j w⟩ respectively.

Thus the words /dīr dar dōr dūr dār/ listed above will be spelled: ⟨djr⟩; ⟨dr⟩; ⟨dwr⟩ or ⟨dr⟩; ⟨dwr⟩; ⟨dr⟩.

These rules, clearly, are motivated by the phonetic similarity of approximants /j w/ to close front spread and back rounded vowels. Indeed, Hebrew scribes may conceivably have heard these vowels as diphthongal, [ɪj ej ɔw ow]. Note that the usage of ⟨j w⟩ as *matres* was phonetic rather than phonemic. The distinction between e.g. /ī/ and /ē/ was clearly contrastive, but the same *mater* had to do duty for both. On the other hand, the distinction between /ī/ and /i/ was at most marginally phonemic, but /ī/ was written as ⟨j⟩ while /i/ was ignored, perhaps because it was a lax, [ɪ]-like vowel lacking a timbre reminiscent of [j].

Rule 4: Because the consonant /h/ scarcely ever or never occurs word-finally in Hebrew (cf. Lambdin 1973, p. xxv n.), it is available for unambiguous use as a *mater* in that position, and it is used to indicate the long vowel not indicated by ⟨j⟩ or ⟨w⟩, namely /ā/. Thus e.g. /malkā/ 'queen' is ⟨mlkh⟩.

The writing of word-final /ā/ as ⟨h⟩ is obligatory, as a special case of a further rule:

Rule 5: Word-final vowels must be indicated by a *mater*.

Rule 5 overides Rule 1; one of the short vowels, /e/, does occur word-finally, and a word like /šāde/ 'field' is written ⟨šdh⟩, not *⟨šd⟩. Rule 5 has a clear rationale. Provided one knows that some vowel occurs in a given position, familiarity with the morphological patterns of Hebrew will commonly tell one which vowel it is; and the presence of a consonant-letter will normally reveal the presence of a following vowel, since consonant-clustering is very limited in Hebrew. However, it is quite usual for a word to *end* with a consonant, so without Rule 5 the reader could overlook an entire syllable (such as the common feminine suffix /-ā/ in the word for 'queen').

Internally in a word, /ē ō/ are sometimes written and sometimes not: e.g. /lōṭ/ 'wrapper' can be ⟨lwṭ⟩ or ⟨lṭ⟩, /ḥēq/ 'lap' can be ⟨ḥjq⟩ or ⟨ḥq⟩; but there are conventions settling the matter for particular vocabulary items or particular inflexional patterns: thus /šēm/ 'name' is always ⟨šm⟩ rather than *⟨šjm⟩, and the -ō-ē- vowel-pattern which marks the active participle is regularly written with ⟨w⟩ for /ō/ but with /ē/ unmarked. The vowels /ī ū/ are always written, irrespective of their position in the word; /ā/ cannot be written except when word-final.

A further letter, ⟨ʔ⟩, is used in a way that makes it resemble a *mater* although historically it was not one. At an early stage in the development of Hebrew as a spoken language, word-final glottal stops were dropped: /lōʔ/ 'not', /nābīʔ/ 'prophet', /dūdāʔ/ 'basket' came to be pronounced /lō/, /nābī/, /dūdā/. However, the glottal stop is still 'underlyingly' present in such words if they can take a suffix beginning with a vowel (such as the masculine plural suffix /-īm/), since in this case the glottal stop (not being word-final) is retained in the pronunciation: /nəbīʔīm/, /dūdāʔīm/. (Compare /nəbī, nabīʔīm/ with /nōçrī/ 'Nazarene, Christian', plural /nōçrīm/, which never had a glottal stop in its pronunciation.) Partly for this morphophonemic reason and partly because of the conservatism of Hebrew orthography, ⟨ʔ⟩ continued to be written in words from which it had been dropped in speech: 'prophet' and 'basket' are written ⟨nbjʔ⟩, ⟨dwdʔ⟩, and 'not' is written ⟨lʔ⟩ even though the glottal stop is never pronounced in this word since it takes no suffixes. (Compare the many word-final consonants in written French which in modern spoken French are pronounced only in liaison or not at all.)

The system of *matres* resolves some graphic ambiguities only at the cost of introducing others. The use of ⟨j⟩ as a *mater* enables e.g. /ʕīr/ 'city' to be distinguished from /ʕār/ 'enemy', but creates the new possibility of confusing /ʕīr/ with /ʕajir/ 'young ass'. On balance so-called *plene* writing – writing with *matres* – is less phonologically ambiguous than writing without *matres*, but plenty of ambiguity remains.

Nevertheless, users of Hebrew script have never felt a need to adopt a more complete phonographic system for ordinary purposes. For certain extraordinary purposes – originally, for preserving the language of the Bible itself as accurately as possible – they have a system of 'pointing' the consonantal script, that is of supplementing it with tiny dots and dashes below, above, and within the consonant-letters, to indicate those aspects of the pronunciation which are left vague by the consonantal orthography. This system gives a very precise indication of pronunciation, extending even to matters such as primary and secondary stress, which is phonologically determined in Hebrew. (The pointing system currently used was evolved in the +9th and +10th centuries, as part of the process by which the Masoretes defined and preserved Biblical Hebrew pronunciation.)

But, apart from the Bible, the only written materials that are normally pointed in modern Israel are reading-books for young children (who are not yet familiar enough with the structure of the language to identify words from the clues given by unpointed consonantal script), and, interestingly, poetry. In poetry words are put together in creative, unexpected ways, so that familiarity with the usual patterns of the language apparently does not always suffice to allow the Hebrew reader to identify words in a poem conveniently from the consonantal script alone. (Likewise, James Barr remarks (1976, pp. 81–2) that the Hebrew equivalent of a nonsense-text such as Lewis Carroll's *'Twas brillig, and the slithy toves* . . . would have to be pointed. An English reader encountering a word like ⟨brillig⟩ or ⟨slithy⟩ knows quite certainly that it is not English, but a Hebrew reader faced with unpointed transcriptions of Hebrew nonsense-words would feel puzzled and unsure of what was being written.)

Ordinary handwritten or printed Hebrew prose contains exclusively the consonantal script, with vowels indicated only by *matres*. The reader identifies the words using the information supplied by the consonant letters, by his understanding of the subject-matter (which makes some words more probable than others in a given context), and by his knowledge of the characteristic morphological and syntactic patterns of the language, which impose strong constraints on the possible distribution of vowels. (Barr (1976, pp. 89–90) points out that the reader's need to recognize word-patterns was allowed for by the practice of leaving spaces between words from a very early period, while in European orthographies word-spacing only became normal about +1000 (Cohen 1958, p. 423). Biblical Hebrew orthography even uses a hyphen to mark cases where 'phonological words', i.e. the domains relevant for application of the stress rules, comprise more than one word in the morphological sense.)

In order to give the reader a sense of how far in practice the vowel-less nature of the script creates difficulties for the reader of Hebrew, I shall illustrate the problems of interpretation posed by ten words chosen at random from a passage of modern written Hebrew (I selected the penultimate word in each of ten successive lines from an advertisement for a dictionary).

Notice that one can in principle distinguish two tasks that a reader might set himself: 1, to work out which of the various words of the language a given sequence of letters stands for; 2, to work out what vowels should be understood as occurring between the consonants represented by the letters on the page. Normally a reader's main aim will presumably be 1, that is to 'read for meaning'. Some psychologists have propounded theories of reading which would imply that the Hebrew reader must achieve 2 as a necessary precondition for achieving 1, but this is highly controversial and the balance of evidence seems to be against it (Downing and Leong 1982, pp. 160–73). One might alternatively suppose that, if a reader knows a given word through reading rather than through having heard it spoken, then, in order to understand a passage containing the word, all that matters is that he works out that the letters he is seeing are intended to represent that word rather than any other – whether he knows every detail of its vocalism would be irrelevant for comprehension. If that is right, then my discussion of the clues available to the reader concerning vowels no doubt exaggerates the size of the problems facing the reader in practice. (I should add that the contemporary Israeli reader will in any case convert the written words not into the pronunciations discussed below but into the modern Hebrew pronunciations; however, the general principles illustrated by my examples are unaffected.)

For each sample word I begin by transliterating its written form.

1 ⟨nwš?jm⟩ The letters ⟨-jm⟩ at the end of a word will almost always stand for the masculine plural suffix /-īm/. Although /n/ occurs in some prefixes, /w/ is very rare as the first consonant of a triliteral root; therefore ⟨w⟩ is likely to be a *mater*. The only stem spelled ⟨nwš?⟩ is /nōśē/ 'topic', active participle of the root √nš? 'to lift', so the word is /nōśə?īm/ 'topics'.

2 ⟨hw?⟩ This is /hū/ 'he', so common a word that no problems of recognition arise.

3 ⟨hmlwn⟩ In a word of several letters beginning with ⟨h⟩ the probability is high that, as here, ⟨h⟩ represents the definite-article prefix /ha-/. (If several words together begin with ⟨h⟩ this interpretation is virtually certain, since Hebrew adds the prefix to each element of a definite nounphrase, i.e. 'this good man' becomes in Hebrew 'the-man the-good the-this'.) In this case the correct reading is /hammillōn/ 'the dictionary', which in context is obvious enough (the succeeding words translate as ' . . . contains 30,000 entries in alphabetical order'); out of context ⟨hmlwn⟩ could equally well read /hammālōn/ 'the hotel', or /hammēlōn/ 'the melon'.

4 ⟨mqjp⟩ This is /maqqīp/ 'circle', derived from the root √mqp 'concave'. Commonly ⟨m-⟩ is a prefix, but it cannot be taken as such here because there is no root *√qjp or *√qp.

5 ⟨hpʕljm⟩ Again ⟨-jm⟩ shows that we are dealing with a noun or adjective plural, so ⟨h-⟩ is likely to be the definite article. √pʕl is a frequent root meaning 'do'. The only noun or adjective stem derived from it which requires no further letters is /pōʕal/ 'deed'. (The root also gives e.g. /pāʕīl/ 'active', but this requires a ⟨j⟩ *mater* in the second syllable; /pōʕēl/ 'worker' is an active participle, the -ō-ē- pattern of which is conventionally always written with a ⟨w⟩ *mater* for the /ō/; and so on.) Therefore word 5 is /happəʕālīm/ 'the deeds' (the vowel-changes and gemination of /p/ are automatic with these affixes).

6 ⟨lr?šj⟩ In a five-letter word some of the letters are almost sure to be

prefixes or suffixes, and ⟨l⟩ is a good candidate because it represents the common prefix /l-/ 'to'; in any case, there are restrictions on the consonants which may occur in adjacent positions in Hebrew roots, and these rule out the possibility of a root with ⟨lr . . . ⟩ in the first two positions. Final ⟨j⟩ is often a *mater* representing a suffix /-ī/ or /-ē/ (or, less commonly, a suffix diphthong). The root spelled ⟨rʔš⟩, meaning 'head', is one of the rare Hebrew words in which a word-internal /ʔ/ has been elided ('head' is /rōš/); word 6 is /lərāšē/, the pregenitive form of /lərāšīm/ 'to the heads'.

7 ⟨mṭbʕwt⟩ Just as final ⟨-jm⟩ indicates the masculine plural /-īm/, so final ⟨-wt⟩ indicates the feminine plural /-ōt/. That leaves four letters, none of which can be a *mater*; since roots usually contain at most three consonants, probably either ⟨m⟩ represents a prefix or ⟨ʕ⟩ a suffix. There is no suffix spelled ⟨ʕ⟩; but nominalizing prefixes frequently begin with /m-/, so we expect this word to be formed from the root √ṭbʕ 'to sink, to coin'. That gives three possibilities: /maṭbēʕ/ 'a coin', plural /maṭbəʕōt/; /miṭbāʕā/ 'a mint', plural /miṭbāʕōt/; /maṭbaʕat/ 'a die', plural /maṭbāʕōt/. All of these plural forms would equally be spelled ⟨mṭbʕwt⟩, and only the context shows that in this case the first of them, 'coins', is intended (the word occurs in the phrase /maṭbəʕōt ʔūkəsāpīm/, literally 'coins and monies', i.e. 'currency').

8 ⟨hlšwn⟩ The root √lšn means 'to slander', and ⟨h⟩ can be a verbal prefix; but no form taking that prefix has an /ū/ or ō/ in the last syllable. In any case the context calls for a noun. Therefore the correct reading is the frequent noun /hallāšōn/ 'the language'; no alternative reading is possible.

9 ⟨šl⟩ The very common word /šel/, 'of'. In isolation the word can also be /šal/ 'error'; but 'of' is so much more frequent that no reader is likely to think of 'error' unless the context is incompatible with the reading 'of'.

10 ⟨wbmjħd⟩ Word-initial ⟨w⟩ is virtually always the prefix 'and'. The range of consonants found in Hebrew suffixes is quite limited and does not include /d/, so that letter must be part of the root – in which case the ⟨b⟩ is likely also to be a prefix (it means 'in'). The possibility that ⟨j⟩ is a *mater* need not to be considered, because there happens to be no root *√mħd. The root is √jħd, which (strangely) combines the opposite meanings 'together' and 'apart', and the stem is the word /məjuħād/ 'particular' (i.e. 'set apart'), formed by adding the nominalizing prefix /m-/ to this root. No alternative reading is possible. The word as a whole is read /ʔūbimjuħād/, 'and in particular'; before bilabial consonants the prefix /w/ has the allomorph /ʔū/ and, exceptionally, this case of /ʔ/ is ignored in writing – all allomorphs of 'and' are written ⟨w⟩.

Needless to say, the fluent reader will not consciously go through the deductive reasoning spelled out in detail for our ten example-words. What it means to be a fluent reader is that one has learned to carry out such reasoning unconsciously and rapidly, so that the process of translating from graphs to sense appears subjectively to be quite direct and effortless. Compare the problem of reading an English word such as ⟨taping⟩, as in *Miss Jenkinson is taping a letter for John.* The form is not so common that a reader will necessarily have encountered it in writing before, but a literate Engish-speaker is unlikely to have trouble with it. If we had to spell out the reasoning by which a reader understands the word, it might run more or less as follows. The last letters ⟨-ing⟩ are almost certainly the common participial suffix /ɪŋ/. The letters ⟨tap⟩ in isolation represent /tæp/, and this root can take the suffix /ɪŋ/. However, an English orthographic rule requires consonant-letters other than ⟨v⟩ to be written double when, as here, they occur in words of the native Germanic vocabulary between a checked vowel such as /æ/ and a following vowel. (*Apical* /æpɪkəl/ is not written with double ⟨pp⟩, because it derives from Latin, but *tap* is a native root.) Therefore ⟨a⟩ in ⟨taping⟩ must be given its alternative (non-checked) value /eɪ/: the word is /teɪpɪŋ/. (If we already know from the context that Miss Jenkinson is working with a recording-machine, this reading is all the more obvious – but context is not necessary; the word ⟨taping⟩ is quite readable in isolation.) Of course no fluent reader of English is aware of going through such steps before understanding the word on the page, and nor is a reader of Hebrew.

Although the idea of writing without vowels seems strange to Europeans, plainly it works. Readers of Hebrew do not find themselves floundering indecisively between one interpretation of a written word and another; where alternative readings are possible for a given letter-sequence, normally the context will settle the matter straightforwardly enough. To say this is not to say, though, that Hebrew script is fully as convenient in practice, for speakers of the Hebrew language, as our script is for English-speakers. By contrast with the orthography of any European language, Hebrew script is strikingly lacking in redundancy.

'Redundancy' is a technical term referring to a measurable property of any system of communicable messages or 'signals' (Shannon and Weaver 1949, pp. 25–6). A system possessing relatively high redundancy is one where, in an average signal, the identity of any given part of the signal is relatively easy to predict given the rest of the signal. Suppose that a policeman telephones to give you details of a suspect who needs to be looked out for, but because the line is bad you hear only some of the letters and numbers as they are spelled out: you hear that the suspect's name is F*ANK DAW*ON and his car registration is OWY 9*8P. You will have little difficulty guessing that the name is 'Frank Dawson'; but you will be completely stumped when it comes to filling in the missing element of the registration. This is because English personal names form a system with high redundancy, whereas car registration marks form a low-redundancy system.

The relevance of this concept to the study of writing systems has to do with the idea that fluent readers do not normally examine all the graphic material that is physically present in a text. Strategies may differ in different circumstances, but it seems probable that in much of our reading we do not act like Baconian scientists, cumulatively registering all available evidence and then proceeding unerringly to the one conclusion that fits all that evidence. Rather, we act more like Popperian scientists: we sample pieces of the evidence and make guesses about the identity of the words we are looking at, checking more of the available visual evidence only if we encounter reasons to believe that our first conjecture was mistaken (Goodman 1967; Gibson and Levin 1975, pp. 449 ff.; Hochberg and Brooks 1976; Rozin and Gleitman 1977; though cf. Rayner and McConkie 1977). That is why proof-reading is a difficult task: it forces us to examine elements of the text which normally we would 'see' without physically looking at them, filling them in mentally from our knowledge of the language and our understanding of the contents of the text. Learning to move away from the 'Baconian' to the 'Popperian' style of reading is one of the last, necessary steps in learning to read (Dunn-Rankin (1978, especially p. 125) suggests that it typically begins at about 8 or 9 years of age), and it is one which some individuals find difficult to take. It is a necessary step, because Baconian reading is inconveniently slow – so slow, in fact, that those who read in the Baconian fashion often seem to have difficulty grasping the sense of texts. Plodding along word by word, indeed letter by letter, they presumably forget the earlier part of a sentence by the time they are dealing with the end of it, and so they fail to see the wood for the trees (Norman 1972; Downing and Leong 1982, p. 209).

However, if one is to read in the Popperian fashion, it is necessary for the texts read to contain a fair degree of redundancy; otherwise it will be difficult to make accurate conjectures about their contents on the basis of a limited number of visual soundings. In this respect there is a marked contrast between Hebrew and English writing.

In the first place, as we have seen, the absence of vowel-letters means that, of ten written Hebrew words picked at random, at least three could be read as any of two or more phonologically-different spoken words. Comparable written words exist in English (e.g. ⟨lead⟩, which can be the verb /lid/ or noun /lɛd/) but they are rare; it is quite unlikely that even one such word would occur in a random collection of ten words. Of course the context will normally settle the ambiguities in Hebrew, but the point is that the existence of such words forces one to examine the context more carefully than one would otherwise need to. When a word is graphically unambiguous, it can act as a fixed datum from which parts of the context can be predicted so that they need not be physically examined.

Second, the idea that one reads by sampling parts and predicting the whole is likely to apply not just between words but within them. Whether or not a fluent English reader looks at every word in a text, it is likely that he does not focus on every letter in a word, unless the word is so short that all its letters are focused in a single fixation.[4] But it is much harder for the Hebrew than for the English reader to predict the identity of an unexamined letter from the identities of the other letters in a word.

Let me illustrate this by a small experiment. I picked a random set of ten English words from a running text, to act as a comparison with my sample of ten Hebrew words; in each word of either language I deleted one letter chosen at random, and then worked out for each language what proportion of the missing letters could unambiguously be restored if the word was taken in isolation from context. Ten-word samples are too small to place great reliance on the numerical results, but the general trend is clear. In the English case only the three shortest words of the ten yielded ambiguities: ⟨*y⟩ could be *my* or *by*, ⟨*he⟩ could be *the* or *she*, ⟨*f⟩ could be *if* or *of*. The seven longer words, ⟨*riting, g*ographic, wer*, thro*gh, resul*ing, inacces*ible, C*erokee⟩, all remain unambiguous. In the Hebrew sample the situation is reversed: only three of the longest words failed to yield ambiguities when this procedure was applied (even leaving aside the ambiguities that already existed for some of the words before any letter was removed). I cannot find any second reading for the words ⟨*wš?jm, hpʕl*m, wbm*ħd⟩. But ⟨h*?⟩ could be ⟨hj?⟩ /hī/ 'she'; ⟨mqj*⟩ could be ⟨mqjq⟩ /miqqīq/ 'from a castor-oil plant'; ⟨*ṭbʕwt⟩ could be ⟨hṭbʕwt⟩ /haṭṭabaʕōt/ 'the rings'; and so on.

Another way of looking at this is to notice that the paragraph from which my ten Hebrew words were chosen, which is an advertisement printed in Hebrew and English, contains 70 words in the English version totalling 407 letters, while the Hebrew version contains 60 words totalling 285 letters. (In each case I ignore punctuation, hyphens, and a numeral which occurs in both texts.) The difference in number of *words* is merely a trivial consequence of the fact that elements such as 'the' and 'to' are separate words in English but prefixes in Hebrew. But the difference in number of *letters* means that each occurrence of a Hebrew letter is on average almost half as important again in determining the meaning of the text in which it occurs as is the occurrence of an individual Roman letter in the English text. It is therefore less easy for the reader of Hebrew than it is for the reader of English to skim a text and reconstruct its contents from observation of a small proportion of its letters.[5]

All this might simply mean that Hebrew script offered a convenient way of packing information densely into a given area of paper, if the individual letter-shapes were highly distinctive so that the identity of a group of letters could easily be determined at one brief glance. The lack of redundancy in Hebrew orthography, while forcing the reader to sample a higher proportion of the graphemes in a text than when reading English, would not imply more samplings to recover a like amount of meaning, which is what matters from the point of view of reading efficiency. However, Hebrew letters are not distinctive. Although the Hebrew alphabet has only 22 letters, as opposed to the 52 letters of the upper and lower case Roman alphabets (Hebrew script has no upper/lower case contrast), Hebrew letters resemble one another much more than Roman letters do.

One of the most important elements making for visual distinctiveness in Roman script is the presence of 'ascenders' in letters such as ⟨b f k t⟩ (as well as the dots of ⟨i j⟩) and 'descenders' in e.g. ⟨g p y⟩, which stand out from the body of a word and make for greater recognizability. This is why highway authorities who produce road-signs that have to be read at speed have abandoned upper-case lettering, normal in Britain until the 1960s, which lacks ascenders and descenders. Dina Feitelson (1967) points out that British experts on the teaching of reading have urged that words lacking ascenders and descenders, such as ⟨run, now, cream⟩, should be avoided in the initial stages because of their non-distinctive outlines. Yet in the Hebrew alphabet, if we leave aside the special word-final allographs, only one letter, lāmed, has an ascender, and one letter, qōp, has a descender. It is true that most of the word-final allographs have descenders, but the fact that these are restricted to word-final position means that they are of relatively little help in recognizing words. If in rapid reading one sees a descender on a Hebrew letter, it tells one in effect 'Unless I am part of a ⟨q⟩ you are at the end of a word' – but the latter piece of information is signalled anyway by the very salient feature of blank space immediately to the left.

Apart from the matter of ascenders and descenders, Feitelson further points out that many groups of different Hebrew letters are strikingly similar in shape:

רדך החת גנכב יון סם

Many Hebrew letters consist largely of a horizontal at the top and a vertical at the right, and the Hebrew alphabet is poorly supplied with unique subcomponents comparable to the eye of a Roman ⟨e⟩, the curved roof of an ⟨f⟩, the barb of an ⟨r⟩, etc. (cf. Shimron and Navon 1980, p. 12). Although in one sense it is true that meaning is packed densely in a page of Hebrew script, it is packed in a form which makes it difficult to extract: each letter of a word counts, but the letters are not very recognizable.

One might suppose that these characteristics of Hebrew script were an idiosyncratic aberration, perhaps connected with the fact that for many centuries the script was used principally for ceremonial purposes where practical speed-reading considerations were irrelevant. Interestingly, however, the problems I have outlined in relation to the letter-shapes of Hebrew script occur even more strikingly in Arabic script, the appearance of which is very different.

Certain groups of letter-shapes in the original Semitic alphabet were so simplified in the development of Arabic script that their forms became wholly identical: thus ⟨z⟩ merged with ⟨r⟩, ⟨p⟩ with ⟨q⟩, ⟨g⟩ with ⟨ħ⟩ḫ, ⟨n + bj⟩ all fell together in shape except that ⟨n⟩, ⟨j⟩ have distinctive word-final allographs. (I identify the letters by reference to their original values; some of the phonemes have acquired different pronunciations in Arabic, but that is beside the point here.) The degree of confusion created was such that a system of dots had to be introduced in writing Arabic to differentiate letter-shapes that had merged (Diringer (1968, p. 216) dates the invention of the dot-system to the early +8c): thus in modern Arabic script the visual difference between ⟨n t b j⟩ has nothing to do with differences between the original shapes of the letters, and rests purely on the fact that they are written with respectively one dot above, two dots above, one dot below, and two dots below. (The diacritic dots which distinguish Arabic consonant-letters are separate from the pointing system for specifying vowels, which is also available in Arabic script but, as in Hebrew script, is not normally used.)

True, when the dots are written (as they invariably now are) they make the letters of Arabic script distinctive enough. However, one might well have expected *a priori* that cultural evolution would never have allowed a system of signs, whose practical value depends purely on their distinctiveness, to reach the point at which a remedy as *ad hoc* as the dot system became necessary (and if any script was to suffer this fate one would not have expected it to be a script that already contained as little redundancy as vowel-less Semitic script).

The point is strengthened by the fact that the system of special word-final allographs is taken further in Arabic script than in Hebrew. A feature of Arabic script is that it has only a cursive form; there is no style of writing in which the letters of a word are disconnected, even printed Arabic imitates the continuous, flowing motions of handwriting. Users of the Roman alphabet tend to see handwritten forms as convenient but imperfect 'performance' deviations from the underlying 'ideal' forms represented by print. Perhaps because Arabic script does not suggest such a point of view to its users, it has gone further than most scripts in developing different allographic variants of letters for use in different graphic environments. About two-thirds of the letters of the Arabic alphabet have special word-final forms, and the difference between these forms and the corresponding non-final allographs is greater than in Hebrew script, and much greater than the differences between many contrasting pairs of Arabic graphemes: see Figure 15 for examples. The consequence is that, perhaps even more than in the Hebrew case, much of what is visually salient in a page of written Arabic is linguistically quite non-significant: it merely marks the ends of words which are in any case marked more obviously by blank spaces.

There is some experimental evidence (Gray 1956, p. 59) tending to suggest that readers of Hebrew and Arabic make rather longer eye-fixations than readers of European languages. The evidence is admittedly far from over-whelming, but for what it is worth the result conforms to what would be expected on the basis of the factors I have discussed. Each sampling of a text has to be more thorough, and therefore takes longer, if the graphemes have few distinctive elements buried amid a mass of non-distinctive visual material.

Arabic script has one advantage, from the writer's point of view, which in a small way may do something to offset its disadvantages from the reader's point of view. (I leave out of account the great beauty of Arabic script, which has probably been a powerful factor determining its development in practice.) Because of the adaptations made in the letter-shapes to facilitate cursive writing, Arabic script can be written rather quickly; when one adds the point that the vowel-less structure of Semitic scripts requires fewer letters than in English to express a given message, the fact that sequences of Arabic letters

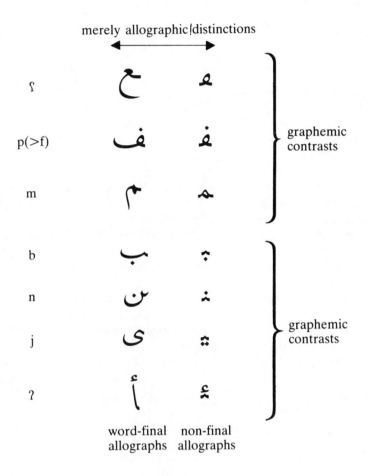

Figure 15

are fast to write means that the script may approach the speediness of a system of shorthand.

Even this virtue is lacking in Hebrew script, however. While Arabic script has *only* a cursive form, Hebrew script has *no* cursive form. There are conventional handwritten letter-shapes which diverge from the shapes used for printing (they are more visually distinctive than the printed shapes, and include more ascenders and descenders). But these manuscript forms are normally written separately: there is no system of writing long letter-sequences with a continuous motion of the pen. The English word *alphabet*, containing eight letters, is commonly written with only one lifting of the pen between beginning and end (to make the cross-stroke of the ⟨t⟩). Its Hebrew equivalent /ʔālepbēt/ is written with six letters ⟨ʔlpbjt⟩, but its handwritten form would standardly involve seven separate pen-strokes:

alphabet   אלפבית

alphabet   אלפבית

Modern Israeli Hebrew is a very young language, and several aspects of its orthography are changing fast. It is noticeable, for instance, that contemporary Hebrew spelling has taken to using many more *matres* than is normal in standard Biblical Hebrew, often writing short vowels as well as long with *matres*; for instance, the word /məjuħād/ (see example 10, p. 91 above) would nowadays be spelled ⟨mjwħd⟩ rather than ⟨mjħd⟩. (The text I quoted my example-words from was printed in 1961.) Although, as we have seen, *matres* create ambiguities as well as resolving them, on balance more *matres* mean less ambiguity. New fonts of type are being designed which increase the visual contrasts between letters, and handwriting is becoming more cursive. If these trends continue and become accepted as norms, written Hebrew may evolve into a system much less different from European scripts than it has traditionally been.

That said, it does seem fair to describe the traditional standard Hebrew script as a relatively cumbersome writing system. Its adoption by the founders of a highly-developed nation, all of whom were familiar with other forms of writing, must be explained in terms of emotional considerations to do with history and religion. In the linguistics of spoken as well as of written language such non-rational factors often weigh more heavily than matters of practical convenience.

6 The Graeco-Roman alphabet

The transition from consonantal writing to writing in which vowel-phonemes are symbolized on the same footing as consonant-phonemes occurred, uniquely, when the Semitic alphabet was adapted to write Greek.

After the collapse of Mycenaean civilization in the −13c the Greeks lost the art of writing for a matter of centuries; in the Classical period, when they were writing alphabetically, the Greeks had no knowledge of the fact that their ancestors had once used a different, syllabic form of writing. Greek tradition dated the adoption of the alphabet to the First Olympiad, i.e. −776. The archaeological evidence is reasonably compatible with this general date for the first Greek use of the alphabet, and it is supported by L. H. Jeffery (1961, p. 21). Other scholars have argued for an earlier date; for instance Diringer (1968, p. 359) suggests that −1000 would be nearer the mark.

It is fairly sure that the version of the Semitic alphabet encountered by the Greeks was that used by the Phoenicians. This would be probable *a priori*, because the Phoenicians were the one Semitic nation who travelled and traded overseas, but in any case the Greeks are known to have called their alphabet 'Phoenician letters'.

At an early stage in the history of Semitic writing, two divergent traditions of forming the letter-shapes had arisen: an 'Eastern' or 'Aramaic' script, from which e.g. the Arabic and modern Hebrew alphabets descend, and a 'Western' or 'Canaanite' script which was used by the Phoenicians and, originally, by the Jews (Hebrew began to be written in Aramaic rather than Canaanite letters after −300). Aramaic script was characterized by relatively extreme degeneration of the original letter-shapes: note, for example, that the modern Hebrew ʕajin has reduced a complete circle to a pair of strokes open at the top. The Canaanite script encountered by the Greeks remained closer to the source; to this day upper-case Greek letters are much more similar than modern Hebrew or Arabic letters to the forms of the original Semitic alphabet.

According to Jeffery (1961, p. 6) the alphabet must have been transmitted to the Greeks just once, rather than being borrowed independently by different groups of Greeks in contact with Semites at different times and places. After the Greeks had acquired the alphabet, many local variations of it evolved in various parts of the Greek-speaking world, differing in shapes and Greek values of some Semitic letters and with respect to various supplementary letters invented by the Greeks themselves; but there are too many coincidences between these variants not to suppose that the original adaptation to the Greek language happened once only. These locally-varying versions of the Greek alphabet can be classified into a 'Western' and an 'Eastern' group. After the early period of diversification there ensued a period of convergence, during which areas which used other versions of the alphabet gradually discarded them in favour of the Ionic version, one of the 'Eastern' group, which became accepted as standard throughout Greece by about −350. This is essentially the classical Greek alphabet that we know today.

Most of the Greek consonant-letters derive their values from the Semitic ancestor-script in a straightforward way. In some cases letters were used for slightly-different consonants because Greek lacked a sound precisely equivalent to the Semitic value of a letter. Thus, consider the Semitic letters for pharyngalized stops. Greek contained no such sounds. The letter ṭēt for /tˤ/ was used by the Greeks, in the form Θ, for a separate, non-pharyngalized phoneme /tʰ/. One might have expected that the Greek letter Ϙ, formed from qōp, would have stood analogously for Greek /kʰ/; instead, it was used to mark a purely allophonic difference in Greek. As in many other languages, /k/ in Greek varied in its precise place of articulation depending on the following vowel; and the Greeks wrote Ϙ for the relatively back allophone of /k/ found before back vowels, keeping K (from kāp) for the allophones of /k/ occurring before central and front vowels. This contrast between two ways of using letters for pharyngalized stops may be explainable in phonetic terms: since pharyngalization involves retraction of the tongue root, a pharyngalized /tˤ/ is a /t/ with a secondary articulation (and may therefore have been heard by the Greeks as comparable to /t/ with the rather different extra feature of aspiration), while a 'pharyngalized velar' will often in practice just be a simple stop formed rather further back than the ordinary velar position. After the −6c the logic of the phonemic principle asserted itself so that back allophones of /k/ were also written with K, and the letter Ϙ, called by the Greeks 'koppa', did not survive into the Classical period.

The development that was really significant and novel was the Greek use of six Semitic letters, ⟨ʔ h w ħ j ʕ⟩, to represent vowels. Let me defer for some pages a detailed analysis of the Greek vowel system, and say simply that the Semitic letters were used roughly as follows: ʔālep for Greek /a/, hē for /e/, wāw became two letters of slightly-different shapes ⟨FY⟩ standing respectively for /w/ and /u/, ħēt was used either for /h/ or for an /e/-like vowel, jōd for /i/, and ʕajin for /o/.

Of the six Semitic letters in question, only wāw had a value, /w/, which also existed as a phoneme in Greek, and one of the two Greek letters developed from wāw retained this value. (The Greek phoneme /w/ was eliminated in the later development of spoken Greek, so that the letter F, like Ϙ, became obsolete in the Classical Greek alphabet.) The pharyngal sounds [ħ ʕ] and the glottal stop [ʔ] did not occur at all in Greek, and [h j], though they did occur, had a marginal, scarcely-phonemic status.

On the other hand, distinctions between vowels were far more crucial in

Greek than in Semitic languages. Greek is a European language: it uses vowel-distinctions heavily to make lexical contrasts, and only to a minor extent for grammatical purposes. Thus in Greek script an indication of vowels is both important for communication, and also does not lead to the confusion that could be caused by a vocalized Semitic script in which the graphic appearance of a lexical root would vary widely depending on grammatical inflexion. Furthermore, Greek words often begin with vowels; and, while sequences of two or more vowels were virtually unknown in Semitic languages, in Greek a word such as /sumbouleuousi/ 'they advise' is quite normal.

All these are reasons why it was desirable for Greek to be written with vowel-letters, if it was going to be written in a segmental script at all. But there remains a question about how the redundant Semitic letters were adapted to this purpose. Some scholars have supposed that this was the result of a conscious plan by a clever Greek scribe. I feel sceptical about that idea. It seems easier to imagine the reinterpretation of the letters as having happened automatically as a consequence of the learning of the letter-names and the acrophonic principle by speakers of a language with a non-Semitic phonological system (cf. Jeffery 1961, p. 22). In general, the Greek *names* of the letters are simply the Semitic names modified to make them pronounceable in Greek: thus Semitic kāp became Greek kappa, since words may not end in /p/ in Greek. (I shall quote Greek letter-names in their ordinary English spelling rather than in a scientific transliteration.) In Greek the letter-names are of course meaningless, but the relationship between names and letter-values is retained: K is called kappa, and its value is /k/, the first sound of kappa. Any teacher of phonetics knows how difficult a layman finds it to hear a sound which does not occur in his own language. One can readily imagine a scenario something like the following. A Greek sees a Phoenician using a mysterious system of written marks and asks for an explanation. The Phoenician (who, incidentally, probably called the first letter /ʔalp/ – the /e/ of Hebrew 'ʔālep' is epenthetic) begins, 'This mark is called ʔalp – no, not "alp" – ʔalp, ʔalp, can't you hear, ʔʔʔalp!', while the bewildered Greek perceives only the [alp], and ends up calling the letter 'alpʰ-a' *and using it for* /a/ since by the acrophonic principle that will now seem to him to be its proper value. This would explain the Greek use of Semitic ⟨ʔ h ħ ʕ⟩ as vowel-letters, without the need to attribute any special linguistic sophistication to the first Greek user of the alphabet, assuming (not implausibly) that the vowels in the Phoenician names of these letters were something like the Greek vowels for which the letters came to be used. And the phonetic similarity between the vowel /i/ and the approximant /j/ is such that, again, the adaptation of jōd would seem to have required no particular act of intelligence.

The only one of the letters in question for which this account is known to be over-simplified is ħēt: in this case it seems that the Greeks identified the Semitic /ħ/ with the [h] which is one of the possible ways of beginning a Greek word whose first phoneme is a vowel (cf. p. 64), and the reinterpretation of ħēt as a vowel-letter occurred not when it was transmitted from Semites to

Greeks but, later, when it was transmitted from one group of Greeks to another whose dialect lacked [h]. In the classical Greek alphabet H, from ḥēt, was used for a vowel akin to /e/; but the fact that other Greeks had used this letter for [h] was reflected in the identity of the diacritics classically used to mark the word-intial [h] v. zero opposition. The so-called 'rough and smooth breathing' marks, as in ⟨ἁ⟩ /ha/ v. ⟨ἀ⟩ /a/, derive graphically from Ⱶ and ⱶ, i.e. two halves of H. (The early Greek use of H for [h] also explains this use by the Romans.)

An aspect of the original Greek use of vowel-letters which does suggest conscious thought is the creation of two letters from the one Semitic letter wāw, in order to distinguish the Greek vowel /u/ from the consonant /w/. The vowel-letter derived from wāw, being an extra letter, was added at the end of the alphabet, after tāw.

Later, different Greek communities created further supplementary letters, always adding them to the end of the current alphabetical order. Ignoring some of these which did not survive into the classical Greek alphabet, the letter Φ was invented for /pʰ/); X was used in the Western group of alphabets for /ks/ and in the Eastern group for /kʰ/; Ψ was used in the Western group for /kʰ/ and in the Eastern group for /ps/; and Ω was created to differentiate long, open /ɔ/ from short, close /ŏ/ – hence the names o-micron, o-mega, 'little o' and 'big o', for O, Ω respectively. (The names e-psilon, u-psilon for E, Y mean 'bare e', 'bare u' – the term 'bare' indicated a vowel without a preceding [h] sound.) Since the Ionic alphabet belonged to the Eastern group, the letters X, Ω had their Eastern values in the Classical Greek alphabet.

The Semitic alphabet had letters zajin, sāmek, çādē, and šīn, standing for five sibilant phonemes, /z s sᵒ ṣ ś/. Greek had only two sibilant phonemes, namely /s/ and a phoneme which in modern Greek is pronounced [z], but at the time of the adoption of the alphabet was probably an affricate [dz] (Allen 1968, p. 55), which is how I shall transcribe it. The four Semitic letter-shapes yielded four Greek letters at the corresponding places in the alphabetical order: Z Ξ M Σ. Of these, Z represented Greek /dz/. Ξ was used for /ks/ in Ionic and some other local alphabets, though ignored in the alphabets which used X for /ks/ (Jeffery 1961, p. 36). M from Semitic çādē (called in Greek 'san') and Σ from Semitic šīn (in Greek, 'sigma') seem to have been used interchangeably for /s/; as time went on some local alphabets used only san, others only sigma. (The fact that san did not survive into the Classical alphabet permitted ⟨m⟩ from Semitic mēm, originally written with five strokes, to lose one of them and thus coincide in shape with the obsolete san.)

The lack of correspondence between Semitic and Greek sibilant phonemes seems to have led to a confusion between letter-names. As letter-shapes, the forms Z Ξ M Σ occur in the same places in the alphabetical sequence as the Semitic letters from which they derive. But the name 'sigma' for Σ seems to derive from sāmek rather than šīn; it may be likewise that 'san' derives from zajin, and perhaps 'zeta' for Z from çādē.

Figure 16 compares the original Semitic alphabet with the letter-shapes, letter-values, and letter-names of the classical or 'post-Eucleidian' version of the Greek alphabet, as used in Athens after −402. Items within brackets had become obsolete by that period.

The Greeks naturally followed Semitic practice by writing from right to left, but from a very early period – possibly from their first use of the alphabet – they usually wrote inscriptions of several lines not all right-to-left (as the Semites did, and still do) but in so-called *boustrophedon* ('ox-turning') style, alternately right-to-left and left-to-right in successive lines as furrows are ploughed, so that there were no big jumps between the end of one line and its continuation. This method gradually gave way to the system we use today of writing consistently left-to-right, which was standard by the Classical period. (Jeffery (1961, pp. 47–8) claims that the left-to-right direction is physically more natural for right-handed people, so that once *boustrophedon* accustomed people to this direction of writing it could not fail to become universal.) In *boustrophedon* writing the shapes of the individual letters were reversed with the direction of writing, so that letters in any one line were the mirror-image of those in adjacent lines. Thus, when the left-to-right direction became standard, the final letter-shapes were the reverse of those inherited from Semitic script (in Figure 16, compare e.g. B, E, N with their Semitic counterparts).

The Greek alphabet was not a perfect, complete reflection of the phonemic system of spoken Greek. It approached fairly close to that ideal, however, and the respects in which it failed to attain it are easy to understand.

To begin by disposing briefly of an oddity which is not so much a shortcoming in the system as an unnecessary luxury: it is natural to wonder why the alphabet should have included special graphemes for /ks ps/, which phonetically speaking are clusters of quite distinct consonants. (Some sounds, e.g. affricates or diphthongs, are commonly transcribed by pairs of phonetic symbols while having some claim to be single sounds from the articulatory point of view; but there is no sense in which /ks ps/ can be described as less than two segments each.) The answer seems to be that /ks ps/ were the only consonant clusters that could occur at the end of a syllable in Greek (cf. p. 69), and this led the Greeks to perceive these clusters as belonging together more tightly than others, and thus as deserving their own graphemes. (One may well find it surprising that this feeling was strong enough to motivate the invention of new letters, but such was the case.)

Two consonant-phonemes had alternative allophones: /r/ was voiceless [r̥] initially and in certain other positions, though voiced elsewhere, and /s/ was voiced [z] before voiced consonants though voiceless elsewhere (Allen 1968, pp. 39–41, 43–4). In each case a single grapheme, respectively P and Σ, covered both members of the phoneme, just as in English the plain and velarized allophones of the /l/ phoneme are both covered by the grapheme ⟨l⟩.

✗	ʔālep /ʔ/	A	alpha /ă, ā/
ϑ	bēt /b/	B	beta /b/
∧	gīmel /g/	Γ	gamma /g/
⊳	dālet /d/	Δ	delta /d/
∃	hē /h/	E	epsilon /ĕ/
Y	wāw /w/	(F	wau /w/)
I	zajin /z/	Z	zeta /z/
ⱶ	ḥēt /ḥ/	H	eta /ǣ/
⊕	ṭēt /ṭ/	θ	theta /tʰ/
ⱬ	jōd /j/	I	iota /ĭ, ī/
ⱦ	kāp /k/	K	kappa /k/
ℓ	lāmed /l/	Λ	lamda /l/
ⱳ	mēm /m/	M	mu /m/
ⱨ	nūn /n/	N	nu /n/
ⱪ	ṣāmek /s/	Ξ	xi /ks/
o	ʕajin /ʕ/	O	omicron /ŏ/
ⱬ	pē /p/	Π	pi /p/
ⱱ	çādē /sᵖ/	(M	san /s/)
ⱷ	qōp /kᵖ/	(Ϙ	koppa /k/)
ⱶ	rēš /r/	P	rho /r/
w	šīn /ŝ, ś/	Σ	sigma /s/
✝	tāw /t/	T	tau /t/
		Υ	upsilon (/ŭ, ū/ʹ>) /ў, ȳ/
		Φ	phi /pʰ/
		X	chi /kʰ/
		Ψ	psi /ps/
		Ω	omega /ɔ̄/

Figure 16

Let us turn now to a detailed examination of the vowel-system and its graphic representation.

Following Allen (1968, ch. 2), we may reconstruct the system of pure vowel phonemes in Attic Greek as follows. (My choice of phonetic symbols differs from Allen's in certain respects.)

long				short		
ī	ȳ	ū		ĭ	y̆	
ē					ɛ̆	ŏ
	ǣ ɔ̄					
	ā				ă	

These phonemes were represented by Greek letters as follows:

ī ĭ	ȳ y̆	ē	ɛ̆	ǣ	ā ă	ɔ̄	ŏ	ū
I	Y	EI	E	H	A	V	O	OY

A sound-change occurring shortly before or during the Classical period had fronted /ŭ ū/ to /y̆ ȳ/, so the letter Y automatically came to stand for these fronted sounds. The phoneme /ē/ resulted from the merging of an earlier contrast between /ē/ and /ei/; while these sounds still contrasted, the pure vowel was written, like its short counterpart, with E, but after the merger the digraph EI (which had been phonetically appropriate for the diphthong) was used for all cases of the new /ē/ phoneme. Likewise, /ū/ in the Classical period was the product of a merger between earlier /ō/ and /ou/; while these sounds contrasted /ō/ was identified with /ŏ/ and written O, but after the merger the digraph OY which had been phonetically appropriate for /ou/ was used for all cases of the new phoneme /ū/.

(There were also various diphthongs in /-i -u/ in Attic Greek, and these were written with ⟨-I -Y⟩; the letter Y continued to retain the value /-u/ for writing diphthongs after it had shifted to the value /y/ as a pure vowel.)

Thus Greek script distinguished vowel quality but not vowel quantity. Long and short vowels were normally written alike. The fact that /ē ɛ̆/ are distinguished as EI E despite differing chiefly in quantity, is an accidental by-product of the fact that many cases of /ē/ derived historically from a diphthong; /ŏ ɔ̄/ were written with separate letters, but they may well have differed in quality as much as in quantity.

It is tempting to argue that vowel quantity is ignored in Greek orthography because, although it is contrastive in Greek – e.g. /dănŏs/ 'a debt' contrasts with /dānŏs/ 'parched' – it is phonologically unimportant, either in Greek in particular or perhaps more generally. One cannot base such an argument on the fact that other alphabetic orthographies, such as that of Latin, also ignore phonological vowel-quantity contrasts, because it may be that the reason why Latin script – and hence some other orthographies which use Roman letters – fail to mark vowel-quantity is that the Roman alphabet was borrowed from the Greeks. But, looking beyond the range of scripts that descend from the Greek alphabet, there does seem to be a general tendency to avoid marking quantity contrasts. We shall return to this matter in Chapter 7 (p. 133). As in Chapter 4 I shall normally omit short-vowel marks in Greek examples cited below.

Greek also had a quantity contrast in consonants, as in /oȓos/ 'rump' v. /oȓos/ 'mountain'. In the early days of Greek writing long and short consonants were not distinguished, but by −500 Attic writing distinguished long consonants by writing them double (Allen 1968, p. 10). It is no doubt for this historical reason that, to this day, orthographies and scientific phonetic transcriptions which mark a quantity distinction in consonants invariably use the device of singe v. double symbols, whereas long vowels are commonly indicated by adding a diacritic to a single vowel symbol.

The alphabet lacked a symbol for the velar nasal [ŋ] and represented it by Γ, i.e. ⟨g⟩. The distribution of [ŋ] was extremely limited (it occurred only before nasals and /g/), and it came close to being an allophone of /g/; so this graphic treatment was reasonable even though, according to Allen (1968, pp. 36–7), [ŋ] must in the last analysis be accorded separate phonemic status because of a few contrasts such as [εŋgenǣs] 'innate' v. [εggonos] 'offspring'. The former word is derived by prefixing /en-/ 'in', and the latter by prefixing /εk-/ 'out of', to stems beginning with /g-/, to which the prefix consonants assimilate. They were commonly distinguished in spelling by writing the former ⟨εgg . . . ⟩ but the latter, in accordance with its derivation, ⟨εkg . . . ⟩.

This is a case where the desire to avoid ambiguity leads to 'deep' rather than 'surface' orthography being used at an earlier period than was normal. Allen points out that [εg-] from underlying |εk-| was spelled ⟨εg⟩ before ⟨b d⟩ (where the possibility of interpreting ⟨g⟩ as [ŋ] does not arise) until the −1c. In general, when assimilation rules or other phonological rules lead to conflicts between deep and surface phonemic forms, Greek orthography tended more often than modern English orthography to reflect the surface facts and ignore morphological structure. Consider, for instance, the fact that the preposition /syn/ 'with' regularly assimilated its /n/ to following consonants in compound words such as /syl-logos/ 'a gathering', /sym-ptōsis/ 'a coincidence', and the assimilated segments were written ⟨l⟩, ⟨m⟩, etc. rather than, in accordance with derivation, ⟨n⟩ – as if we were to spell the English word *input* as ⟨imput⟩, which is how we pronounce it. Or consider the spelling of the consonant clusters that arise, regularly, in various perfect passive forms of a root such as /prāg-/ 'do':

1st person sing.	pε-prāŋ-mai
2nd person sing.	pε-prāk-sai
3rd person sing.	pε-prāk-tai
2nd person plur.	pε-prāk^h-t^{h}ε

Each of the clusters /ŋm, ks, kt, k^{h}t^h/ straddles the boundary between root and suffix; they are spelled respectively ΓΜ, Ξ, ΚΤ, ΧΘ. This is rather as if the English words *optic, optics, optician, opticist* were to be spelled ⟨optik, optix, optishan, optisist⟩.

The final respect in which classical Greek orthography is less than fully complete has to do with 'accent'.

It is commonly said that ancient Greek had a system of 'tonal accent' based on pitch, which later (probably in the early centuries of the Christian Era) gave way to a system of 'stress' accent. It is difficult to know how to interpret this statement, since the fact is that in languages described as using 'stress' rather than 'tone', such as English, a chief phonetic exponent of 'stress' is high pitch. If there is a clear distinction between stress and tone, it is a structural rather than a phonetic distinction: in a tone language the choice of pitch or pitch-contour on any one syllable is more or less independent of the choice for any other syllable of the same word, while in a stress language just one syllable in each word has primary stress and the location of this stress heavily influences the levels of stress on other syllables of the word (McCawley 1970). In this sense Ancient Greek was a stress language rather than a tone language: the tonal pitch-pattern of a word was wholly determined by the location of one relatively high-pitched element, the only significant complication being that for tonal purposes long vowels were treated as sequences of two short vowels either of which could bear the high pitch. (Certain diphthongs introduce a problem that will be ignored here: see Allen 1968, p. 114 n. 2; Sommerstein 1973, p. 125.)

Position of accent was sometimes distinctive: we find minimal pairs such as /tómos/ 'a cut' v. /tomós/ 'cutting, sharp', or /lýysai/ 'to have loosed' v. /lyýsai/ 'he would have loosed'. But the contrasts realized by accent in Greek are almost exclusively grammatical (lexical contrasts such as /pʰɔɔ́s/ 'man' v. /pʰɔ́ɔs/, a contracted form of /pʰáos/ 'light', are very rare), and even in the grammatical domain the functional yield of accent is quite low. Sommerstein (1973, ch. 5) presents a set of accentual rules for Greek which, he says, permit accent to be predicted unambiguously in the great majority of words. It is therefore not surprising to find that accent was ignored by classical Greek orthography. Again it may be that this deficiency in Greek orthography is ultimately the cause of the widespread feeling among users of alphabetic scripts today that stress-marking is an inessential luxury – so that while the failure of English orthography to provide a way of distinguishing /θ/ from /ð/ is seen as a real shortcoming, lack of marks for stress (which is probably at least as important as the θ/ð contrast in English phonology) is seen as a trivial matter. Among modern European languages Spanish is unusual in using an orthography which scrupulously indicates position of stress.

As in the case of Hebrew script, the Greeks too in due course supplemented the orthography described here with diacritic marks indicating many of the aspects of pronunciation ignored by their main writing system, such as accent and the allophonic distinction between voiced and voiceless /r/. Unlike Hebrew pointing, the 'Byzantine' system of diacritics for Greek gradually came to be adopted as a standard part of the orthography. However, it seems possible that the period during which this happened coincided with the period when many of the phonetic contrasts indicated by the diacritics were ceasing to be part of the living spoken language, so that the Byzantine system may always have been more a technical philological device than a phonographic orthography in the ordinary sense. We shall not discuss it.

Segmental script is for Western readers the most familiar type of writing, and it is illustrated by classical Greek orthography about as well as it could be by any other example. But, since the writing system we ourselves use descends from the one we have been examining, it will be appropriate in the rest of this chapter to look in detail at how our script has come to have its present form.

The Romans acquired the art of writing about a century after the foundation of the city of Rome in −753. In the −7c Rome was still a small place, and the dominant culture in that part of Italy was Etruria, to the north of Rome. (Later, as Rome's strength grew, it gradually absorbed the Etruscans until by −200 Etruria no longer existed as a political entity.) The Etruscans spoke a non-Indo-European language about which only a limited amount is now known; and they had borrowed a Western version of the Greek alphabet (with H standing for /h/ rather than a vowel, and X standing for /ks/ rather than /kʰ/).

One fact that is known about the linguistic structure of Etruscan is that voice was non-contrastive in stop consonants: the sounds [b d g] either did not occur at all or, if they did, they were mere allophonic variants of [p t k]. This meant that the Etruscans had no use for the Greek graphemic contrasts between ΠB, TΔ, KΓ and in due course the letters BΔ were given up.

At the time when the Romans encountered Etruscan writing, these letters were still included in their alphabet, so that the Romans were able to use them for the voice contrast which exists in Latin as it does in Greek. (When people encounter writing for the first time, they are often understandably slow and cautious about discarding elements of the system which serve no purpose with respect to their own language.) However, in the case of the velar letters the Etruscans had already rationalized the system they had taken over from the Greeks. We have seen that early Greek writing used the letters K Ϙ for different allophones of the /k/ phoneme. The Etruscans took this logic further: since they did not need Γ to stand for a separate voiced consonant, they used it too for an allophonic variant: they wrote Ϙ for the back allophone of /k/ found before /u/ (their language had no /o/), K for the neutral allophone found before /a/, and Γ – the shape of which evolved into C – for the front variant of /k/ found before /i e/.

When the Romans first borrowed the alphabet, they took over this method of using C K and Q (i.e. Ϙ); but they soon abandoned K as redundant, and they came to reserve Q not for the ordinary /k/ before /u/ but rather for the 'labio-velar' phoneme /kʷ/ that occurred in Latin as it did in early Greek (p. 63), and which the Romans wrote ⟨QV⟩ – so that e.g. /kʷī/ 'who' contrasted in writing with /kuī/ 'to whom' as ⟨QVI, CVI⟩. The Romans had no knowledge of the fact that C had once been reserved for /g/, so they used C for both of their phonemes /k g/.

Another letter which the Romans inherited via the Etruscans but had no use for was Z for /dz/; Latin had no /dz/-like sound. In the −3c the freedman Spurius Carvilius Ruga (the first Roman to open a fee-paying school) remedied the lack of graphic differentiation between /k g/ by adding a stroke to C to make a new letter G for /g/, and he inserted this new letter in seventh position in the alphabet, replacing the useless letter Z.[1] Evidently the order of the alphabet was felt to be such a concrete thing that a new letter could be added in the middle only if a 'space' was created by the dropping of an old letter.

At this point, then, the Romans had a 21-letter alphabet: A B C D E F G H I (K) L M N O P Q R S T V X. All vowel-letters covered long as well as short vowels, and the letters I V were used for semivowels /j w/ as well as for vowels /i u/. (Greek F for /w/ had been adapted by the Etruscans to write /f/, a sound lacking in Greek – the Etruscans perceived /f/ as similar to a voiceless /w/ and wrote it FH or simply F and the Romans followed them, never using F for /w/.) K was used only in a few words which retained an archaic orthography (just as there remained some archaic uses of C for /g/, e.g. the name *Gaius* was abbreviated ⟨C.⟩); /kʷ gʷ/ were written ⟨QV GV⟩, and X was used for the cluster /ks/. Otherwise the alphabet was almost perfectly phonemic (Allen 1965).

One discontinuity with earlier versions of the alphabet, for which the Etruscans were responsible, related to the names of the letters.

We saw that the Greeks took over most of the Semitic names, although in Greek these have no meaning. The Etruscans simplified things, rather in the manner of an English child who spells *cat* 'ker-a-ter'. Vowel-letters were named by their own sound; most of the consonant-letters were named by adding the most neutral Etruscan vowel, /e/, to the respective consonant to give names such as /pe, te/ for P, T. (Because of the special usage of C K Q these had to be named /ke ka ku/.) Continuant consonants were named simply by pronouncing the consonant without a vowel: L was 'lll', S 'sss', and so on – again a common practice with modern children; and these names were eventually turned into phonologically-respectable words by prefixing a vowel, /el es/ as opposed to /pe te/. (X was /eks/ rather than /kse/ because in Latin – and Etruscan? – unlike Greek, /ks-/ as an initial cluster was impossible.) With two exceptions to be discussed below, the resulting 21 letter-names are the direct ancestors of our English names, having undergone the regular sound-changes of late Latin and English which caused e.g. Latin /ge/ for G to become our /dʒi/ just as Latin /genius/ became our /dʒiniɪ/, *genie*.

In the −2c Rome conquered Greece, and the relatively sophisticated culture and thought of the Greeks, and with it the Greek language, proceeded to massively infiltrate Roman life (indeed, this process had begun well before Roman hegemony over Greece). Many Greek words were borrowed into Latin; consequently, the Romans needed to write two Greek sounds which Latin lacked, namely /y/, and /z/ from earlier Greek /dz/. The Romans had inherited Greek upsilon, via the Etruscans, in the form V, but for the Romans this still stood for its original Greek value /u/; so they formed a new letter Y, imitating what had become the standard Greek shape for upsilon; and the Greek Z likewise was copied into the Roman alphabet at the end. Hence our name /zɛd/, from Greek zeta, and the German *ypsilon* or French *y-grec* for Y (the etymology of the English name /waɪ/ is obscure).

Further developments in the alphabet were a consequence of phonological developments in Latin and its descendant languages. The sound /h/ dropped out of the Romance languages, which caused a problem for the name of H (which, as a grapheme, was retained). What seems to have happened is that, so long as early Romance-speakers retained some ability to make an [h] or [h]-like sound, they made increasingly desperate and emphatic attempts to utter a name including such a noise: [ahha] passed into [axxa] and finally resulted in the pronounceable if not very appropriate name /akka/. Just as Latin *vacca* 'cow' gave Norman /vatʃe/ and modern French /vaʃ/ *vache*, so /akka/ gave Norman /atʃe/, which by the sound-laws of Middle and Modern English yielded our name /eɪtʃ/, while simultaneously developing into Modern French /aʃ/.

The Latin approximants /j w/ developed into obstruents in the modern Romance languages: Latin /juːdikem/ 'judge', /wiːtam/ 'life' are Italian /dʒuditʃe/, /vita/, French /ʒyʒ/, /vi/. The double use of V for /u v/ was inconvenient for speakers of Germanic languages, which had a /w/ phoneme distinct from /v/, so in the +11c they began to indicate /w/ by writing V double; in due course VV, 'double /u/', came to be seen and written as an independent grapheme, W. In the +16c speakers of Romance languages also found it awkward to use the same letters I V both for vowels /i u/ and for very different consonants. The cursive, minuscule form of capital V was ⟨u⟩, so this was used to form a new capital letter U while V gave a new minuscule ⟨v⟩, thus splitting V into two letters. Likewise, ⟨I i⟩ had swash allographs (cf. the medieval practice of writing e.g. 13 as ⟨xiij⟩), and these were elevated to the status of a separate grapheme ⟨J j⟩, whose English name /dʒeɪ/ is perhaps formed by analogy with the adjacent K to avoid homonymy with the name of G. (According to Updike (1922, vol. 1, pp. 22–3 n. 2), the differentiation of U, V, and W was not complete in England before the 19c.) It is noteworthy that no less than five of our 26 letters, namely F, U, V, W, Y, all descend ultimately from the same letter, wāw, in the Semitic ancestor-alphabet.

Perhaps more interesting than the issue of how the alphabet came to contain 26 letters is the study of how the letter-shapes have developed since Roman times – a study which is relevant to decisions that have to be made in everyday life now.

For the Romans, the 'basic' shapes of the letters were the forms used for inscriptions cut on stone – 'capitals' as we call them nowadays. Unlike Greek monumental lettering, which was characteristically monoline (i.e. there was no variation of thick and thin in different parts of a letter), the monumental capitals of Imperial Rome had light, oblique stress – that is, the line of a letter such as O varied smoothly in width, being narrowest at the eleven o'clock and five o'clock positions, and widest at the points 90° from these. In this respect the men who chiselled lettering on stone were influenced by the variation of line that occurs naturally when letters are written in ink with a broad nib. Imperial Roman capitals were also characterized by serifs much more pronounced than were normal in Greek lettering. Again this may represent an influence from handwriting, but serifs are held to make an important contribution to both the beauty and the legibility of lettering: they arrest the eye at the end of an unconnected line, and 'eas[e] . . . the combination of separate letters into whole words' (Morison 1972, pp. 8–9). The inscription on Trajan's Column (+214) is often cited as an example of monumental Roman lettering at its finest (see Figure 17).

In handwriting, and even for less formal public inscriptions, various less-authoritative, more cursive styles of lettering evolved. The term 'cursive' may be misunderstood: so far as is known, even in the most informal styles of handwriting each letter was formed separately, as in Hebrew handwriting (p. 97). But the outlines of individual letters were simplified in various ways, and most letters could be produced by a single stroke of the pen; and, significantly, a 'minuscule' hand developed in which letters differed in height, some having ascenders and others descenders (Updike 1922, vol. 1, p. 45).

In the ancient world as in the modern, the medium was an important part of the message. Different styles of lettering had their own political and cultural associations and were appropriate for different kinds of text; and, after the break-up of the Roman Empire, the picture was further complicated by the development of diverging 'national hands' in various parts of Europe: Italian semi-cursive minuscules, the spidery Merovingian script of France, the rounded 'Insular' or Anglo-Irish hand, and others. About +800 the Carolingian hand was developed in the Frankish empire, possibly evolved on the basis of the Anglo-Irish hand under the influence of Alcuin of York who organized the reform of education under Charlemagne. Over the next few centuries Carolingian script spread throughout Europe, replacing local hands everywhere except in Ireland (Irish has been printed in type based on pre-Carolingian, Insular models until the present generation).

The graphic unity created by the success of Carolingian script began to break up again in the 12c. By the 15c two important rival styles of writing had developed out of the Carolingian hand. 'Humanist' script was an attempt to reconstruct the handwriting of Classical Rome, but in practice remained relatively close to the Carolingian original: it was the script of the Renascence, of secular learning and the study of classical antiquity, and thus primarily of Northern Italy; while 'gothic', or black-letter, was the script of the Church, of medieval as opposed to modern world-views, of France and Germany. Humanist letters were rounded, wide, and written with a fine pen; gothic letters were written with an extremely broad pen held at a sharp angle to the

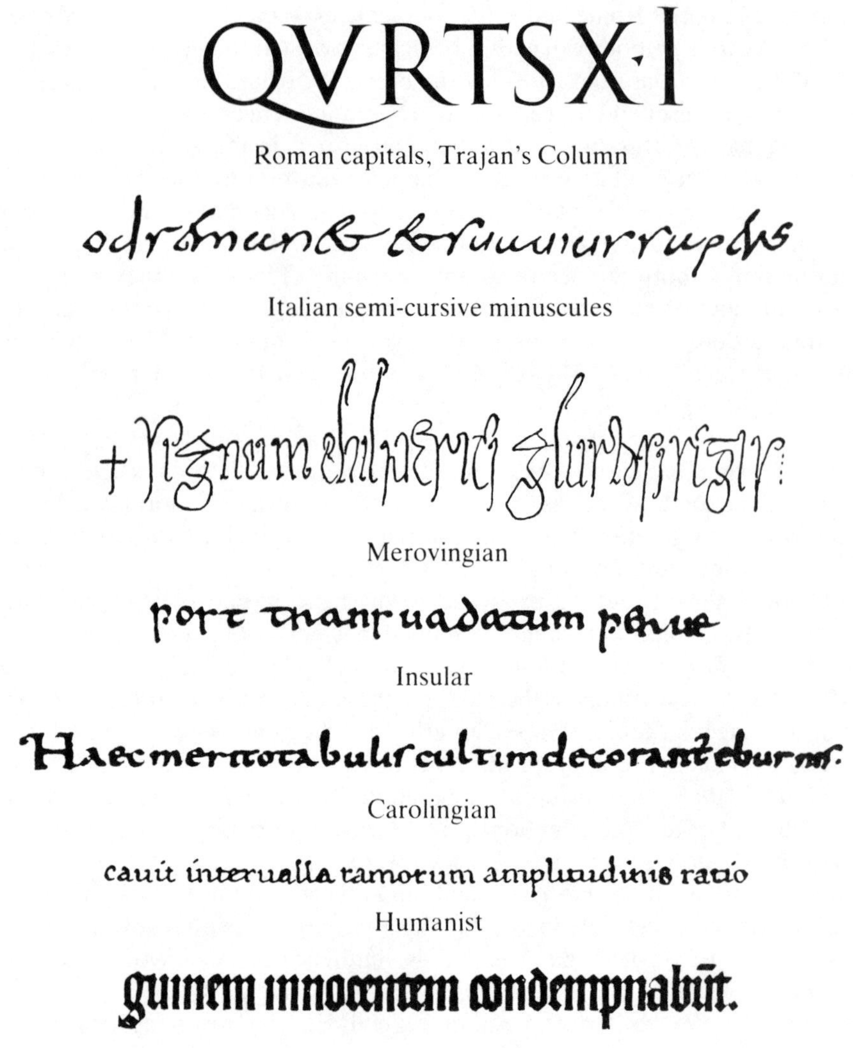

QVRTSX·I

Roman capitals, Trajan's Column

odrómanb bruwururupds

Italian semi-cursive minuscules

† Yĩgnum ehlyeycĩ glurbyĩrẽyĩ

Merovingian

porc tnanr uadatum penue

Insular

Haec mertotabulrcultrimdecoranteburnr.

Carolingian

cauit interualla ramorum amplttudmis ratio

Humanist

guinem innocentem condempnabiit.

Black-Letter

Figure 17

horizontal, were narrow, and contained few curves – in many gothic alphabets an ⟨o⟩, for instance, was a wholly curve-free, tall, narrow hexagon.[2]

Such was the situation when printing was introduced to Europe. Printers, naturally enough, imitated the styles of lettering current in handwriting, and thus made relatively permanent the range of styles that happened to exist when their craft arose. German printers usually printed in gothic; Italian printers often used humanist fonts, which became known as 'roman' because of the belief that they reflected Classical Roman script.

Although gothic type was much commoner than roman in the early years of printing (and was still almost universally used in Germany until it was condemned by Adolf Hitler in 1941 (Morison 1972, p. 323)), in Britain it was given up for all but a few marginal purposes in the 17c (Johnson 1966, pp. 44–5), and we shall consider it no further. What is relevant for the practical purposes of those who deal with the printed word today are the varieties of letter-form which have evolved within roman script. Obviously we cannot separately consider each of the thousands of faces which have been cut during the five centuries of typographical history, but this huge number of individual faces can be classified into a small set of families whose characteristics are easily described. We shall consider only 'book-faces', that is type-faces designed for printing continuous text, as opposed to 'display faces' used for printing single words or short phrases on posters, in headings, or in similar positions; display faces are very diverse indeed, and in many of them legibility is a subsidiary consideration.

The first important developments in roman type were structural. Originally, the distinction between 'capital' (or 'majuscule') and 'minuscule' letters had been essentially a difference in style of writing: some documents would be written in capitals, others in minuscules. In any text it was common for certain key letters, such as the first letters of sentences and/or of names, to be emphasized by being written larger and perhaps in a somewhat different, more formal, though essentially similar style. The system of combining minuscules with majuscules of a contrasting style began to grow up in the Carolingian hand of the early Middle Ages, but was not fully formalized until the 15c Italian developers of roman type designed fonts which combined an upper case modelled on monumental capitals with a lower case imitating minuscule handwriting. Thus, in roman type, most letters differ quite markedly in shape as well as size between upper and lower case: compare ⟨A a⟩, ⟨D d⟩, ⟨E e⟩, etc. Alphabets which share this feature today, such as the modern version of the Greek alphabet, do so because they borrowed the idea from roman type; and other alphabets (e.g. the Cyrillic script used for Russian, which was created on the basis of the Greek alphabet of the +9c) lack the feature: in modern Russian typography most capitals are merely larger versions of the lower-case letters.

A further structural development was the co-ordination of italic and roman fonts. 'Italic' type began life in 1501 as simply a different style of type, modelled on Italian handwriting which was more cursive than the hand represented by ordinary roman minuscules. One book would be printed in roman, another in italic. At first the difference referred only to the lower-case letters, since capitals were by definition formal while italics were by definition cursive. Fairly soon, however, printers began to cut sloping upper-case letters to match the slope usually found in italic minuscules. Not until the mid 16c, in Paris, were roman and italic treated as 'fellow halves of a single design' (Morison 1973, p. 70), to be mixed in the printing of a single text with italic reserved for such purposes as emphasis and differentiation.

Alphabets other than roman have no parallel graphic distinction: a word to be emphasized in a German text printed in gothic, or in a Hebrew text, is set with spaces between the letters – a less salient distinction.

Once italic and roman had been co-ordinated, roman type as a symbolic system had become what it is today. It remains to consider the various letter-forms which have instantiated the system. Roman book-faces can be classified into three main families: in chronological order, these are 'Old Face', 'Modern Face', and 'Sans-Serif'.[3]

Old Face types (many of which are in fact new, such as Stanley Morison's Times New Roman of 1931, the type used in the present book) are relatively close to the original shape of roman type. (Those faces which are closest of all to Humanist handwriting are usually distinguished from Old Face as 'Venetian': their letters have thin lines but wide bodies, so that they are uneconomical of space, and they are seen only rarely, usually in fine editions of poetry and the like – though J. R. Firth's *The Tongues of Men* (1937) was printed in the Venetian face Centaur (1470).) An Old Face has fairly light, oblique stress; serifs are bracketed, and those at the upper end of verticals are oblique.

Apart from Times, already mentioned, some Old Faces in common current use are Imprint (1912), Bembo (1495), and Garamond (1621). (Here and below, dates quoted are for the earliest type of which the contemporary type named is identifiably a descendant. Thus, the type produced by the Monotype Corporation in 1929 and named by it 'Bembo' is not identical to the type which the 15c printer Aldus Manutius cut and used to print Pietro Bembo's *De Aetna,* but the former is consciously a 20c 'interpretation' of the latter.) The *Journal of Linguistics* was set in Imprint until 1980. Gilbert Ryle's *The Concept of Mind* (Hutchinson, 1949), and the English edition of Sir Karl Popper's *Logic of Scientific Discovery* (Hutchinson, 1959), are set in Bembo. The Penguin Classics editions of Plato are in Garamond. For examples of these and other faces mentioned below, see Figure 18.

Modern Face is one of the products of the spirit of rationalism which swept through all aspects of French culture in the 18c. The first type of the class now called Modern, the so-called *romain du roi*, was produced by a committee of the Académie des Sciences charged by Louis XIV in 1692 with the task of creating new types for the Imprimerie Royale; these were eventually completed in 1745. The committee approached its task in a highly theoretical way, planning at one stage to define each letter-shape on a grid divided into 2304 tiny squares like the pixels of a modern computer graphic display.

Old Face letters have oblique, bracketed serifs, because that is how serifs are naturally formed when letters are written by hand. The Académie des Sciences found it irrational to let the mechanics of penmanship dictate the design of printing type: in Modern Face, serifs are perfectly horizontal (i.e. at right angles to the lines they terminate), and usually unbracketed. 15c type-casting techniques had not allowed letter-shapes to include very thin lines, since they would break in use; Modern Face exploited superior 18c technology by introducing extreme stress contrast, with hairline serifs and upstrokes and thick downstrokes; and, since the obliqueness of Old Face stress was another hangover from the natural way of holding a pen, in Modern Face the stress was made vertical (i.e. the thinnest parts of an ⟨O⟩ are at the twelve and six o'clock positions).

Venetian

Let me ask you a riddle. If you can guess it during the seven days of the feast, I will give you 30
Centaur

Old Face

Let me ask you a riddle. If you can guess it during the seven days of the
Bembo

Let me ask you a riddle. If you can guess it during the seven days of the
Garamond

Let me ask you a riddle. If you can guess it during the seven days of the feast, I will g
Imprint

Let me ask you a riddle. If you can guess it during the seven days of
Times

Transitional

Let me ask you a riddle. If you can guess it during the seven days of the feast, I will
Fournier

Let me ask you a riddle. If you can guess it during the seven days of
Baskerville

Let me ask you a riddle. If you can guess it during the seven days of the feast, I wi
Bell

Modern Face

Let me ask you a riddle. If you can guess it during the seven days of the feast, I w
Bodoni

Let me ask you a riddle. If you can guess it during the seven days of the feast, I
Didot

Let me ask you a riddle. If you can guess it during the seven days of the feast, I will
Walbaum

Let me ask you a riddle. If you can guess it during the seven days of the feast, I
Monotype Modern

Sans Serif

Let me ask you a riddle. If you can guess it during the seven days of
Helvetica

Let me ask you a riddle. If you can guess it during the seven days
Univers

Let me ask you a riddle. If you can guess it during the seven days
Optima

Figure 18

Although the *romain du roi* was reserved for royal use, French typographers began to cut faces which shared its novel features, and Modern Face became increasingly popular throughout Europe during the 18c and early 19c. It was resisted for some time in Britain: in the later 18c British typographers created 'Transitional' faces having a more vertical and somewhat heavier stress than Old Face but retaining oblique, bracketed serifs. Such faces include the beautiful Baskerville (1757) and Bell (1788). (Baskerville is the face of Noam Chomsky's *Aspects of the Theory of Syntax* (1965) and my *Liberty and Language* (1979), and was used for the journal *Linguistic Inquiry* until 1976; Bertrand Russell's *Autobiography* (1967–9), and the lettering on the Wellington £5 note, are in Bell.) But by the early years of the 19c the tide of fashion overwhelmed this country too, and throughout that century most printing – for several decades, virtually all printing – was in Modern Face. Many Modern fonts are relatively narrow-bodied, and have ascenders and descenders that are short relative to x-height: both of these features make them economical of paper. Three of the better-known early Moderns are Bodoni (*c.* 1767), Didot (*c.* 1784), and Walbaum (*c.* 1805). (Bodoni and Didot are scarcely or never used as book faces in Britain, and the Monotype Bodoni which is used for some purposes is much less 'extreme' aesthetically than the 18c original; but Bodonis and Didots closer to the original are common in France – one book using Bodoni is the 1955 edition of Henri Maspero's *La Chine Antique* (Imprimerie Nationale, Paris), and Marcel Cohen's *La grande invention de l'écriture* (Klincksieck, Paris, 1958) is in Didot. Walbaum is occasionally used as a book face here, e.g. for the one-volume English edition of the *I Ching* (Routledge, 1968), and for Mollie Panter-Downes's book on Swinburne, *At The Pines* (Hamish Hamilton, 1971).)

In the 20c, Monotype created a new series of Modern fonts, less extreme than the original Moderns, which are still widely used for technical printing, particularly in America. Leonard Bloomfield's *Language* (Holt, 1933) is in Monotype Modern, and until 1976 (when it changed to Times) the journal *Language* used the same face.

The initial success of Modern Face was a matter of pure fashion. Interestingly, the professionals tended to oppose it in France, as well as in Britain. Updike (1922, vol. 1, p. 243) quotes the younger Fournier (designer of a fine Transitional face, *c.* 1740) as remarking 'Must there be so many squares to make an O that is round'; Johnson (1966, p. 78) quotes a remark made in 1828 by a British typefounder regretting that popular taste had forced him to melt down thousands of pounds' worth of type superior to what replaced it. As printers began to revert to Old Face in the later 19c and early 20c, though, Modern Face came to be seen as a practical type suitable for serious, scientific writing, while Old Face was felt to be more appropriate for literary texts in which aesthetic considerations were paramount.

However, the chief practical virtue of any type is legibility, and the allegations repeatedly made against Modern Face were not merely that it appeared mechanical and ugly but also that it was harder to read than Old Face. Already in 1800 a certain *citoyen* Sobry complained in Paris that whereas Old Face emphasized the parts of letters which differentiated them from one another, Modern Face with its heavy vertical stress emphasized the parts that are common – in this respect Modern Face is somewhat reminiscent of gothic.

Since the great revival of fine typography which occurred in Britain in the first half of the 20c, Modern has been relatively little used here; the role of 'unmarked' face, which once belonged to Monotype Modern, seems to have passed to Times. Indeed, the connotations of the styles have changed to the point that Modern Face is now associated with a Victorian 'period' atmosphere, so that for instance the 1970 edition of Sir John Betjeman's *Collected Poems* (Murray) is set in Monotype Modern. Routine use of Modern Face lingered later in the USA, and in France where the extreme original Moderns are still common.

Rationalism in typography has manifested itself anew in the 20c, however, in the promotion of Sans-Serif types. Sans-Serif letters, as the name implies, have no serifs; they are usually monoline (although some Sans faces, such as Optima (1958), have slight stress), and they tend to simplify letter-outlines into assemblages of a few geometrical elements, so that for instance a Sans ⟨a⟩ will often be 'single-storeyed': ɑ. The most widely used Sans faces at present are Helvetica and Univers (both 1957).

Sans faces were originally developed in the 19c purely as display faces; lower-case Sans are not known to have existed before 1850 (Johnson 1966, p. 159). Although necessarily austere, Sans type used for display purposes can have great beauty: outstanding in this respect is Edward Johnston's Railway Type (1916), used throughout the London Transport system for the lettering of notices, destination-boards, and the like.

Between the wars, however, as part of the general movement in the arts associated with the 'Bauhaus', German and Swiss typographers began to elevate Sans to the role of a book face. Sans type, stripped as it was of all unnecessary frills, was advocated as the proper lettering for twentieth-century man, liberated by Freud from his complexes. Morison (1972, p. 336) suggests that Sans was seen as a democratic, anti-élitist style. In late 20c Britain Sans is still far rarer than serifed type as a book face, but it is becoming commoner. In my experience it tends to be used particularly in works discussing urgent 'current affairs' issues, in which it is important to convince the reader of the up-to-date, radical outlook of the writer. Thus, the first two books on my shelves which I find to be set in Sans are H. Lindsay Smith, *Anatomy of Apartheid* (Khanya, Germiston/Transvaal, 1979), and Rhodes Boyson (ed.), *Goodbye to Nationalisation* (Churchill Press, 1971).

One wonders whether this typographical policy is not counter-productive; I am fairly sure that the chief subliminal effect of Sans text in my own case is to reduce the perceived authority of the printed word. Furthermore, the legibility problem already discussed in connection with Modern Face appears subjectively to be much acuter in the case of Sans. Stanley Morison (1973, p. 98) regarded the superior legibility of serifed type as too obvious to discuss.

Particularly open to question is the practice, currently widespread in British primary schools, of using Sans for children's initial reading-books. The rationale seems to be that the letters *read* by children should be as close as possible in outline to those they are learning to *write* (cf. Watts and Nisbet 1974, p. 33); obviously children writing with modern instruments will not be producing serifs, and they will not be making outlines like the traditional printed shapes of ⟨a⟩ or ⟨g⟩, so the faces in their reading-books incorporate forms such as ⟨ɑ g⟩. The effect, however, is to produce a kind of print with minimal distinctiveness of letter-shapes: it is somewhat reminiscent in that respect of Hebrew script. A page of a contemporary children's basic reading-book is a sea of circles, arcs, and straight lines – 'balls and sticks' – unrelieved by any stress contrast or quirkiness of individual letters. Children tend to confuse left and right; ⟨b d⟩, ⟨p q⟩ in these faces are formed quite symmetrically, which must surely aggravate that tendency (cf. Downing and Leong 1982, p. 56), whereas in a serifed face such letter-pairs are not symmetrical. (It is noteworthy that ball-and-stick writing was rejected by the typographer, Edward Johnston, whose ideas had triggered its invention in 1913 (Myers 1984, p. 336).)

Already in the 16c French typographers invented a somewhat bizarre type, 'Civilité', which was motivated largely by the principle that childen ought to learn to read from print that was as close as possible to handwritten forms (Johnson 1966, p. 138). This principle seems less than axiomatic. One would be glad of hard evidence that the special type now used in teaching literacy in Britain actually promotes that aim, rather than hindering it as I suspect it may.

There is in fact a dearth of hard evidence on any of the issues raised here. The psychology of typography is an under-studied subject, and I must make it clear that the subjective impressions of relative legibility discussed above, though widely shared, cannot at present be supported by scientific evidence. The chief published attempt to investigate the legibility of different styles of type is still Paterson and Tinker (1932). Comparing the speed at which texts printed in ten different faces were read, Paterson and Tinker failed to find any consistent differences between the Old and Modern faces. The one Sans face was read relatively slowly, but the difference was not statistically significant; the only significantly slow faces were American Typewriter (a printing type which imitates the equal-width lettering of typewriting) and, far slower still, Cloister Black (a gothic face). More recently Sir Cyril Burt claimed (1959) to have established legibility-differences between Old, Modern, and Sans which confirmed the subjective impressions discussed here, but it is clear (Hartley and Rooum 1983) that this work suffers from the same failings as other published research by Burt and cannot be taken seriously. E. C. Poulton (1965) failed to find significant legibility-differences between the three families of fonts. (See also Spencer 1969, and, on a fascinating side-issue, Bryden and Allard 1976.)

I find the current lack of interest in the psychology of typography surprising, considering how all-important the printed word is in any kind of academic work. (Much more research is being done on issues concerning layout of texts, such as forms or technical material containing headings and subheadings – see e.g. Hartley (1980), Twyman (in press); and it is probably true that, for such texts, layout is far more significant than typeface as an influence on legibility.) It appears that academics are by and large inclined to take the form of their written materials for granted, and that decisions about type-faces are usually determined, even today, purely by considerations of aesthetics, fashion, and cost. Michael Brady (1981, p. 207) complains that 'A great deal of research on font design . . . is depressingly subjective'. Since the role of writing in our civilization shows no sign of diminishing in importance, this lack of scientific interest in it seems unfortunate.

7 A featural system: Korean Han'gŭl

Korea is a fairly small and very distant country, but it is a country of great significance for the linguist in two respects. It was in Korea, in the 13c, that the Chinese invention of printing from movable type was first seriously exploited; and in the 15c a Korean created for the use of his countrymen a wholly original and quite remarkable phonographic script, nowadays called Han'gŭl, which has been described as 'perhaps the most scientific system of writing in general use in any country' (Reischauer 1960, p. 435), or more simply as 'the world's best alphabet' (Vos 1964, p. 31).

Any discussion of writing in Korea must begin by considering the relationship between the cultures of Korea and China.

China was the first civilization to emerge in East Asia; accordingly, when neighbouring nations such as the Koreans, the Japanese, and the Vietnamese began their own climb from barbarism towards civilization, they inevitably looked towards China as the ancient fount of culture and to a large extent borrowed its institutions and inventions rather than creating their own from scratch. There is a sort of parallel in Europe: since the Renascence, European nations have looked towards the ancient cultures of Greece and Rome to provide a source and precedent for everything from theories of political life to words for new ideas such as *helicopter* or *audiovisual*. But the analogy is weak; for many reasons, China loomed far larger on the mental horizon of the satellite nations in East Asia than did the Classical Mediterranean civilizations in the mind of the post-Medieval European. In the European case, the Classical civilizations had died long before the new one was born; modern Greece and Italy are small and not very powerful nations which can scarcely claim to inherit more continuity with Classical Greek or Roman culture than can many other nations. Furthermore, the two Classical European civilizations were very different from one another; and, while the contributions of Greece and Rome were perhaps complementary rather than opposed, Christianity has provided a rival, Asiatic source of cultural authority which in many ways was incompatible with the Classical heritage. In East Asia, matters were quite otherwise. Far from dying out, Chinese civilization has grown more or less continuously, in population, geographical spread, and cultural complexity, from its beginnings to the present day; modern China is both by far the most populous State in the world and the possessor of the oldest living civilization. Furthermore, it was a characteristic of Chinese culture from an early stage to be monolithic, highly centralized, unwilling to recognize any value in cultural diversity. And for a peripheral East Asian nation such as Korea there was no other external source of culture whatever; everything came from China. Even the few institutions, such as Buddhism, which the Chinese themselves borrowed from elsewhere came to the Koreans only after having been thoroughly digested and reshaped by the Chinese.

Politically, the satellite nations of East Asia contracted very diverse relationships with China at different periods; but culturally China was, for all of them at all times, the sun round which they revolved as minor planets. And if this was true for Japan, Vietnam, and other lesser States, it was true most of all for Korea. During much of Korea's history, the aim of Korean education was quite explicitly to make Korea a *Sohwa*, a 'Small China'. In some ways Korea became a better realization of Confucian Chinese cultural norms than China itself ever was. One consequence of this cultural dependence of Korea on China was that the Korean language was not much written until recently.

As a spoken language, Korean is quite different from Chinese. It belongs to an entirely separate language-family, the Altaic family; within this family, Korean is related relatively closely to the Tungusic languages such as Manchu, more distantly to Mongolian, and more distantly still to Turkish and to less well-known languages such as Chuvash. Not only is Korean genetically unrelated to Chinese, but the two languages are very different in type. Chinese is an 'isolating' language whose words consist of one or more invariant monosyllabic roots; Korean is an 'agglutinating' language containing polysyllabic roots which take a fairly complex range of grammatical suffixes. The grammatical order of words is quite different in the two languages: for instance, Chinese places verb before object and preposition before noun as in English, while Korean puts the verb at the end of the clause and uses 'postpositions' rather than prepositions. Korean is much more different from Chinese than one European language is from another. Nevertheless, until the 20c the normal medium of written communication in Korea was the Chinese language. To be educated meant to study Chinese language and literature; until recently a Korean scholar would have been less likely to write in Korean than would his counterpart in medieval Europe to write in his own native language rather than in Latin.

Naturally, the Korean language borrowed vocabulary from Chinese on a massive scale, adapting Chinese roots to Korean habits of pronunciation; in modern spoken Korean, the grammar is purely Korean and the commonest words are formed from native Korean roots, but the majority of items listed in a large dictionary are 'Sino-Korean', i.e. Chinese words in Korean pronunciation. Indeed, the relationship between the two languages is such that *any* Chinese word automatically counts in its conventional Sino-Korean form as a word of Korean. If an English-speaker creates a neologism, say in order to name some technological innovation, from a Latin or Greek root not previously used in the English lexicon then he normally feels obliged to explain and justify his coinage briefly, but Chinese words are used freely in Korean without any such 'naturalization ceremony'. Sino-Korean vocabulary is by no means restricted to learned usage, as Classical-derived vocabulary tends to be in English. For instance, virtually all Korean personal and place names are Chinese rather than Native Korean; and there are many grammatical environments where Sino-Korean rather than Native Korean numerals have to be used, although in other environments the Native numbers occur.

The prestige of the Chinese language in Korea was so great that, even in its Chinese-influenced form, the Korean language was not much used as a written language before the 1880s. After their conquest of Korea in 1910 the Japanese encouraged the use of their own written language; thus only since the Second World War has Korean been for as long as a generation a standard national written language in general use.

But that does not mean that Korean was not written at all until a hundred years ago. As early as +600 or thereabouts the Koreans were beginning to adapt Chinese script to write their own language, and throughout subsequent Korean history the native language was used in certain kinds of writing, though normally relatively low-status, 'unofficial' writing (mainly poems and novels).

The Chinese script, as we shall see in Chapter 8, is logographic, and consequently not particularly easy to adapt for the purposes of transcribing a language other than the one for which it was invented. Several relatively cumbersome methods were used to solve this problem. We shall not examine these methods in detail here, since they are paralleled almost exactly by the methods the Japanese used, and most of which they still use today, to solve the same problem with respect to their own language – these will be examined at length in Chapter 9. (It is no coincidence that Koreans and Japanese used the same devices in order to write non-Chinese languages in Chinese script: the Japanese originally borrowed Chinese culture from Korea rather than directly from China, and Koreans taught the Japanese how to write.) In Korea these clumsy systems were eventually made obsolete by the creation of the far more efficient Han'gŭl script, the logic of which owes nothing at all to China (and which the Japanese never copied, since by the 15c they had ceased to look to Korea as a source of cultural loans). At present Korean is still sometimes written in a mixed script which uses Chinese graphs for Sino-Korean words as well as Han'gŭl for Native forms; but North Koreans now write exclusively in Han'gŭl, and South Korean usage is moving in the same direction although older South Koreans still use the mixed script. In this chapter we shall examine the pure Han'gŭl script, as used by North Koreans and most South Koreans.

The Han'gŭl script was created by King Sejong (reigned 1418–50), who assembled a group of scholars for the task in a 'Bureau of Standard Sounds'. (It is usually supposed that Sejong's role in the creation of Han'gŭl was a purely managerial one. However, Lee Ki-moon (1977, p. 61) suggests that

Korean tradition may be correct in asserting that the King invented the script personally. I shall write as if that were so, simply for ease of exposition.) The script was completed in 1444, and promulgated two years later in a book entitled *Hunmin Chŏng'ŭm*, 'The Standard Sounds for the Instruction of the People' (translated in Zachert 1980), and this title was also the official name for the script itself. (The script immediately became very unpopular with the educated classes, who saw it as a trivialization of the serious and difficult task of writing in Chinese; they disparagingly called the script *ŏnmun*, 'vernacular writing', and this was the term normally used until the name *han'gŭl*, 'great script', was adopted early in our own century as a move to upgrade the status of the system.) *Hunmin Chŏng'ŭm* makes it clear that the motives for creating Han'gŭl included not only the disinterested aim of promoting cultural activity but, as elsewhere, the desire of the State to control the citizenry: 'Those who practise the sciences are suffering from the fact that it is difficult for them to make their ideas known, and those who run prisons are in difficulties because indictments and evidence are incomprehensible.'

The script is reckoned by the Koreans as containing 28 'letters' in its original form; four of the 28 are now obsolete. But, unlike the letters of the Roman alphabet or its congeners, those of Han'gŭl have systematic internal structure correlated with the phonetic-feature composition of the phonemes. In this respect Han'gŭl is very like Pitman's shorthand (p. 41), and quite unlike any other script known to me that is used as the ordinary writing-system of a society.

The Korean analysis of the script into 28 (now 24) letters is not in fact the most enlightening way of presenting it to a newcomer, since some combinations of these letters are better treated as separate graphic units. In what follows I shall begin by discussing the subset of the original system which is still in use, arranged so as to display its linguistic logic rather than in accordance with Korean tradition.

Before presenting the alphabet, I should make some preliminary remarks about Korean phonology. In Korean, the primary distinction of manner among obstruent consonants (stops, fricatives, affricates) is not voicing, as it is in many European languages, but rather the distinction of 'tense' versus 'lax' (or 'fortis' v. 'lenis'); a 'tense' consonant involves greater muscle-tension and higher air-pressure than its lax equivalent (Kim 1965). At most places of articulation Korean has two tense obstruents and one lax obstruent, the tense obstruents being respectively unaspirated (i.e. voice-onset is simultaneous with release of the consonant-closure) and heavily-aspirated (it follows from the definition of 'tense' that if a tense stop is aspirated the aspiration will be heavy, because the air-pressure is high). Taking bilabial as a typical place of articulation, I shall symbolize the three phonemes as /p*/ (tense unaspirated), /pʰ/ (tense aspirated), and /b/ (lax). Voice-onset timing is non-distinctive among lax obstruents, which are voiced at some positions in a word and voiceless at other positions; indeed, each lax obstruent has a range of several different allophones in complementary distribution with one another. In my transcriptions I shall ignore these allophonic differences, as does the Han'gŭl script (which in this respect is phonemic rather than phonetic). I shall use the major visual distinction which the IPA alphabet provides between pairs of symbols such as ⟨p b⟩, ⟨t d⟩ etc. in order to symbolize the major Korean phonological distinction of tense v. lax. Futhermore I shall write /c/ (with asterisk or superscript ⟨ʰ⟩ as appropriate) and /ɟ/ for palato-alveolar affricates, IPA [tʃ dʒ] (in the 'Middle Korean' of the 15c it is likely that these sounds were dental affricates [ts dz], cf. Lee 1977, p. 108).

Otherwise IPA symbols are used with their standard values, though as usual cardinal symbols are used for sounds which, no doubt, are not precisely at cardinal positions – the transcription portrays a neat, 'ideal' phonological system which lies behind a somewhat messier phonetic reality.

The Han'gŭl symbols for simple phonemes are shown in Figure 19.

Consonants

	bilabial	apical	sibilant	velar	laryngal
lax continuant	ㅁ	ㄴ	ㅅ		ㅇ
	m	n	s		q (see p.126)
lax stop	ㅂ	ㄷ	ㅈ	ㄱ	
	b	d	ɟ	g	
tense aspirated stop	ㅍ	ㅌ	ㅊ	ㅋ	ㅎ
	pʰ	tʰ	cʰ	kʰ	h
tense continuant			ㅆ		
			s*		
tense unaspirated stop	ㅃ	ㄸ	ㅉ	ㄲ	
	p*	t*	c*	k*	
liquid		ㄹ			
		l			

Vowels

	front			back		
	spread		rounded		spread	rounded
close	i ㅣ				ɯ ㅡ	u ㅜ
mid	e ㅔ		ø ㅚ		ɤ ㅓ	o ㅗ
open	æ ㅐ				a ㅏ	

Figure 19

The major graphic distinction is between vowels and consonants: vowels are based on long horizontal or vertical lines with the addition of small distinguishing marks, consonants are represented by more compact, two-dimensional signs.

The consonants are divided into five families corresponding approximately to what a Western phonetician would call 'places of articulation'. (I have supplied my own labels for the rows and columns of Figure 19, as the terms used in *Hunmin Chŏng'ŭm* do not correspond to those standard in 20c Western phonetics.) From a strictly phonetic point of view it may seem odd to separate off the 'sibilants' as a column parallel to the others, as these fricatives and affricates are made at or near the same place of articulation as the apical stops in the second column. Phonologically, however, this treatment makes good sense for a language such as Korean, which has consonants involving friction only in one area of the mouth – Korean has no [f] or [x], for instance. At that area, Korean distinguishes much the same set of 'manners of articulation' as at any of the stop positions, so the sibilants are appropriately treated as a separate sound-family.

Taking the lax rows as basic, we find that the five consonant-families are represented by (highly stylized) pictures of the articulations involved. Thus, the symbols for /n/ or /d/ show the tongue-tip raised to touch the front of the palate, while the symbol for /g/ suggests the back of the tongue touching the rear of the palate – like the writers of modern phonetics textbooks, King Sejong evidently visualized the speaker as facing left. It may be less easy to see the /m/ symbol as portraying the lips, but it is relevant that this sign is identical to the Chinese graph for 'mouth', which was originally a picture of a mouth. The /s/ sign represents a tooth, and the two columns which I have labelled 'sibilants' v. 'apicals' are called in the *Hunmin Chŏng'ŭm* 'tooth sounds' and 'tongue sounds'. (One may feel sceptical about whether this was an appropriate way to characterize the articulatory difference between the two sound-families in Middle Korean; but, even if Sejong had succeeded in understanding that the real phonetic distinction of the 'tooth-sounds' was turbulence in the airstream, it is difficult to see how he could have symbolized such an intangible phenomenon graphically.) Lastly, the circle on which the 'laryngal' graphs are based represents the throat in cross-section; I shall take up the question of the phonetic reality of this column below.

Until recently it was controversial whether the forms of the Han'gŭl graphs were in fact motivated as I have described them here, rather than being mere arbitrary simple shapes, some of which happened accidentally to look appropriate in terms of articulatory phonetics. This question was resolved in 1940 with the discovery of the original draft of the *Hunmin Chŏng'ŭm*, which included a section explaining the logic of the forms in the terms I have just given. In this respect, then, Han'gŭl is even more phonetically systematic than Pitman's shorthand (in which the correlation between phonetic and graphic features is entirely arbitrary); Han'gŭl exemplifies a type of phonetic transcription which Abercrombie (1967, p. 116) supposes to be unusable in practice despite its theoretical attractions.

Stop as opposed to continuant articulation is shown by adding a horizontal

The fact remains that, as we shall see in later chapters, phonographic scripts often seem to be considerably 'deeper' than the allophonic or even phonemic level. (Like the motivated/arbitrary contrast, the deep/shallow contrast is a gradient rather than all-or-none distinction, and one which applies to different components of an orthography separately – a given writing system may well be deep in its representation of one aspect of a spoken language but shallow in its representation of another aspect.)

The points I have been making about a deep/shallow distinction in phonology are in principle equally applicable to grammatical analysis. Consider, as a very simple example, the word *du* in French: this would commonly be described as the 'surface' manifestation of an 'underlying' sequence of morphemes *de le*. In standard French orthography, a phrase such as /aʃte dy pɛ̃/ is written ⟨acheter du pain⟩. But it is easy to imagine a hypothetical orthography which recorded the underlying morphemes and wrote the same phrase ⟨acheter de le pain⟩. Such an orthography would be grammatically 'deeper' than standard French orthography, and the grammatical depth of a script would be an issue independent of its phonological depth – even a logographic script could be deep or shallow in this sense.

In practice, however, the depth issue arises only with respect to phonology. I know of no script, whether phonographic or logographic, that is at all deep grammatically, though phonographic scripts differ considerably in their phonological depth.

We have now drawn all the theoretical distinctions necessary for an introductory investigation of the linguistics of writing. The chapters that follow will apply these conceptual tools in a series of case-studies.

line at the top of the symbol. Perhaps because the /m/ graph is already well-supplied with horizontals, an exceptional solution is adopted in the bilabial column and /b/ is symbolized by what was historically the earlier form of the square Chinese 'mouth' graph. Tense aspirate articulation is shown by doubling the horizontal line, though again an exception is made in the bilabial column and a special symbol is provided for /pʰ/. Tense unaspirated articulation is shown by doubling the whole lax symbol. (One of the respects in which my presentation of the Han'gŭl system varies from the traditional analysis is that the Koreans do not count the tense unaspirated symbols as separate letters – they are regarded as pairs of the lax letters.) The unique liquid phoneme is shown by adding an angular mark to the basic apical symbol.

One of the most interesting points in connection with the consonants concerns the circular symbol, which I transcribe ⟨q⟩ as a purely arbitrary convention. The grapheme ⟨q⟩ has two values: it represents either the velar nasal [ŋ] or no consonant at all. Logically one might expect the velar nasal to be represented by the /g/ symbol minus its top stroke; but no such sign exists in Han'gŭl. The reason why [ŋ] is not treated on a par with the other nasals undoubtedly has to do with the fact that [ŋ] is a sound of limited distribution in Korean: as in English, it can occur at the end of a syllable but never at the beginning, and accordingly it tends not to be perceived as an independent phoneme in its own right. (The latter assertion is certainly true of English-speakers' perceptions of their language, and we may infer it to be true also for Koreans.) Han'gŭl is written with the phoneme-symbols grouped into syllables, as we shall see below; the rule is that ⟨q⟩ represents [ŋ] at the end of a syllable but zero at the beginning. It is illegitimate to write a syllable without a consonant-symbol preceding the vowel; if no consonant occurs, ⟨q⟩ must be written (though a syllable *ending* with a vowel will have no mark corresponding to the absence of final consonant).

One reason why this is interesting is that it is closely reminiscent of a famous linguistic debate about the phonemic status of [ŋ] in English and German (Chao 1934, p. 46; Trubetzkoy 1958).

In both of these languages, the sound [ŋ] is in complementary distribution with [h]: [h] occurs only preceding the vowel of its syllable, [ŋ] only following the vowel. It would in principle be possible, therefore, to treat the two sounds as allophones of a single phoneme, say '/x/', and to transcribe English words such as *hat, behave, song, singer* as /xæt/, /bə'xeɪv/, /sɒx/, /'sɪxə/. Linguists writing about European languages have usually taken this to be an absurd proposal, feeling that although the two sounds happen to be in complementary distribution they clearly have nothing to do with one another; and they have argued that the criteria for phonemic analysis ought to include a test of 'phonetic similarity' for the allophones of a phoneme, precisely in order to rule out this kind of analysis.

Now in the Korean case there is no question of [ŋ] being equated with [h] – Han'gŭl provides clearly distinct symbols for these sounds. But those Korean syllables that have no other initial consonant commonly begin with a voiced laryngal continuant that we may transcribe [ɦ] (Lee 1977, pp. 151–2), which is ignored in conventional romanizations of Korean for the same reason that conventional orthography ignores the glottal stops of German words such as *ʔEisen, Theʔater* – namely, because the Roman alphabet provides no convenient symbol for it. The sounds [ɦ] and [ŋ] are in complementary distribution in Korean just as [h] and [ŋ] are in English, and the arguments for and against regarding them as allophones of a single phoneme would be quite parallel in the two cases. We might suspect that the Han'gŭl use of a single circle symbol for both [ɦ] and [ŋ] implies that the equation between an initial laryngal sound and final [ŋ], which has struck Western linguists as absurd, was for Koreans natural: that [ɦ] and [ŋ] are members of a single Korean phoneme /q/.

The facts are more complicated than this, however. The original version of Han'gŭl had four graphemes based on the circle shape, corresponding to four syllable-initials (zero, glottal stop, /h/, /ŋ/) which contrasted in 15c Chinese – as in e.g. /ĭ/ 'barbarian', /ʔĭ/ 'doctor', /hī/ 'hope', /ŋī/ 'doubt'. Sejong wished to provide distinct spellings for these sounds when they occurred in Sino-Korean loans, even though the contrasts between the three other than /h/ were lost in Korean pronunciation; compare the way that the Romans, when borrowing words from Greek, adopted a letter Y to represent the Greek /y/ sound even though in Latin this sound fell together with that of I. The four Chinese initials were written as in Figure 20:

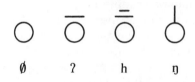

Figure 20

Notice that the original /ʔ/ symbol fits in terms of its shape into the 'lax stop' row of Figure 19: for Sejong it seems that the proportion ∅ : ʔ : h was analogous to, say, m : b : pʰ, and this has some phonetic logic – no horizontal, one horizontal, and two horizontals represent respectively no interruption, momentary interruption, and prolonged interruption of voicing. On the other hand the vertical stalk of ⟨ŋ⟩ is a unique element, like the angular top of ⟨l⟩, implying that [ŋ] was not seen as analogous in manner of articulation to any of the other consonants. (Again there is a possible phonetic justification for this; in Korean [ŋ], unlike [m] or [n], is in certain circumstances reduced to mere nasalization of the preceding vowel.)

At an early stage in the history of Han'gŭl the ⟨ʔ⟩ grapheme was given up, since the Chinese distinction between initial [ʔ] and zero initial was alien to Korean ears. Likewise ⟨ŋ⟩ came to be used only where [ŋ] is pronounced in Korean (namely at the end of syllables), a tendency reinforced by the fact that initial /ŋ/ was disappearing even in Chinese. Chinese words that were originally pronounced with zero, /ʔ/, or /ŋ/ initial, when used as Sino-Korean loans, all came to be written with initial ⟨∅⟩.

If a syllable lacked a final consonant, although in theory ⟨∅⟩ could be written in final position, the *Hunmin Chŏng'ŭm* had itself recommended writing nothing. When /ŋ/ occurred finally, the rules for grouping the graphemes of a syllable (to be discussed below) meant that the grapheme ⟨ŋ⟩ had to be squeezed underneath other graphemes: this inevitably led to shortening of its stalk, so that it came to look more like ⟨∅⟩. Thus the two graphemes ⟨∅⟩ and ⟨ŋ⟩ came to be used in complementary distribution with one another and at the same time came to look increasingly alike; so naturally they were confused. By the 17c (Lee 1977, pp. 231–2) the two graphemes were for practical purposes merged into one.

All this might be taken to imply that the double usage of ⟨q⟩ is not, after all, very good evidence that Korean speakers mentally equated [ŋ] with a phonetically very different initial consonant. It might be said that the dual use arises through a series of pure historical accidents, comparable to the accidents which cause ⟨C⟩ to have the values /k/ and /s/ in English (sounds which are psychologically distinct for English-speakers). On the other hand, it is remarkable that from the beginning of Han'gŭl script the sound [ŋ] was symbolized with a graph based on a circle, representing the throat and hence appropriate for [ɦ] or [ʔ], rather than on the curve used in the velar letters. There are several passages in the *Hunmin Chŏng'ŭm* which seem to express doubt about the phonological status of [ŋ].

(For completeness, I should mention that the third consonant symbol which is no longer used in modern Han'gŭl was a triangular mark standing for a native Korean sound conventionally transcribed /z/, which has since dropped out of the language. There were also a number of special devices for indicating further Chinese consonants that Korean lacked, e.g. Chinese /x/ was indicated by a double ⟨h⟩.)

Let us turn now to the vowels. Here the Han'gŭl system provides six basic vowel graphs, those for the back vowels and for the vowel /i/. Each of these is made up of a horizontal or vertical line, to which in four cases is added a distinguishing mark – originally a dot close to the line, now turned into a second short line projecting from the base-line at right-angles. (The fact that the distinguishing mark for ⟨u⟩ is made as long as the horizontal base-line when the letter is written in isolation has to do with the fact that the aesthetics of Han'gŭl script, and the technique of writing it with brush on paper, were taken over from the Chinese, even though in its logic it is a purely Korean invention. It happens that a horizontal stroke with a short tick *above* it, as in Han'gŭl ⟨o⟩, is a standard graphic element in Chinese writing, but a horizontal stroke with a vertical tick *below* it is not possible in Chinese script so the vertical was lengthened into a T-shape, which looks less grotesque to Chinese-trained eyes.) Originally there was a seventh basic vowel, written with a simple dot, standing for a phoneme conventionally transcribed /ʌ/ which no longer occurs in the spoken language.

The front vowels other than /i/ are written with miniature versions of the corresponding back vowels added to the /i/ symbol. (The Koreans do not count these as separate letters but as pairs of basic vowel letters.) In other words, we might say that the vertical stroke is not so much a symbol for the phoneme /i/ as for the feature of front vowel-quality in general: with a miniature back-vowel symbol it represents the front version of that vowel, in isolation it represents the frontest of all vowels, namely the close front vowel /i/. (It might seem odd to symbolize front vowels by attaching a small back-vowel symbol to a large frontness-marker, rather than vice versa; but this arrangement produces unambiguous symbols, while the alternative method would have been likely to lead to confusion particularly with some of the diphthong symbols to be introduced shortly.) The front vowels other than /i/ were not originally assigned separate graphemes because, when Han'gŭl was created, they were diphthongs: /e æ/ derived from /ɤi ai/ in the late 18c, /ø/ from /oi/ more recently.

The graphic relationship between front and back vowels is plain. One might suppose, though, that there is little logic in the choice of symbols to represent the six 'basic' vowels (seven including the obsolete /ʌ/). Phonetically, this is true. Phonologically, however, the symbols reflect a system of a quite surprising kind.

Like other Altaic languages, Korean is a 'vowel-harmony' language. This means that most of its vowels fall into one of two classes, such that all the vowels of a given word must be drawn from one class or the other but not from both. If a root has vowels from Class A, then a grammatical suffix will contain a Class A vowel; with a root containing Class B vowels, the same grammatical suffix will show the corresponding vowel from Class B (the vowels in the two classes pair off with one another). In most Altaic languages this system is very salient and well-defined. It happens that modern Korean has lost all but a few traces of vowel-harmony (a fact which may be connected with the massive borrowing of Chinese words into Korean; two-syllable Chinese compounds contain all kinds of vowel-combinations violating Korean harmony rules, and must therefore have made those rules hard to maintain). However, the Middle Korean spoken in the 15c still possessed vowel-harmony. The vowels /ɯ u ɤ/ formed one class, whose members paired off respectively with /ʌ o a/ in the other class; /i/ was a 'neutral' vowel which could occur with vowels of either class. Thus, for example, the topic-marking suffix was /-ɯn/ after roots containing vowels of the first class, /-ʌn/ after roots containing vowels of the second class, and /-ɯn/ or /-ʌn/ interchangeably after roots containing /i/:

bom+ʌn	'as for spring'
sjɤm+ɯn	'as for the island'
jib+ʌn ⎫ jib+ɯn ⎭	'as for the house'

Comparable examples could be given to demonstrate the correspondence of /o/ with /u/ and of /a/ with /ɤ/.

Sejong associated the relatively close and relatively open vowel-classes with the Chinese philosophical terms *yin* and *yang*, representing the female and male principles respectively and correlated with the first two elements of the mystical trinity Earth, Heaven, and Man. The vowel /i/, being phonologically neutral, was associated with Man, who mediates between the *yang* of Heaven and the *yin* of Earth. Of the shapes used to make up the vowel-symbols, the dot stands for Heaven, which is round; the horizontal stands for Earth, which is flat; and the vertical stands for Man, who is upright. Sejong further postulated that a symbol containing a dot over or 'outside' (to the right of) a line was to be classed as *yang*, a symbol with a dot under or 'inside' (to the left of) a line was *yin*. This gives the system shown in Figure 21, in which the vowels pair off precisely as required by the vowel-harmony rules. This talk of *yang* and *yin* is certainly a very different style of phonetics from that usual in British linguistics departments, but it serves to capture the phonological relationships between Korean vowels very neatly.

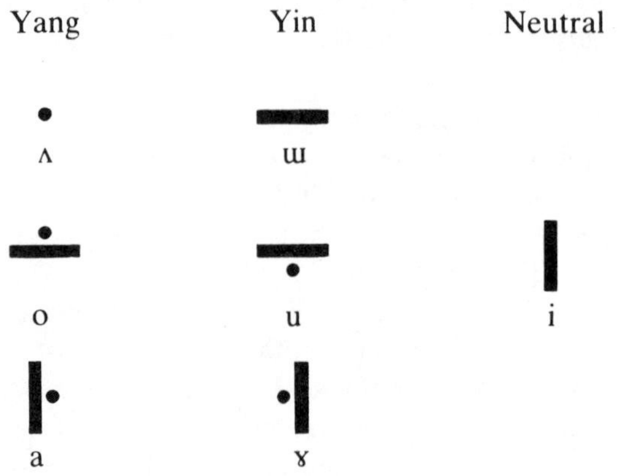

| Yang | Yin | Neutral |

Figure 21

(*Hunmin Chŏng'ŭm* introduces astrological concepts also in connection with the consonant letters, but I do not discuss this since it is not relevant to the functioning of the script.)

Han'gŭl also has a number of diphthong symbols, as shown in Figure 22. For diphthongs in /j-/, the rule is: double the distinguishing dot of the basic vowel-symbol (and, in the case of /j-/ preceding a front vowel, take the corresponding diphthong with a back vowel and add a miniature version of it to the frontness-marking vertical stroke). The four graphs made by doubling the dot of a back vowel-symbol are treated as separate letters by the Koreans. This rule which indicates a /j-/ diphthong by doubling the dot could not be used to indicate diphthongs /ji/, /jɯ/ (since the symbols for /i/, /ɯ/ have no dot) – but that does not matter since Korean has no such diphthongs.

		ㅠ	ㅟ		ㅢ
		ju	wi		ɰi
ㅖ	ㅕ	ㅛ	ㅖ	ㅕ	
je	jʌ	jo	we	wʌ	
ㅒ	ㅑ		ㅙ	ㅘ	
jæ	ja		wæ	wa	

Figure 22

Diphthongs in /w-/, like front vowels, are indicated by combinations of phoneme-symbols. Indeed, one point worthy of note is that Han'gŭl fails to make a clear graphic distinction between pure vowels and diphthongs: in particular, by the logic of the system the /wi/ graph might equally well be pronounced [y] (a fronted /u/). At first blush this looks like a defect in the script, but it is not. Korean actually has free variation between [wi] and [y] (and also between [we] and [ø], and between [wæ] and [œ] – Kim 1968, p. 517), so it is quite appropriate for the script not to mark the pure-vowel/diphthong distinction. (Han'gŭl does provide alternative writings for [we] and [ø]; but in this case, unlike the other two pairs, there is an etymological basis for the distinction and it is still maintained by some speakers, although it is merged for most.)

It was mentioned above that, in its treatment of lax obstruent consonants, Han'gŭl is phonemic rather than phonetic. In its treatment of diphthongs in /w-/, on the other hand, Han'gŭl may seem to be narrowly phonetic rather than phonemic. Before the close and mid vowels /i e ʌ/, the semivowel /w/ is written with a miniature ⟨u⟩; before the open vowels /æ a/, /w/ is written with a miniature ⟨o⟩. It is probably true in any language that semivowels are a little less close before very open vowels than they are before other vowels, but the difference is slight and would often be overlooked even by phoneticians. However, according to Vos (1964, p. 34), the reason why Han'gŭl makes this distinction is not in order to record fine phonetic detail but rather in order to conform to the vowel-harmony rule – to write ⟨ua⟩ rather than ⟨oa⟩ would be to mix *yin* and *yang*, whereas the spellings ⟨uʌ⟩ and ⟨oa⟩ are all-*yin* and all-*yang* respectively.

The diphthong /ɰi/ has a marginal status in Korean, but when it occurs it is written as shown at the right of Figure 22.

Rather than being written in a linear sequence like letters of European alphabets, Han'gŭl symbols are written grouped into syllables. The reason for this is no doubt historical, having to do with Koreans' familiarity with Chinese script: a syllable-sized grouping of Han'gŭl symbols looks somewhat like a Chinese graph, having a roughly comparable degree of visual complexity, and, since each Chinese graph is pronounced as one syllable, it seemed appropriate for Han'gŭl writing to be organized into similar-sized units. Whatever the historical cause of the system, it might be argued that by using a small number of basic graphic units and arranging them into syllable-sized perceptual groups Han'gŭl succeeds in reconciling two contradictory desiderata for a writing-system: the fewness of the basic graphic elements makes Han'gŭl easy to learn, while the large size of the perceptually-salient units makes it efficient to read.

The rule for assembling Han'gŭl phoneme-symbols into syllables is as follows. If the vowel of the syllable is based on a vertical line, place the preceding consonant to its left, and if the vowel is based on a horizontal line place the preceding consonant above it; in either case place a following consonant, if any, below the middle of the resulting group. This produces syllabic groupings which are squarish, like Chinese graphs, rather than unduly strung out on the horizontal or vertical dimensions. Some examples are shown in Figure 23. While the order of elements within a syllable-grouping is fixed, the syllables may be written one after another in different directions. Traditionally the Chinese system of vertical downward columns was used, but this has now been replaced, in all genres of handwritten and printed texts except newspapers, by the European system of left-to-right horizontal rows.

The passage of continuous text in Figure 23 is reproduced from the article 'Passives in English and Montague Grammar' by Ik-Hwan Lee in the December 1981 issue of the Korean linguistics journal *Ŏhak Yŏn'gu*. (In scholarly material of this kind containing many foreign names and technical terms they are written in the Roman alphabet, though in other kinds of text they will be transliterated into Han'gŭl: in the Korean title of Ik-Hwan Lee's article the name 'Montague' is written in Han'gŭl as ⟨mon-tʰæ-gju⟩.)

Apart from consonant and vowel contrasts, Middle Korean possessed 'suprasegmental' contrasts of pitch and of vowel-length.

Modern Standard Korean no longer uses pitch distinctively; but Middle Korean had what appears (Chang 1982, ch. 5) to have been a 'pitch-accent' system very similar phonologically to that of ancient Greek (p. 107 above). (The authorities disagree about how high the 'functional yield' of this system was; cf. Lee 1977, p. 168, and Chang 1982, p. 188.) While the pitch-accent system existed, the contrast between low, high, and rising pitches which realized it was indicated in Han'gŭl script by adding zero, one, or two dots respectively at the left of the written syllable.

The contrast between long and short vowels, on the other hand, has never been indicated in Han'gŭl writing (and I have not indicated it in my transcriptions of Korean). There are various possible explanations for this. Although length is still contrastive today in most Korean dialects, including the standard dialect of Seoul, this contrast seems to be one of relatively low functional yield (Martin 1951, §1.32). While pitch-accent was still marked in writing, furthermore, the yield of a graphic mark of length would have been even lower, since rising-pitch syllables (like syllables marked with a circumflex in Greek orthography) always had long vowels: only in high- and low-pitched syllables would such a mark have been non-redundant. Finally, it is tempting to speculate that contrasts of phonological length (and perhaps suprasegmental

바다	⟨ba-da⟩	/bada/	'sea'
나무	⟨na-mu⟩	/namu/	'tree'
하늘	⟨ha-nɯl⟩	/hanɯl/	'sky'
바람	⟨ba-lam⟩	/balam/	'wind'
부엌	⟨bu-qɤkʰ⟩	/buɤkʰ/	'kitchen'
빨강	⟨p*al-gaq⟩	/p*algaŋ/	'red'
서울	⟨sɤ-qul⟩	/sɤul/	'Seoul' (capital of S. Korea)
평양	⟨pₕjɤq-qjaq⟩	/pₕjɤŋjaŋ/	'P'yŏngyang' (capital of N. Korea)

4. 몬태규 문법에서의 수동규칙

지금까지의 논의는 수동규칙이 어휘적 단계의 작동인 국면도 있음을 증명하려고 했다. 앞에(2절 참조) 논의 한 대로 Chomsky와 Wasow 등은 어휘적 수동과 통사적 수동의 두가지의 필요성을 주장한다. 여기서 통사적 수동이란 이동규칙을 포함하고 있으며 문장 단계의 작동규칙이다. Bach나 Keenan은 문장 단위 작동으로서의 수동 규칙은 문제가 많음을 지적하고,[3] 따라서 구절단계의 수동규칙의 타당성을 보이려 하고 있다.

Figure 23

contrasts in general) may simply be less noticeable than segmental contrasts to speakers of languages which include them. There are many other cases where a script ignores length contrasts (cf. Justeson 1976, pp. 61, 65, 71). We have seen for instance that Hebrew script ignored length in consonants and that Linear B ignored length in vowels and consonants alike; classical Greek script ignored contrastive length in most vowels even after the adoption of the Byzantine system of diacritics, despite being in other respects a meticulously complete sound-recording system. (Likewise few phonographic scripts indicate stress even when it is unpredictable – though Spanish and Italian orthographies are exceptions.) It used to be axiomatic in linguistics that small perceptual differences between phonemes do not exist – that the very fact of phonological contrast between two sounds guarantees that competent speakers will hear the distinction clearly. But we now know that this is untrue (Labov *et al.* 1972, ch. 6). I suggest that scripts commonly ignore contrasts of length because they are perceptually less salient than, for instance, contrasts of vowel quality. (Length is not always ignored, of course; e.g. Czech orthography marks it consistently.)

   This, then, is the Han'gŭl script as an inventory of graphemes. At this point it is worth pausing to re-emphasize what a prodigious achievement it constitutes. Not only the principle of writing phonemes in terms of their constituent features, and the outlines of the individual graphemes, but even the very principles on which Sejong analysed syllables into component sounds were entirely original. Sejong was familiar with the Chinese tradition of phonological analysis, but his decision to divide syllables into what we know as vowels and consonants represented a sharp break with that tradition. So remarkable an achievement was Han'gŭl that some Western scholars to this day argue that it must have been developed on the basis of an earlier model. Gari Ledyard (1966), for instance, urges that Sejong based Han'gŭl on the ḥPhags-pa alphabet then used for Mongolian. But Ledyard argues this largely by interpreting a remark in the *Hunmin Chŏng'ŭm* as a deliberately cryptic reference to Mongolian writing, and this argument seems contrived. It may well be true that Sejong knew of ḥPhags-pa and other phonographic scripts in use in East Asia, but those scripts were all segmental: they offer no precedent for Han'gŭl.

Even more interesting than the structure of the Han'gŭl graphemes, from the point of view of current controversies in Western linguistics, is the history of the changing orthographic conventions that have governed the use of Han'gŭl, during its five centuries of existence, with respect to the distinction between 'deep' and 'shallow' approaches to writing (pp. 43–5).

When a spoken language includes rule-governed morphophonemic alternations, one way of defining the range of possibilities (as we saw in Chapter 2) is to posit a sequence of phonological rules which apply so as to derive the pronunciations of morphemes in particular environments from single, invariant 'underlying forms'. Such rules tend to reflect the history of the language to which they apply. Consider, for instance, the morphophonemic alternations in French whereby many words that are written with final consonants have the consonant pronounced in speech when a word beginning with a vowel follows, but not otherwise: /pətit elɛv/ 'small pupil' v. /pəti garsɔ̃/ 'small boy', /groz elɛv/ 'fat pupil' v. /gro garsɔ̃/ 'fat boy', etc. A simple way of stating these alternations is to choose the forms with the final consonant as underlying forms, and to state a rule 'Consonants drop when not immediately preceding a vowel'. (To be a satisfactory description of French this rule would have to be made more precise, since not all final consonants drop in the same way, but let us leave that point aside for our present purposes.) The reason why modern spoken French can be described by such a rule is that, historically, the words in question were at one time invariably pronounced with the final consonants (as they are still written in standard French orthography), and at a certain time the language changed so as to drop consonants when they preceded other consonants or were final in their phrase.

Because efficient morphophonemic rules tend to coincide with historical sound-changes, a 'shallow' phonographic script which remains fixed over a long period during which the associated spoken language undergoes many changes will often end up as a 'deep' script through simple inertia, as it were. The orthographies of both French and English are very far from being surface phonographic scripts, and they reflect many aspects of the medieval or early modern periods of the respective spoken languages which are no longer heard in their modern standard forms; most linguists take it that this is purely a consequence of orthographic conservatism.

However, one school of linguists, the 'generative phonologists' (Sampson 1980a, ch. 8), claim that morphophonemic rules have current psychological validity: that speakers store their vocabulary in their minds in terms of invariant 'underlying' root-shapes, and apply morphophonemic rules in order to derive the appropriate pronunciations when they speak.

This claim is highly controversial. The fact that traditional orthographic systems such as those of English and French seem to represent the 'underlying' forms of morphemes rather than their (often strikingly different) surface pronunciations is one category of evidence sometimes cited in its favour; it is suggested that this fact is not merely a consequence of orthographic conservatism, but rather that speakers are able to use such orthographic systems conveniently just because the spellings of words correspond to the forms stored in a speaker's mental lexicon. From this point of view, a reformed English or French orthography which corresponded more closely to the surface phonetic facts of the modern language might actually be *less* convenient for its users. According to Chomsky and Halle (1968, p. 49), 'conventional [English] orthography is . . . a near optimal system for the lexical representation of English words'.

Chomsky and Halle go so far as to claim that the mental representations of some English roots contain sounds which never occur in *any* English surface forms. For instance, they argue that the root of *right, righteous* must contain an underlying velar fricative |x| which is foreign to the surface phonology of English, though it is recorded by the ⟨gh⟩ of the conventional spelling (which is thus, in this respect, very 'deep'). We know, of course, that the sound [x] was pronounced in words such as *right* in Middle English, and that they were originally written with ⟨gh⟩ for that reason. But Chomsky and Halle argue that the presence of a latent |x| in these words can be established purely on the evidence of synchronic alternations in the modern language, implying that the velar fricative continues to be a psychological – although not a phonetic – reality in these words. (The argument for underlying |x| is complex; it has to do with facts such as the presence of an /aɪ ~ ɪ/ alternation in *expedite* ~ *expeditious* v. the absence of an analogous alternation in *right* ~ *righteous*.) From the viewpoint of the generative phonologists, the difference between Middle and Modern English phonology has not been the loss of a phoneme /x/ but the addition of a new phonological rule which prevents that phoneme surviving from underlying into surface forms.

It should be of particular interest in connection with this theory, then, if we can find standard orthographies which are relatively 'deep' and where we can demonstrate that this characteristic is not simply the result of inertia or conservatism in face of historical sound changes, as is likely to be the case for English and French spelling.

We have already seen hints, in the discussion of Greek spelling (p. 106), that a phonographic script may evolve in ways that make it 'deeper' independently of any historical developments in the associated spoken language. In the case of Korean script such an evolution is very striking.

In order to explain this, I must first sketch the morphophonemics of spoken Korean. Korean possesses a fairly rich set of rule-governed alternations, many of which already existed when Han'gŭl was invented. It is not easy to state one authoritative set of phonological rules for Korean: not only are there many small differences between regional dialects, but the authorities some-times disagree with one another about the facts of a given variety of the language. (Kim-Renaud 1975 and Chang 1982 survey the literature.) But the set of rules stated below can be taken as covering most of the well-established patterns of alternation in standard Seoul Korean.

Most of these rules can be arranged in a linear sequence: often a given underlying form will be changed by several of the rules successively before attaining its surface pronunciation. There is also one rule, which I shall call Rule X, that applies whenever a pair of segments arises to which it is applicable – Rule X can apply to underlying forms or to forms at any point along the path to the ultimate surface pronunciations. Rule X governs the coalescence of pairs of adjacent phonemes into single phonemes:

$$(X) \quad \left\{ \begin{array}{c} /d/ \\ /b/ \text{ or } /g/ \end{array} \right\} \text{ coalesces with } \left\{ \begin{array}{c} \text{any} \\ \text{a homorganic} \end{array} \right\} \text{ following}$$

obstruent, to form an obstruent identical with the second element of the pair, except that if this was lax the resulting consonant will be tense unaspirated; and any lax stop coalesces with a preceding or following /h/ to make a tense aspirated stop.

'Homorganic' means 'made at the same place of articulation'. Thus for example, /gg/ becomes /k*/, /bp^h/ bcomes /p^h/, /db/ becomes /p*/, /gh/ and /hg/ become /k^h/ – but /bd/, for example, is unaffected.[1]

To state the ordered sequence of rules, I must give a general principle about the placement of syllable-boundaries in Korean. A consonant immediately followed by a vowel (or by a sequence of /j/, /w/, or /h/ plus vowel) will always belong with that vowel as the beginning of its syllable; any other consonant will belong to the syllable of the preceding vowel. Thus, at least at the underlying level, it is possible to have more than one post-nuclear consonant (i.e. consonant following the vowel of its syllable), but at most one pre-nuclear consonant (not counting /j w h/). Note particularly that the presence of a morpheme boundary is not relevant to phonetic syllabification. The nomina-tive of the noun /mal/ 'word' is /mal+i/, where the plus-sign indicates the boundary between the root morpheme and the case suffix; but the phonetic syllable-boundary is as shown by the dollar-sign in /ma$li/.

The sequential rules can now be stated as follows:

1 A post-nuclear tense consonant becomes lax.

Thus underlying |nat^h| 'piece' and |nad| 'grain' fall together as /nad/. The underlying difference between them comes out when a suffix beginning with a vowel is added (so that the root-final consonants become pre-nuclear): for example, with the accusative suffix |ɯl|, /natʰɯl/ contrasts with /nadɯl/. Similarly, |nopʰ| 'high' with suffix |da| gives /nobda/ 'is high', and with suffix |ɯn| gives /nopʰɯn/ 'high (adj.)'; |bak*| 'outside' in isolation is /bag/, but with suffix |e| is /bak*e/ 'except'.

2   A post-nuclear sibilant becomes a stop.

Thus underlying |nacʰ| 'face' (which becomes /naɟ/ by Rule 1), |naɟ| 'day-time', and |nas| 'sickle', also fall together as /nad/; cf. the accusative forms /nacʰɯl/, /naɟɯl/, /nasɯl/. Likewise |is*+da| 'exists' $\xrightarrow{1}$ /isda/ $\xrightarrow{2}$ /idda/ $\xrightarrow{X}$ /it*a/, cf. |is*+o| 'he exists' which is /is*o/.

3   In a sequence of two post-nuclear consonants, delete the second if it is coronal, otherwise delete the first.[2]

Thus the root |gabs| 'price' gives /gab/, accusative /gabsɯl/; |anɟ+da| 'sits down' is /anda/, cf. |anɟ+hi+da| 'sets down' $\xrightarrow{X}$ /ancʰida/; |ɟɤlm+da| 'is young' is /ɟɤmda/, cf. |ɟɤlm+ɯn| 'young (adj.)' which is /ɟɤlmɯn/. After Rule 3 has applied, no syllable has more than one post-nuclear consonant.

4   Except when following a vowel, /l/ becomes /n/.

Pre-nuclear /l/ exists only in Sino-Korean or other non-native loans, but there are many such cases. Thus the Sino-Korean morpheme |lo| 'old' is /lo/ in /ɟolo/ 'premature decay', but /no/ in /noin/ 'old man'. (Likewise English *lamp* has been borrowed into Korean as /nambo/.)

5   Word-initial /n/ is deleted before /i j/.

Thus |ni| 'tooth' and |li| 'mile' fall together with |i| 'two' as /i/; |njɤ| 'female' lacks its /n/ in /ɟɤɟa/ 'woman' but |nam+njɤ| 'male and female' is /namnjɤ/.

6   A stop becomes a nasal before a nasal.

Thus |buɤkʰ+mun| 'kitchen door' is /buɤŋmun/. Likewise |bæg+li| 'a hundred miles' $\xrightarrow{4}$ /bægni/ $\xrightarrow{6}$ /bæŋni/; |ab+log+gaŋ| 'Yalu River' $\xrightarrow{X}$ /ablok*aŋ/ $\xrightarrow{4}$ /abnok*aŋ/ $\xrightarrow{6}$ /amnok*aŋ/; |os+mada| 'all garments' $\xrightarrow{2}$ /odmada/ $\xrightarrow{6}$ /onmada/; |ljug+sib| 'sixty (i.e. six-ten)' $\xrightarrow{4}$ /njugsib/ $\xrightarrow{5}$ /jugsib/ but |sib+ljug| 'sixteen (ten-six)' $\xrightarrow{4}$ /sibnjug/ $\xrightarrow{6}$ /simnjug/.

In addition to these morphophonemic rules, a complete statement of Korean phonology would include rules governing allophonic variation in certain phonemes, whereby for instance lax stops are voiced intervocalically, and /l/ is realized as a flap [ɾ] in certain positions. No version of Han'gŭl writing has ever taken any notice of these purely allophonic differences (despite the fact that to a non-Korean ear the differences are quite large, so that the romanization systems which various European nations use to transliterate Korean for everyday purposes invariably make distinctions between the allophones of the lax stops and of /l/). It is difficult to know whether these allophonic differences already existed in the 15c; but there has never been more than one Han'gŭl grapheme to cover the pair of sounds [r] and [l], or a family of sounds such as [b], [p'], and [pº]. This is not surprising: the orthographies of European languages behave very similarly. Our own script is incapable of showing any distinction between plain [l] and velarized [lʷ], or between aspirated and unaspirated stops.

With respect to the morphophonemic rules, on the other hand, which involve alternations between contrasting phonemes rather than between allophones of single phonemes, Han'gŭl conventions are now very different from what they were originally.

It seems likely that Sejong intended his script to be used as a 'shallow' system. *Hunmin Chŏng'ŭm* comments, for instance:

⟨bʌis-goɟ⟩ is 'pear blossom', ⟨Øjɤz-Øɯi-gacʰ⟩ is 'fox fur'; but, since the letter ⟨s⟩ can equally well be used in such cases, only ⟨s⟩ should be used.

That is, the four final underlying consonants |s ɟ z cʰ| in the words quoted all fall together at the surface (as /d/); so they may as well be written alike. (Postnuclear /d/ was written ⟨s⟩ rather than ⟨d⟩ because underlying |s| is far commoner in final position than underlying |d|.)

Indeed, *Hunmin Chŏng'ŭm* even includes instructions for transcribing sounds that occurred only in non-standard dialects or children's speech, which suggests that users of Han'gŭl were expected to hug the phonetic ground quite closely. Lee Ki-moon (1977, pp. 137, 140) confirms that 15c and 16c orthographic usage in general followed this lead. Spelling reflected the surface results of applying phonological rules, so that a given root would appear now in one orthographic form, now in another. Thus, |gabs| 'price' with case-suffixes |i|, |do|, pronounced /gabsi/ and (by Rule 3) /gabdo/, would be written ⟨gab-si⟩, ⟨gab-do⟩; |gipʰ| 'deep' with conjugation-suffixes |ɯni|, |go|, pronounced /gipʰɯni/ and (by Rule 1) /gibgo/, would be written ⟨gi-pʰɯ-ni⟩, ⟨gib-go⟩. In Han'gŭl, phoneme-signs are grouped into syllables; one of the consequences of the choice of the 'surface' approach to writing was that orthographic syllable-boundaries (indicated in my transcriptions by hyphens) represented phonetic rather than morphological divisions – the final consonant of a root was written as part of the suffix when the suffix happened to begin with a vowel.

From the start, the surface approach was not adopted with total consistency. There are sporadic examples in works published within a year or two of the promulgation of the Han'gŭl system which distinguished in writing between the various underlying post-nuclear sibilants merged by Rule 1, and cases where the effect of Rule 6 was ignored in writing (so that e.g. |mid+nɯn| 'believing', pronounced /minnɯn/, might be written ⟨mid-nɯn⟩ rather than ⟨min-nɯn⟩). But in general the rule was that the written graphemes corresponded to the spoken phonemes.

After the 16c, however, Han'gŭl orthographic conventions broke down. In the 1590s the Japanese ruler Hideyoshi invaded Korea as a preliminary to an (ultimately unsuccessful) attempt to conquer China. This invasion had a destructive effect on Korean society from which the country did not fully recover for centuries, and one consequence was that it became much more difficult to maintain nationwide written norms – particularly as the circle of users of Han'gŭl script was widening. The 17th and subsequent centuries brought successive changes to the spoken Korean language, many of which required some adaptation of previous spelling-conventions; in practice the result was deepening orthographic confusion. The matter was taken in hand only in the early 20c, when the rise of Korean nationalism led to a raising of the status of Han'gŭl script and the foundation in 1921 of a Korean Language Research Society to examine such questions.

At present there are some minor differences in spelling-conventions between North and South Korea (see Martin 1968), but in the main both half-nations now follow the rules laid down in a *Guide for the Unification of Korean Spelling* published by the Korean Language Research Society in 1933. The philosophy behind these rules derives from the ideas of Chu Si-gyŏng (1876–1914), the father of modern Korean linguistics (it was Chu, incidentally, who coined the name *han'gŭl* for the script previously known as *ŏnmun*). That philosophy is precisely opposite to the orthographic principles of the 15c.

Chu Si-gyŏng's ideas about language were strikingly reminiscent of recent 'generative' linguistic theories (Lee 1981). While drawing a strict distinction between synchronic and diachronic analysis, Chu believed that linguistic forms were to be treated as possessing two levels of structure both grammatically and phonologically. Grammatically, the surface structure of a sentence conceals a 'hidden meaning' (generative linguists would say 'deep structure'); and, phonologically, the 'temporary form' which a root displays in a given morphological environment will often differ from its fixed 'original form'. Orthography should reflect the 'original form' of roots, ignoring the consequences of the various phonological rules that affect them.

This principle has been applied consistently to modern Korean orthography so that, now, alternations between variant pronunciations of a given root are ignored in writing unless they are irregular, i.e. not predictable by general phonological rules. Orthography is 'deep' rather than 'shallow' (and thus the phonological transcriptions of Figure 23 should strictly have been enclosed in vertical bars rather than solidi).

A pair of forms such as /gabdo/, /gabsi/ (see above) will now be written not as ⟨gab-do⟩, ⟨gab-si⟩ but as ⟨gabs-do⟩, ⟨gabs-qi⟩: the root has a consistent written form, because the underlying |s| is written even where Rule 3 eliminates it in speech. Orthographic syllable-division is now morphological rather than phonetic: the /s/ of /gabsi/ belongs phonetically to the following syllable, but semantically it is part of the root and it is written as such. (When consonant-clusters such as /bs/ are written as part of a single syllable they are placed side by side, like the two halves of the graphemes for tense unaspirated stops.) In some cases the spelling of a word will be very different indeed from its pronunciation: /it*a/ 'exists', /amnok*aŋ/ 'Yalu River' (see p. 137

above under Rules 2 and 6) are written respectively ⟨qis*-da⟩, ⟨qab-log-gaq⟩.

On the other hand, the alternation between /d/ and /l/ found in cases such as |dɯd+da| 'hears' – which by Rule X becomes /dɯt*a/ – v. |dɯl+ɤs*+da| /dɯlɤt*a/ 'heard' is irregular, like the /f ~ v/ alternation in English *wife ~ wives, half ~ halves*; many other Korean roots in |-d| do not have allomorphs in /-l/, just as English roots like *reef, laugh* do not change their /f/ to /v/. So these Korean forms are spelled ⟨dɯd-da⟩, ⟨dɯl-qɤs*-da⟩.

One consequence of the shift from phonetic to morphological syllable-division is that, since 1933, the grapheme ⟨q⟩ in initial position has become a purely abstract 'place-holding' element of the script. We saw on p. 127 that it was possible to regard initial ⟨q⟩ as standing not for zero but for the sound [ɦ] which commonly occurs in a syllable having no other initial consonant. But, if a word like |gabs+i| is written ⟨gabs-qi⟩, there is no longer any question of identifying ⟨q⟩ with [ɦ]. The principles of Korean syllable-structure mean that the word is *pronounced* /gab$si/, with /s/ acting as initial consonant of the second syllable. The sound [ɦ] could not possibly occur in this word; ⟨q⟩ occurs in writing purely because the orthographic rules require every written syllable to begin with some consonant-sign.

I should stress that the 1933 orthographic system represented a decision to write synchronic underlying pronunciations; it was not an archaizing decision to write obsolete surface pronunciations, as (to some extent) we do in English script. Often these two principles would yield similar spellings; but sometimes their results differ, and in such cases modern Korean orthography is deliberately un-archaic. For instance, after the invention of Han'gŭl the phoneme /ʌ/ disappeared from the spoken language by merging with other vowels. This meant that the sign ⟨ʌ⟩ no longer represented a distinct phoneme, but it was still used distinctively in writing (just as we distinguish between the vowels of *meat, seal, mead* and *meet, wheel, seek* in writing despite the fact that the spoken vowels in the two sets of words have been identical since the late 17c). Before 1933 a word like /salam/ 'person', from Middle Korean /salʌm/, was still written ⟨sa-lʌm⟩. An archaizing orthography would retain such spellings; but, since the mergers between /ʌ/ and other vowels left behind no synchronic alternations in the spoken language, there is no ground for positing a synchronic underlying |ʌ| in modern Korean and accordingly the 1933 reform abolished the ⟨ʌ⟩ grapheme – /salam/ is now written ⟨sa-lam⟩. Other, comparable examples could be quoted.

In 1949 a further orthographic proposal was published in North Korea (Xolodović 1958) which, had it been adopted, would have moved Korean orthography even further in the direction of the abstract, 'deep' approach. We have seen that certain Korean morphophonemic alternations are irregular: for example, there are a number of roots like 'hear' (p. 140) which have allomorphs in /-d/ alternating with allomorphs in /-l/, but the majority of Korean roots ending in either of these phonemes do not exhibit such alternations. One can always turn an irregular alternation such as this into a regular one, by postulating that at the underlying level the root contains some third phoneme, different from both of the phonemes entering into the alternation, which is always changed into one or the other of the alternating phonemes by rules designed for the purpose. In English, for instance, we could make the *wife/wives* type of alternation regular by treating a root such as *wife* as, say, underlying |waɪɸ| rather than |waɪf| (whereas *reef* would be |rif|), and positing the following rules: 1 the bilabial fricative |ɸ| (though not the labiodental fricative |f|) becomes voiced before voiced sounds; 2 bilabial fricatives (subsequently) become labiodental. This, in essence, is how Chomsky and Halle argued for an |x| in English (though that case is relatively complex). The 1949 proposal used this approach not as a technical device of academic linguistic analysis but as a route towards an improved everyday orthography for Korean.

Six sounds were defined as occurring in Korean underlying forms (though they are never actually pronounced in Korean); graphemes were created to represent them (in some cases obsolete Han'gŭl graphemes were revived, in other cases the shapes were new), and in each case phonological rules governing the behaviour of the novel underlying phoneme were defined in such a way as to capture some class of common but irregular morphophonemic alternations. Thus, the behaviour of roots like 'hear' was handled by reviving the obsolete grapheme ⟨z⟩, defined as standing for a 'voiced apical fricative', and specifying that |z| becomes /l/ between vowels and /d/ before most consonants (the rules had to be a little more complex than this to handle certain other alternation-phenomena not discussed here). This allows us to spell /duɯt*a/ 'hears', /duɯlɤt*a/ 'heard' as ⟨duɯz-da⟩, ⟨duɯz-qɤs*-da⟩; and now the root 'hear' is regular and obeys the principle of constancy of graphic shape.

Again it should be stressed that there is no intention here of making contemporary orthography reflect history. In the case I have quoted, the new grapheme ⟨z⟩ is a revival of a grapheme which occurred in the original Han'gŭl system and stood for a consonant which may well have been a voiced apical fricative. But the historical /z/ never turned into /l/ between vowels, and it did not historically occur in the root 'hear'; when the historical /z/ ceased in the 16c to be part of the living language, it simply dropped (i.e. merged with zero). The |z| of the 1949 proposal was a purely theoretical, synchronic construct.

In fact the 1949 proposal was not put into practice. But the fact that such a scheme can be seriously considered demonstrates how far some Korean linguists have been from accepting the axiom which often passes in Europe for common sense, that the best practical orthography is one that assigns graphemes one-for-one to the phonemes of the spoken language. The orthography actually in use in Korea, let alone the one proposed in 1949, are closer in spirit to the generative phonologists' views about ideal orthographies.

At the same time, it is not at all clear that the history of Han'gŭl spelling-conventions supports the generative phonologists' psychological theories about the form in which speakers store their vocabulary in their memory. If the generative phonologists are right about this, it ought to follow that 'deep' orthography will be relatively natural, so that a society which acquires the use of a phonographic script will begin by writing underlying forms. A move towards shallow writing would come, if at all, only as speakers with increasing phonetic sophistication gradually learn to perceive consciously the effects of the phonological rules which they apply automatically to their stored forms when they speak. But the historical movement, in the case of both Greek and Korean orthographies, was the reverse of this. Spelling began with a surface approach and became gradually deeper – even setting aside the cases of 'inertial deepening' resulting from failure of the orthography to adapt to historical sound-changes.[3] (I have discussed the move from shallow to deep Han'gŭl spelling as if it were a sudden switch brought about by Chu Si-gyŏng single-handed, but Lee Ki-moon (e.g. 1977, pp. 234–5) suggests that movements in that direction had been occurring in previous centuries.)

It may possibly be that there are practical advantages in deep as opposed to shallow phonographic systems (this is a question to which Chapter 10 will return). If so, however, those advantages must surely be ones that accrue not to every speaker of the relevant language *qua* competent speaker, but rather to those people who in addition to speaking the language fluently have acquired some understanding of its structural properties (cf. Mattingly 1972). For linguists of the generative school, to be a competent speaker of a language *is* to have acquired knowledge of its structure; but this equation is a questionable one. (I have criticized logical fallacies in generative phonologists' arguments for psychologically-real 'abstract phonology' elsewhere: Sampson 1975.)

In this connection it is interesting to compare the views of Lee Ki-moon (the foremost contemporary Korean linguist) and Frits Vos (a leading Western Koreanist) on the relative merits of old and new Han'gŭl usage. For Vos (1964, pp. 39–40) the move from shallow to deep spelling was an unqualified improvement. The old system by which underlying final tense consonants were written phonetically as lax consonants 'was intended as a simplification of the writing system, but actually complicated the study of the language to a large extent'. The fact that word-sets such as 'piece', 'grain', 'sickle', 'daytime', 'face' (p. 137) were all written alike when not followed by a suffix was a 'disastrous' result. Conversely, Lee (1963, p. 23) deplores the modern deep spelling: 'It represents every morpheme by a single form of writing, choosing the base form as a representative shape . . . . This is contrary . . . to the principles of phonemic orthography . . . [and] As a result, Korean orthography has become a very difficult one to learn, to read and to write.'

Do these judgements perhaps reflect the differing standpoints of foreign student and native speaker respectively? For someone who studies a language as an outsider, even if he becomes extremely proficient, mastery of its rules of automatic phonological substitution is commonly one of the hardest skills to acquire (and, from a scholar's point of view, one of the least valuable).

When such a person reads the language he wants to see what meaning-units are on the page, and it is merely a nuisance to him if these are disguised by the effect of various phonological processes. The native speaker, on the other hand, comes to written language with a perfect grasp of how forms are pronounced; he may in some cases be scarcely aware of links between allomorphs of a single root which are obvious to a philologically-minded professor. When the generative phonologists praise English orthography, it may be that they are unconsciously making value-judgements appropriate to their own very specialized role as professional linguists (though even from that point of view their assessment is questionable, as we shall see in Chapter 10), while Lee Ki-moon may be speaking for the mass of his countrymen who have no special interest in technical linguistic studies.

It is possible to be sceptical not only about the modern Han'gŭl spelling-conventions but about the advantages of the Han'gŭl type of script in general.

The special characteristic of Han'gŭl is that it is based on phonetic features rather than on complete segments. In Korean (as in any language) a largish number of segmental phonemes are built up by combining a smaller number of features in different ways, so a featural script should have the virtue of fewness of graphic units to be learned. One might claim that theoretically Han'gŭl comprises just fifteen distinctive graphic elements: the five outlines for places of articulation, four manner-of-articulation modifications, outlines for the three *yang* vowels and ⟨i⟩ together with the principle for converting *yang* into *yin* outlines, and the principle for depicting diphthongs in /j-/. Admittedly there are complications such as the irregular outlines of bilabial stops; but, even so, there will still be many fewer Han'gŭl graphic elements than there are segmental phonemes in Korean (thirty including /j w/).

However, it is not at all clear that a script involving only fifteen graphemes is in practice markedly easier to learn than one of thirty graphemes, particularly when the small inventory is achieved at the cost of requiring the learner to analyse sound-segments into their constituent features. It could be argued that memorization of the shape of the graphemes is only a trivial part of the whole task of learning a phonographic script, so that size of grapheme-inventory would not be a sensitive factor in the design of such a script. Indeed, one may doubt whether Koreans do in fact commonly learn or perceive their script in terms of the featural principle that was used to construct it. We saw in Chapter 2 that Pitman's shorthand is based on the same featural principle, but I believe that British stenographers usually learn the outlines for the various phonemes as separate units, paying little or no attention to the logic by which the outlines are determined; similarly, Koreans regard Han'gŭl ⟨n⟩, ⟨d⟩, ⟨tʰ⟩ etc. as separate individual 'letters' rather than as partly-identical graphic composites.

Furthermore, while the fewness of Han'gŭl graphic elements may conceivably offer an advantage for learnability, it carries an offsetting disadvantage for readability. In Chapter 5 we saw that distinctiveness in the written shape of linguistic forms is a desideratum from the reader's point of view. The fact that Han'gŭl uses so few graphemes means that there is little for the eye to fasten on in a page of Korean writing: everything is composed of the same few simple geometrical shapes repeated over and over again.

In fact, although I suggested earlier that the Han'gŭl system of recording features individually but grouping them visually into syllables offers Koreans the best of both worlds (few units to learn, but many different visually-salient outlines), it would be equally possible to argue that in present-day circumstances this compromise between the featural and syllabic principles represents the *worst* of two worlds. Because Korean phonology allows little variety of syllable-structure (almost all written syllables will be of CVC or CV structure), the syllables which are the perceptually-salient elements of the script are not really very diverse in visual outline. On the other hand, the fact that 'letters' are built up into syllables in two dimensions, rather than being strung out linearly, makes for difficulties in printing. Pieces of Han'gŭl movable type have to comprise entire syllables, not individual 'letters'; so a printer has to have many hundreds of 'sorts' in each font rather than just two or three dozen.

But it would be inappropriate to end this chapter on a negative note. Any disadvantages which Han'gŭl may have relative to a phonemic script containing more diverse graphemes are fairly marginal; the script clearly functions with quite acceptable efficiency for those who use it. Indeed, when in Chapter 9 we come to compare the solution the Koreans have evolved for the problem of recording speech visually with the solution reached from precisely the same starting-point by the Japanese, we may well marvel at the outstanding simplicity and convenience of Han'gŭl. Whether or not it is ultimately the best of all conceivable scripts for Korean, Han'gŭl must unquestionably rank as one of the great intellectual achievements of humankind.

8 A logographic system: Chinese writing

The Semitic alphabet, viewed as an enduring and developing historical phenomenon of which Arabic, Roman, or Cyrillic scripts are individual representatives, is one of the two great systems of writing which between them provide the media of most of the world's written language. We turn in this chapter to the other of these systems, the Chinese. Until fairly recently in the history of writing it is likely that Chinese script (even if we consider only the system actually used by the Chinese, ignoring its offshoots such as the Japanese system or the Chinese-derived script formerly used for Vietnamese) was more widespread than all the the Semitic-derived alphabetic scripts put together. It has been estimated, for instance, that up to about the end of the 18c more than half of all the books ever published in the world were written in Chinese. Even today, when Semitic-derived alphabetic writing has spread over an exceptionally wide domain thanks to the sudden spurt in wealth and power which the Industrial Revolution fuelled in some of the nations using that system, Chinese and Chinese-derived writing occupies a very respectable second place in terms of number of users. Most of the scripts that have no historical connection with either Semitic or Chinese systems, of which Linear B and Han'gŭl are two examples, are (or were) used in quite small corners of the world.

It happens that what are historically the two major systems of writing exemplify the two main typological categories of script: whereas the Semitic family is phonographic, the Chinese system is logographic. A graph of the Chinese writing system stands not for a unit of pronunciation but for a morpheme, a minimal meaningful unit of the Chinese language. Since Chinese, like English or any other language, has thousands of morphemes in its vocabulary, the Chinese script includes thousands of graphs, rather than the few dozen found in a segmental, or even syllabic, phonographic script. If two morphemes are pronounced identically (which, as we shall see, happens a great deal in Chinese) they will normally have two separate graphs which may not share even a partial resemblance. To give a single example: one pair of Chinese homophones are the words /çʰuān/ 'parboil' and /çʰuān/ 'leap'. (In my phonetic transcriptions of Chinese, /ç c z̧/ stand for alveolar, alveolopalatal, and retroflex affricates, IPA [ts tç tʂ]. Diacritics as in /ā á ǎ à/ mark the four distinctive 'tones' or pitch-patterns of the language.) These words are written as follows:

汆   踡

çʰuān 'parboil'   çʰuān 'leap'

The two graphs do not look similar to the untutored eye, and this impression is correct – there is no relationship between them. The European expectation that homophones, such as English *can* 'be able to' and *can* 'metal box', will normally be written alike, and that a special explanation is needed when homophones such as *meet* and *meat*, or *doe* and *dough*, are written differently, is alien to the Chinese method of writing. That is not to say that similarities between the shapes of Chinese graphs never correspond to similarities between the pronunciations of the morphemes they represent; we shall see that correspondences of this kind do play a part in the organization of Chinese writing. But although it not infrequently happens that morphemes which sound the same or similar are written with partly similar graphs, there is nothing regular about this; very often, as in the case just illustrated, there is no relationship between the graphs for words which are perfect homophones. The European idea that from a knowledge of the pronunciation of a word one should be able to make at least a good guess at how to write it would seem bizarre to a Chinese.

In the above paragraphs, I have been playing somewhat fast and loose with the terms *word* and *morpheme*, the reason being that the distinction between these two concepts is not as clear-cut for Chinese as it is for European languages. Chinese, as a spoken language, has a number of interrelated special features which are quite relevant to an understanding of how Chinese writing works. (For a description of the Chinese language, see Kratochvíl 1968.)

First, Chinese is a language in which syllables are clearly demarcated from one another phonologically. In English it is normally straightforward to *count* syllables – *river* has two, *philodendron* four; but very difficult to specify where one syllable stops and the next starts – does the /v/ of *river* end the first syllable or begin the second? should the /ndr/ of *philodendron* be split /n$dr/ or /nd$r/? Indeed, questions of the latter category may well be pseudo-questions for a language like English: the truth may well be that the /v/ of *river* should be treated as belonging to both syllables equally. This sort of thing does not occur in Chinese: in that language, any consonant can easily and unambiguously be identified either as closing one syllable or as opening another, so that the boundaries between syllables are obvious. (One reason why this is so is that the set of consonants which can occur post-vocalically in Chinese is almost disjoint from the set which can occur initially.)

Secondly, morphemes in Chinese are co-extensive with syllables: each morpheme is one syllable long, and there are virtually no cases such as *feather* or *elephant* where a single meaning-unit spans more than one syllable, or conversely like the /s/ of *cats* or the /t/ of *height* where a meaning-unit corresponds to a fraction of a syllable. (There are certain relatively marginal phenomena in view of which this statement is not wholly true; but the Chinese writing-system can most easily be understood in relationship to an 'idealized' account of the spoken Chinese language which ignores various small-scale phenomena that disturb the generalizations which are valid for by far the larger part of its structure.)

Third, Chinese is an 'isolating' language; its grammar works exclusively by stringing separate words together, as in English we say *I write, I will write*, rather than by modifying the pronunciation of words as in English *I write, I wrote, he writes*. Clearly, this characteristic is closely related to the two already listed. Most of the inflexions of European languages derive ultimately from what were once independent suffix-morphemes which have influenced the pronunciation of the root and been influenced by it reciprocally so that in many cases one can no longer recognize the identity of the suffixes or separate them phonologically from the roots. Because Chinese morphemes all consist of syllables which are kept phonetically separate from one another, nothing comparable has happened in that language; individual morphemes have modified their pronunciation independently down the ages, but there is virtually no morphophonemic alternation, and no coalescence of roots with affixes.

Finally: although a single word in a European language will often translate into modern Chinese as a sequence of two morphemes, it is difficult to identify these unambiguously as single compound words akin to English *blackbird, interview, overthrow*, because the borderline between morpheme-combinations which are and those which are not established elements of the language is vaguer for Chinese than it is for English – a user of Chinese is relatively free to group morphemes into different combinations. This fact may well be partly a consequence of the different writing-systems: in written English the visual unit is the word, so words are what we learn to regard as the elementary building-blocks whose internal structure we tend on the whole to accept as given, whereas in written Chinese the visual unit is the morpheme – the script does not group pairs of graphs together spatially to show that they go together as a compound, all the morphemes of a sentence are written with equal spacing, so a Chinese sees the morphemes as the units which the language-system supplies and thinks of the combining of morphemes as falling within the domain of individual language-use. (This difference should not be exaggerated – there certainly are very many cases where a particular compound of two morphemes is entirely standardized with its own fixed and idiosyncratic meaning; but such cases might be compared with multi-word idioms in English such as *white spirit*, and in relative terms Chinese morphemes have more freedom of combination than do morphemes of English or other European languages.)

Since morphemes in Chinese are independent units of pronunciation and are the units symbolized independently in the writing system, and since they are relatively free to combine with one another grammatically, the result is that for Chinese there is no very clear notion of 'word' as a unit larger than the morpheme.

All this has been by way of explaining why there is little point in discussing whether Chinese writing should be described as a 'morphemic' or a 'word-based' system. Technically it is morphemic; but, in most cases, words in Chinese can be identified with morphemes. The problem of the very large number of graphs that would be needed if a European language adopted truly word-based writing and therefore had to use quite separate symbols e.g. for *eat, ate, eaten, eats, eating, eater*, etc., or (still worse) for French *mange, manges, mangeons, mangé, mangée, mangés, mangerai, mangeras, mangera*, etc. etc., could not arise in any case in Chinese, since Chinese does not inflect roots. (It seems rather implausible that any language which *did* inflect would adopt a genuinely word-based logographic system; certainly I know of no case.) Because words are scarcely distinguishable from morphemes in Chinese, and because the term 'word' is so much more natural in English than 'morpheme', I shall often allow myself to talk of Chinese graphs as standing for 'words'. However, in cases where a clear distinction can be drawn between morphemes and words in Chinese, it is the morphemes and not the words which are individually symbolized in the script.

I have said enough, I hope, to establish clearly the fact that Chinese writing is a logographic rather than a phonographic system. It is true that the units of script are co-extensive with syllables, which are phonological units; but this is merely an accidental consequence of the fact that in Chinese the minimal meaningful units, or morphemes, happen always to be one syllable long. When a given spoken Chinese syllable stands for different homophonous morphemes, those morphemes will have distinct graphs which will often share no similarities whatever; and on the other hand, a group of Chinese graphs may be very similar in shape but stand for morphemes whose pronunciations are entirely unrelated.

It is necessary at this point, however, to warn against an alternative error, namely that of supposing that Chinese writing is semasiographic, in the sense defined in Chapter 2. This is a very widespread misunderstanding, and has been so ever since Chinese writing became a subject of intellectual interest in Europe. In the 17c in particular there was considerable enthusiasm among European philosophers for the idea of creating a universal philosophical written language, or 'real character', that would cut through the arbitrary inconsequentialities of various natural languages by symbolizing ideas directly, in some fashion related straightforwardly to their logic. Proponents of this concept often appealed to Chinese writing as an existing, if perhaps imperfect, example of such a scheme. Knowlson (1975, p. 25) tells us that:

. . . the majority of the projectors of a common writing or, later, of a character based on philosophical principles referred to the use of these [Chinese] characters as a form of common script in the East. As late as 1681, in his first letter . . . about a universal character, De Vienne Plancy expressed his . . . surprise that Chinese characters had not been adopted throughout the world 'pour le commerce des Nations, puisqu'ils signifient immédiatement les pensées.' . . . [Chinese writing] indicated that the only way to form a script that would be universally intelligible was, to quote John Webster (here echoing Bacon), to use characters 'which are real, not nominal, expressing neither letters nor words, but things and notions.'

This view of the nature of Chinese script is still widely held; it is reinforced by the common use of the word 'ideogram' to refer to Chinese graphs, suggesting that they stand for ideas rather than words.

The truth is, however, that Chinese writing comes no closer than English or any other to 'signifying thoughts directly', or to expressing 'things' rather than 'words'. Chinese script is thoroughly glottographic: it symbolizes units of a particular spoken language, namely the Chinese language, with all its quirks and illogicalities. There are various ways of demonstrating this. One concerns synonyms. Like other natural languages, Chinese contains groups of words which are distinct in their pronunciation and etymology but which mean more or less exactly the same thing. Thus, as it happens, Chinese has four words for 'red'; /xún/, /z̧ʰù/, /tān/, /z̧ū/. So far as I know there is no distinction of meaning whatever between these four words, and accordingly a 'philosophical script' which represented ideas directly and logically would presumably need only one symbol to cover all four of them; but in Chinese they are four quite separate words, and they are written with four distinct and unrelated graphs, 紅 赤 円 朱.

Another point relates to the internal structure of items of vocabulary. All natural languages contain terms comparable to English *buttercup*, which looks as though it ought to be the name of a kind of cup but is in fact a flower. In a 'philosophical script' the symbol for *buttercup* would be related to symbols for flowers rather than utensils; but a morphemic script would spell *buttercup* with the *butter* graph followed by the *cup* graph. Likewise in Chinese /cʰīŋ-pʰí/, literally 'green skin', is a term for 'rogue'; it is written with the ordinary graphs for /cʰīŋ/ 'green' and /pʰí/ 'skin', and the writing gives no clue that the term represents a kind of person. (I give just one example, but such cases are legion.)

Finally, the syntax of spoken Chinese is often idiosyncratic and logically opaque, just as is the case with other natural languages; a philosophical language would replace illogical turns of phrase with simpler and more transparent constructions, but written Chinese reproduces on paper the grammar of the spoken language.[1] Chinese graphs stand for *words*, not directly for 'things' or 'ideas'.

(Incidentally, the fact that synonyms such as the words for 'red' have different graphs in Chinese script exemplifies a major difference between Chinese and Sumerian writing – a point which is worth stressing, since in certain other respects the early histories of Chinese and Sumerian systems were similar. We saw on p. 54 that in archaic Sumerian script a picture representing a mouth stood for a range of different words from that semantic area: 'mouth', 'speech', 'tooth', etc. This sort of thing is unknown in Chinese script. We shall see, below, that in the early stages of Chinese script one graph would be borrowed to stand for a range of different words, but such loan-uses were not based on semantic relationships.)

Having examined the relationship between the units of Chinese writing and the language it is used to write, we turn now to a consideration of the internal structure of the individual graphs. When a script uses only a few dozen separate graphs, the question of how the various shapes are derived is of little more than antiquarian interest; from an English-speaker's point of view the different symbols of the Roman alphabet are just arbitrarily-chosen distinct marks. When a script contains thousands of graphs, on the other hand, their structure becomes very important: nobody could learn such a system unless the graphs were produced by combining a smaller number of distinctive elements in various ways, and it seems implausible that the system could be learned unless there were at least some measure of regularity in the manner in which elements are combined into wholes.

In order to understand the logic underlying the graphs of Chinese, we must approach the subject historically. We cannot go back to the origin of Chinese writing, and indeed we do not know when it began; there are some relics of what appear to be its forerunners which date back to about −2000, but the earliest time from which we have plenty of examples is the period −1400 to −1200, and by then the script was already a highly elaborated system, essentially similar to what it is today. However, although the very early stages of Chinese writing are lost, the oldest examples that we have represent a system that was still fluid and continuing to develop, so that they enable us to reconstruct how the system as a whole emerged. Not until shortly before the beginning of the Christian Era was Chinese writing fixed in every respect as we know it now.

The *shapes* of the graphs and of their component parts changed greatly, mainly because of a change in medium: the earliest inscriptions that have come down to us were incised on bone or metal, and involved naturalistic curves and circles, but the use of brush and ink led, late in the −1st millennium, to curved lines becoming straight or angular, circles becoming squares, etc. As a result, motivated graphs became arbitrary. Probably all the elements of Chinese graphs were pictures of something once; but I cannot think of any graph whose meaning would be recognizable from its modern shape (where 'modern' means later than about −200), unless it were the graphs 一 二 三 which mean 'one, two, three'.

Chinese graphs can be divided into two groups, simple graphs and complex graphs. This division does not refer to their degree of visual complexity but to the rationale of their construction.

Figure 24 illustrates some 'simple' graphs, showing their original form in the first column and the modern form in the second column, followed by the modern pronunciation and an English gloss. In some cases, where the meaning of the word in question has changed over the millennia, I give the original meaning, as being the one relevant to the construction of the graph. (Note that glosses such as 'sun/day', 'river/water', etc., represent single polysemous morphemes rather than homophones: that is, it happens that the Chinese language extends the word for 'sun' to mean a day as a unit of time, as English extends the word 'star' to mean a person of prominence in show business – it is not that Chinese had originally-separate words for 'sun' and 'day' which happened to fall together in sound, as English *meet* and *meat* have come to be pronounced the same though once pronounced differently.)

1		日	ɻ̣ùi	'sun/day'
2		雨	y̌	'rain'
3		水	ṣuěi	'river/water'
4		魚	ý	'fish'
5		人	ɻə́n	'man' (i.e. human being)
6		女	ny̌	'woman'
7		口	kʰǒu	'mouth'
8		目	mù	'eye'
9		眉	méi	'eyebrow'
10		木	mù	'tree'
11		其	cī	'winnowing-basket'
12		子	ç̌ǔ	'child'
13		兼	ciēn	'to have two at once' (hand holding two arrows)
14		若	ɻuò	'yield, conform'
15		東	tūŋ	'east' (sun behind tree)
16		囚	ciōu	'prisoner' (man in cell)
17		好	xàu	'love' (woman and child)
18		奻	nuàn	'quarrel' (two women)
19		言	jén	'flute'
20		辟	pì	'prince'

Figure 24

Some of the graphs in Figure 24 are straightforward pictures of the objects, or salient parts of the objects, for which they stand. (Graph 6 depicts a woman kneeling, showing either her breasts or perhaps her arms as she does housework. Graph 12 shows a human whose head is large relative to body-size.) Others indicate more abstract ideas in a necessarily subtler, more allusive fashion: graph 14 shows a fighter with dishevelled hair kneeling and holding up his hands in surrender. In other cases again the rationale of the graph-shape is now lost; it seems unlikely that we could recognize graph 19 as a flute if we did not know what the graph meant, and we do not know why the form of graph 20 is appropriate for 'prince'.

In all there are in the order of a thousand or so of these 'simple' graphs.

Since it was a near-impossible task to think up a separate pictorial representation for each of the many words of Chinese, scribes resorted to the obvious device of adapting a graph that had been established for a word that happened to be relatively 'picturable' in order to write other words that were pronounced the same or similarly. Here a complication arises in giving examples: the pronunciations of Chinese words that are relevant for these loan-uses of graphs are the pronunciations current at the period when the script was developing, which are often extremely different from the modern pronunciations of the same words. In what follows I use an asterisk to mark pronunciations in so-called 'Old Chinese' (also called 'Archaic Chinese', i.e. the Chinese of about -1000) as reconstructed by Bernhard Karlgren (1957), though I replace Karlgren's phonetic notation with IPA equivalents.[2] Thus, graph 11, *kjəg 'winnowing-basket', was borrowed for *gʰjəg 'his'; graph 13, *kljæm 'to have two at once' was borrowed for *kʰljæm 'dissatisfied'; graph 19, *njăn 'flute' was borrowed for *njăn 'speak', and for *njən 'contented'; graph 20, *pjĕk 'prince' was borrowed for all of the following words: *pjĕk 'thin-sliced', *pjĕk 'jade insignium', *bʰjĕk 'law', *bʰjĕk 'beat the breast', *bʰjĕk 'open', *bʰiek 'inner coffin', *pʰjĕk 'oblique', *bʰjĕg 'avoid'. At this early stage it is probable that there was nothing very fixed and definite about which graphs could be borrowed for which particular similar-sounding words; rather, scribes would simply have adapted the stock of existing graphs to their needs as best they could. The fact that graph 20 had many different recorded loan-uses while some simple graphs had none may reflect the fact that an unusually large number of words sounding roughly like *pjĕk had meanings which Chinese scribes found it difficult to draw pictures for – or it may be a chance property of the particular collection of inscriptions that happen to have come down to us.

If no further principles for the creation of graphs had been adopted, the system would presumably have ended up as a syllabic phonographic system (though with the important special feature that, because Chinese morphemes are one syllable long, each morpheme would have been written with just a single syllabic sign). However, it seems that a system with this degree of ambiguity, in which most graphs could stand for any one of three, four, or even a dozen or more morphemes, was felt to be unsatisfactory. Instead of curing the problem by inventing more simple graphs, which was no doubt impractical because of the abstractness of the morphemes lacking their own graphs and the consequent difficulty of getting fellow-scribes to agree on an appropriate visual image, an alternative solution was adopted. The various similar-sounding readings of a given simple graph were distinguished by supplementing that graph with another graph whose meaning gave a clue to the particular word intended. Thus one of these complex graphs would consist of two parts, which we may call a *phonetic* – the basic graph, standing for a family of near-homophones and originally a picture of one of them – and a *signific*, an element showing the semantic category into which the word in question falls. (Chinese 'significs' are very comparable in their logic to Cuneiform 'determinatives', cf. p. 55, though the latter were written as separate graphic units whereas the elements of a complex Chinese graph are written together as a single visual whole.) This device for creating graphs proved enormously fertile, and the great majority of the eventual stock of Chinese graphs are 'complex' in this sense.

For example (quoting graphs in their modern forms), 其 *kjəg 'winnowing-basket', together with 土 'earth', gives 基 *kjəg 'foundation' – a word whose pronunciation is the same as that of 'winnowing-basket' and whose meaning has something to do with 'earth'. (The reconstructed pronunciation of 土 is *tʰo; but, since the pronunciation of a graph used as a signific is irrelevant, I shall omit this information in what follows.) The same graph with 鹿 'deer' gives 麒 *gʰjəg 'unicorn'; with 示 'spirit/divine' it gives 祺 *gʰjəg 'fortunate'; with 人 'person' it gives 俱 *kʰjəg 'mask'. (Several graphs commonly used as significs are written in special compressed or abbreviated versions of their normal form; in the case just quoted, 亻 is the 'combination-form' of 人 'person'.)

Sometimes the signific system was not adequate to distinguish between words pronounced similarly: two more words which sounded like *kjəg 'winnowing-basket' were *kjəg 'aquatic grass' and *gʰjəg 'beanstalk', and the best signific for both of these was the graph for 'plant' 艸, with the combination-form 艹: 'aquatic grass' and 'beanstalk' are both written 萁. Occasionally such problems were resolved by differences in the orientation of signific and phonetic: it seems that 言 'speak' was felt to be an appropriate signific for both *kjəg 'to plan' and *gʰjəg 'fear', and these words are written respectively 諆 and 誓. But this is quite unusual. More commonly, differences of orientation are in free variation (*gʰjəg 'chess' is written with the 'wood' signific as either 棋 or 棊); but in the great majority of cases orientation of signific with respect to 'phonetic' is fixed, and is commonly determined by the identity of the signific – the combination-form 艹 of 'plant' always appears above a phonetic, 言 'speak' almost always appears to the left of a phonetic, 鳥 'bird' almost always to the right, and so on.

Once the phonetic/signific system was established, a complex graph could itself be used as a phonetic to which further significs were added, making graphs of the structure (P/S)/S. This structure is less common than the structure

P/S, but it is far from rare. For instance, the simple graph 可 *kʰa 'can, be able' enters into the following P/S combinations: with 'wood', 柯 *ka 'axe-handle'; with 'water', 河 *gʰa 'Yellow River'; with 'mouth', 呵 *xa 'scold'; with 'big', 奇 *gʰiæ 'strange'; and the last of these graphs, standing for a syllable with a medial -i-, is as a whole the phonetic in graphs such as 騎 *gʰiæ 'ride' (with 'horse'), 寄 *kiæ 'lodging' (with 'roof'), 綺 *kʰiæ 'patterned silk' (with 'silk'), etc.

To guard against misunderstanding, let me stress that the elements I am calling 'phonetics', and also those I am calling 'significs', also occur as simple graphs: to call a graphic element a 'phonetic' or a 'signific' is to identify the role it is playing within a particular complex graph. A given graph may occur as a simple graph, as a phonetic in one series of complex graphs, and as a signific in another series of complex graphs. For instance, 女 *njo 'woman' occurs as a signific in a large number of graphs for words to do with women's life – with 古 *ko 'ancient' it forms 姑 *ko 'aunt', with 因 *ʔjĕn 'to rest / rely on' it forms 姻 *ʔjĕn 'relationship by marriage', with 某 *məg 'such-and-such' it forms 媒 *mwəg 'matchmaker', and so on; but conversely it acts as phonetic in another series – with 米 'rice' it forms 籹 *njo 'cakes made of rice and honey', with 口 'mouth' it forms 如 *njo 'to agree / resemble', with 氵 combination-form of 水 'water/river' it forms 汝 *njo, proper name of a river. There is, however, an asymmetry: almost every simple graph acts as phonetic in at least one or two complex graphs, and any given phonetic will be used in only a dozen or two dozen complex graphs at most, whereas significs are usually drawn from a class containing a few dozen simple graphs with key meanings such as 'wood', 'metal', 'person', 'bird', 'hand' (for actions), and so forth, and some of these are significs in hundreds of different complex graphs.[3]

In the writing system which ultimately emerged from the processes of borrowing graphs to stand for phonetically-similar words, adding significs to disambiguate such multiple uses, and changing the shapes of graphs until they were wholly arbitrary, it was not always the case that the value attached to a simple graph was the word which had originally motivated its design. For instance, the word written 言 and meaning 'flute' became obsolete quite early in the history of Chinese, so that this graph now stands exclusively for what was originally its loan-use, 'speak' (the graph is indeed a common signific for words having to do with language). In the case of 其 'winnowing-basket' the original value did not become obsolete, but the loan-use 'his' was so much commoner a word that it came to be perceived as the basic value of the graph; 其 now always stands for 'his', and the word 'winnowing-basket' is written with the addition of the 'bamboo' signific: 箕 . And the case of 辟 'prince' corresponds to an unusually complex situation in the modern script: the morphemes meaning 'thin-sliced', 'law', and 'inner coffin' appear to have become obsolete, the 'jade insignium' word is now invariably written with the 'jade' signific, and the other loan-values are *optionally* written with significs ('hand' for 'beat the breast', 'door' for 'open', and so on) but can alternatively be written with the simple graph which also still stands for 'prince'.

In some cases, significs were used to distinguish between diverse senses of a single polysemous morpheme, rather than between homophones. For instance /méi/ 'eyebrow' (Old Chinese *mjər), the word written with graph 9 of Figure 24, has the extended sense 'lintel' (the lintel having been seen as the eyebrow of window or door), but when the word is used in this latter sense the 'wood' signific is added to the basic 'eyebrow' graph: 楣 . Quite possibly this was not perceived by the inventors of the script as a separate, distinct principle for the use of significs; rather, they would often have been unclear about where to draw the line between polysemy and homophony. The distinction, for any language, is essentially a historical one: when a given phonological shape is used for more than one meaning we say that we have distinct homophonous words if we know that at earlier stages the words were entirely separate, but we have a single polysemous word if the various meanings can be shown to have developed out of one original sense. Most speakers of a language have no access to its history and hence no way of drawing this distinction correctly in many cases; thus in English the fact that different spellings are used shows that people take *mettle* and *metal* to be homophones (whereas in fact the meaning of *mettle* developed as a figurative extension of that of *metal*), while conversely many English-speakers undoubtedly take *ear* (of wheat) to be the same word as *ear* (the organ of hearing) whereas in reality these are accidental homophones which derive from words originally pronounced differently. At the period when Chinese script was being developed no Chinese-speakers had any significant access to the earlier history of their language, so it may well not have been obvious to them that the use of /méi/ for both 'eyebrow' and 'lintel' was a case of polysemy. In most cases where the Chinese could perceive polysemies as being separate senses of a single word at the time the script was invented, they used a single graph to cover all the senses even if its signific was appropriate to only one of them; and, once the script was fully evolved (by the beginning of the Christian Era), significs were not changed to reflect subsequent changes in the meanings of words.

For instance, 里 /lǐ/ 'village' (from here on I give modern pronunciations) with 王, the combination-form for 'jade', stands for a homophone 理 /lǐ/, which means 'to cut jade' but much more commonly has the abstract, extended meanings 'to regulate, reason, principle'. Likewise, the same phonetic with 衣 'clothes' is 裏 (this particular signific is commonly separated into two halves with the phonetic inserted as the meat in the sandwich), which stands for a word again pronounced /lǐ/ that originally meant 'lining' (so that 'clothes' was appropriate) but now never means anything more specific than 'inside', 'in'. Again, 雚 /kuàn/ 'heron' with 木 'wood' makes 權 /cʰyán/ '(wooden) weight on a steelyard', hence 'influence, authority, rights': in modern Chinese the original meaning is virtually obsolete. Nobody thinks it odd that 'reason' includes a 'jade' element or 'authority' a 'wood' element; when significs do remain appropriate for the modern Chinese meanings of words, the graphs are that much easier to remember, but very frequently they do not.

When the phonetic/signific system first evolved, significs were added optionally and variably; and there is a danger that by approaching the subject historically I may have given the reader an impression of much greater chaos and complexity than is actually present in the Chinese script as it has existed over the last two millennia. In fact the system was standardized by the beginning of the Christian Era so as to approach reasonably close to the ideal of providing one unambiguous graph for each morpheme in the Chinese language. Certainly there are still cases where a given graph can stand for alternative morphemes, and where a given morpheme can be written in different ways, but such cases are fairly rare. (For the latter kind of ambiguity, compare the way that in English we can choose to write *gaol* or *jail*, *connexion* or *connection*. Graphic variation is commoner in Chinese script than in English, but not overwhelmingly commoner.)

On the other hand, while the relationship between graphs and morphemes comes fairly close to being one-to-one, for modern Chinese it is far more arbitrary than my discussion so far may have suggested.

I have already indicated that, because of the considerable shifts of meaning and changes in material culture that have occurred over the millennia, the significs are nowadays rather unreliable as a guide to the meanings of graphs. Nouns denoting flora and fauna almost always do have the appropriate signific for their category, such as 'plant', 'tree', 'bird', 'fish', or the like; but, at the opposite extreme, verbs have very diverse and unpredictable significs.

In view of the system of 'phonetic' elements, though, the reader might suppose that I am wrong to deny that the script is phonographic. While the script was acquiring its present form in the −2nd and −1st millennia, one might well have called the system essentially a phonographic system, but one which was 'incomplete' in that it did not mark all the phonetic contrasts which played a role in the language, and which added the system of significs as a non-phonographic device to make up for this deficiency. However, Chinese script ceased many centuries ago to be phonographic in any substantial sense. The reason for this is that, while the script has not changed, the spoken language has changed a great deal. We have seen that a given 'phonetic' element could be used to represent each of a range of similar syllables in Old Chinese; during the millennia that separate Old Chinese from the present day there have been many complex sound-changes in Chinese, and very often these have had the effect of exaggerating what were once small differences of pronunciation. (To give just one example: Old Chinese had syllables beginning /kl-, gl-/, and these clusters commonly appear in words whose graphs share a phonetic; after the graphs were fixed, /kl-/ was simplified to /k-/ and /gl-/ to /l-/, so the words no longer alliterate.)

As a result of these semantic and phonological developments, the relationship between morphemes and graphs is by now to quite a large extent opaque. A Chinese-speaker who learns to read and write essentially has to learn the graphs case by case; both significs and phonetics will give him many hints and clues to help him remember, but the information they supply is far too patchy and unreliable to enable him to *predict* what the graph for a given spoken word will be, or even which spoken word will correspond to a graph that he encounters for the first time. From the point of view of a modern speaker, the most important benefit of the phonetic/signific structure is that graphs involving many brush-strokes can be seen as groupings of familiar visual units, rather than having to be remembered stroke by stroke; the original logic behind the phonetic/signific structure certainly is still useful, but its usefulness is limited.

In order to give the reader a feeling for the extent to which the logic behind the graphs is apparent in the modern, everyday use of the language, I have chosen at random a sample of ten graphs to examine. The sample was constructed by sticking a pin into chance pages of a dictionary of the kind which devotes a lot of space to common graphs and little space to rare ones, so that most of the ten graphs are fairly common and just one or two are rather rare. In the analysis below, 'phonetic' and 'signific' are abbreviated 'P' and 'S'. All glosses quoted refer to meanings in current use (hence one or two discrepancies as compared with glosses given earlier for the same graphs), and the pronunciations quoted are the modern ones.

1 召 z̦àu 'summon'. P 刀 tāu 'knife' + S 口 'mouth'. The initial consonant of the P is not very close; on the other hand the complex graph itself occurs as a P in many (P/S)/S graphs (cf. p. 154) for words pronounced /z̦au/, /z̦ʰau/, or /ṣau/, which helps its value to be remembered.

2 前 cʰién 'before'. This was originally a simple graph, and has lost any mnemonic value it may once have had; in its modern form it looks like a combination of 月 'moon' and 刂 combination-form of 'knife' below a near-unique element ⸚. But the word is so common that the lack of transparency in the graph does not matter (just as English-speakers do not have trouble with the irregular spelling of *one*). It may even be an advantage that the overall shape is very distinctive rather than being yet another permutation of standard P and S elements.

3 忽 xū 'suddenly/careless'. This was originally P 勿 ū 'don't' + S 心 çīn 'heart'. No other words with P 勿 begin with /x-/; 'heart' is suitable for 'careless' but not for 'suddenly'. Again a fairly common and distinctive graph (distinctive because 'heart' as a signific usually occurs in a combination-form rather than written in full as here, and also because 勿 is an uncommon and visually-simple P).

4 絮 çỳ 'cotton waste / to line with cotton wadding'. S 糸 'silk' is expected, but P 如 ɽú 'as' is a surprising P (which is a nuisance since the word is of low frequency).

5 關 kuān 'shut'. The element 門 is 'door', and with some imagination one can see the rest as two hands stretching up to fix a bolt or the like. In fact etymologically the interior part of the graph was a phonetic element which is

long-obsolete as an independent graph (it meant 'a pair of tufts of hair on a child's head') and which occurs as P in no other complex graph. Thus the graph gives no clue now about its pronunciation, but again it is very common.

6   廟 miàu 'temple'. This looks as if it were S 广 'building' and P 朝 zِāu 'morning' or zِʰáu 'dynasty' (this latter graph is one of the minority which represent either of two phonetically-distinct words). But in that case the P would be baffling: phonetic elements are usually more reliable with respect to consonants than vowels, but there is no resemblance between the consonants here. Etymologically the graph is actually of the form S + S (a /miàu/ was the building where one performed the morning sacrifice) – but not even an educated Chinese would be likely to know that, so the graph is largely opaque.

7   抒 ṣū 'to strain / pour out' (this word is obsolete in the modern spoken language, but it is still listed in dictionaries as part of the literary language). S 扌 (combination-form of 'hand'), fairly predictable for this meaning, and P 予 ý 'I' – a surprising phonetic, but the same graph is used as P to represent /ṣu/, /zِu/ in a few other P/S combinations.

8   釘 tīŋ 'a nail', tìŋ 'to nail' (this grammatical use of tone now occurs in just a handful of words, but is thought to be a relic of a regular system of inflexion in a prehistoric stage of the language). The S 金 'metal' is wholly predictable, and P 丁 tīŋ 'individual' is natural (though there are other graphs that might have been used as P instead). An easy graph to learn, particularly since – by coincidence – the P element even happens to be shaped rather like a nail.

9   自 ç̀ù 'self', 'from'. A simple graph which has to be learned as a unit; it is extremely frequent.

10   油 jóu 'oil'. S 氵 combination-form of 'water'; P 由 jóu 'cause'; quite straightforward.

So much as an account of how the Chinese writing-system works. A written text in Chinese consists simply of a sequence of graphs corresponding to the morphemes of the sentences, with each graph being written so as to fill a notional square of constant size (so that graphs involving many strokes are written relatively compactly) and spaced equally except where interrupted by punctuation. Since the graphs are not linked to one another as are the letters of a word handwritten in the Roman alphabet, it is easy to write sequences of them in any direction; traditionally they have usually been written downwards in columns beginning at the right, with one-line inscriptions sometimes running horizontally from right to left, while in the People's Republic of China they are now written in the European style in left-to-right rows.

The sample of Chinese script shown in Figure 25 is part of a news item from the *Ming Pao Evening News* (Hong Kong) of 1 July 1983. The headlines, reading from the top right, run: 'British unemployment rate falls to / twelve point five per cent / Fifth successive monthly fall'.

Figure 25

At this point we should very briefly mention recent reforms in Chinese writing, before going on to consider the advantages and disadvantages of the script. Two separate reforms have been introduced under the People's Republic.

In the first place, a new romanization system (i.e. system for transcribing the sounds of Chinese in terms of the Roman alphabet), called *pinyin*, was promulgated in 1958; since 1979 the Chinese have with considerable success urged Western publishers to use this system instead of the various schemes previously used. (This is why, for example, the name 毛澤東 /máu çɤ̌ tūŋ/ is now spelled 'Mao Zedong' rather than 'Mao Tsê-tung'.) There is no doubt that *pinyin* is a more rational romanization system than most others including the 'Wade-Giles' system traditionally used in the English-speaking world, which depended heavily on the use of apostrophes and other diacritic marks that were misunderstood and often omitted in non-specialist publications. Within China, *pinyin* is used for purposes such as specifying pronunciations of graphs in dictionaries, as a device for introducing small children to the activity of reading, and as a supplement to ordinary Chinese script in contexts such as slogans on posters, or place-names on road-signs – the pronunciation in *pinyin* is shown under the Chinese graphs for the benefit of semi-literate and/or dialect-speaking readers who may be able to use this information to deduce the identity of individual graphs with which they are unfamiliar, or to learn the standard pronunciation of words which they pronounce differently.

The most important point in the present context is that it is *not* proposed to replace traditional logographic Chinese writing with *pinyin* or any other phonographic script for general purposes. That was made clear when *pinyin* was promulgated (Chou 1958, p. 17), and is an obvious implication of the other writing reform, which would serve little purpose if the logographic script were about to be swept away.

This second reform has involved changing the shapes of a large proportion of the graphs so as to reduce the number of strokes. Several principles have been employed for this purpose. Sometimes a few-stroked graph for an infrequent morpheme is used to replace a many-stroked graph for a common morpheme pronounced the same way: e.g. 里, traditionally /lǐ/ 'village/mile' (cf. p. 155), is now also used instead of 裏 for /lǐ/ 'in'. In other cases unique or near-unique components occurring within many-stroked graphs are made to stand for the whole graph: e.g. 豐 /fəŋ/ 'abundant' is now written 丰. The most important principle is that various writings which were tradition-ally used as cursive handwritten versions of commonly-recurring elements are now adopted as the standard printed forms; thus 馬 'horse' is now 马, and the combination-form of the 'speak' signific has been changed from 訁 to 讠.

This reform seems misguided; it depends for its justification on the implaus-ible judgement that the most important factor determining the efficiency of Chinese script is the number of strokes involved in the graphs. In reality an at least equally important consideration is the visual distinctiveness of the elements (a point to which we shall return), and in that respect many (though not all) of the reformed graphs are inferior to their predecessors (Downing 1973, pp. 201–4; Leong 1973; C.-C. Cheng *et al.* 1977). The graph for 'horse' used to be fiddly to write in its official form, but it was extremely recognizable and memorable; the new version looks rather similar to a number of other graphs. (The reformed graphs also entail disadvantages of a more technical nature having to do with dictionary look-up.) One would have thought that there was little objection to a system whereby certain complex elements had conventional quick handwritten equivalents but were printed in their full form – users of the Roman alphabet see no problem in the fact that letters such as ⟨a⟩ and ⟨g⟩ are handwritten in ways that deviate considerably from their printed shapes. After an initial period of enthusiasm, the Chinese authorities have now ceased to produce further lists of simplified graphs; and no part of the Chinese-speaking world outside the People's Republic (except Singapore) has accepted them. (This book uses the traditional graphs.)

Logographic script, then, remains a fixture in the Chinese-speaking world. The last question to consider in this chapter is what its good and bad points are as compared with the phonographic system of writing with which most readers will be so much more familiar.

The casual remarks that laymen make suggest that Chinese writing appears to the average Englishman to be almost excruciatingly cumbersome and difficult. Of course it is a very different system from ours, and things that are unfamiliar often seem complex for that reason alone. It has often puzzled me to know whether the common reaction is based on anything more substantial than this, because I cannot myself see that it is justified. Europeans often suppose that it would unarguably be of great advantage to the Chinese for them to abandon their logographic script in favour of an alphabetic one, except that certain special features of the Chinese language unfortunately make it difficult for them to do this. We shall see in due course that there are two considerations which would create great problems for any proposal to write Chinese phonographically. But I defer discussion of these for the moment, since even if the special factors in question did not obtain it is not clear to me that logographic script would be obviously inferior to phonographic script as a solution to the problem of recording language visually.

If one presses the layman to be specific about why he sees Chinese writing as frighteningly complicated, one point often mentioned is its unbounded nature. People used to the 26 letters of our alphabet ask how many 'letters' there are in total in the Chinese script and are startled to be told that the question is unanswerable. But this is a simple consequence of the fact that each word, roughly speaking, has its own graph: to ask how many graphs there are in the Chinese script is like asking how many words there are in the English language, and this is not a question with a well-defined answer. The largest Chinese dictionary, the Kang-xi Dictionary of 1716, includes about 40,000 graphs, but of these the great majority either stand for thoroughly obsolete words or are obsolete variant forms of graphs for current words. (Likewise, most headwords in the *Oxford English Dictionary* are unfamiliar to a contemporary speaker, even though the eight centuries of English covered by the *OED* represent less than a third of the period covered by a major Chinese dictionary.) An average literate Chinese would probably not know, and would not need to know, more than a few thousand graphs – say five or six thousand at most. (This figure may sound low as a measure of a speaker's total vocabulary; but remember that a Chinese graph represents a *morpheme*, and Chinese did not borrow morphemes from other languages to any significant extent. A family of words such as *king, kingly, kingship, royal, royalty, regal, regalia, Rex, Basil, basilica* count as ten separate items in an Englishman's vocabulary, but a comparable family in Chinese would use a single root morpheme compounded with various high-frequency morphemes akin to English derivational affixes.)

Even a few thousand graphs are clearly a lot to learn when compared to the 26 letters of the Roman alphabet (or even to the 80-odd symbols on a European typewriter). In justifying their view that Chinese script is inordinately complex, people make the point that with an alphabetic script there is essentially *nothing* more to learn once one knows the few simple rules for using the letters, together with the pronunciations of the various words to be written (which, as a native-speaker, one has absorbed without conscious effort) – whereas for every single word that a Chinese knows he must separately learn its writing.

It is not true of English, of course, that the spellings of its words follow automatically from their pronunciations – in this respect our orthography has some resemblance to that of Chinese, a theme to be developed in Chapter 10; and in fact few scripts which use the Roman alphabet are close to being 100 per cent 'phonemic' in this sense. Nor is it really true that all our vocabulary is acquired in the effortless, unconscious fashion in which we pick up the common words in childhood; many less-common words are learned through conscious study, involving consultation of dictionaries and the like, and often we meet them first in print and then discover their pronunciation rather than vice versa. Suppose that Chinese morphemes were written down in a phonemic script but were phonologically much more complex than they are: would the situation still seem so awe-inspiring to the European layman? I suspect not. The phonological shapè of a Chinese morpheme is in fact very simple: a single initial consonant, a vowel or at most a diphthong with a tone, and possibly a single final consonant drawn from a very small set of alternatives. In a language which permitted consonant clusters and a wider range of individual consonants, and which allowed morphemes to be polysyllabic, each morpheme might involve almost as much to be learned, in terms purely of pronunciation, as Chinese morphemes involve in terms of pronunciation and writing together. Yet it seems likely that an Englishman who finds it hard to get his mind round the idea that the Chinese morpheme for 'thunder' is:

léi   雷

might be quite unfazed by the news that in some other language 'thunder' is, say:

sprēʃváugli   (spelled as pronounced)

Admittedly, to someone unfamiliar with Chinese graphs they often look so complex in themselves that a morpheme would have to include an implausible number of syllables in order to match their complexity in terms of phonology. But this is a trivial matter of what one happens to be used to. To anyone who can read Chinese, the graph for 'thunder' cited above consists of just two elements, each of which is so familiar that it is difficult for him to see the individual strokes of which they are composed as separate entities.

Goody and Watt (1963, p. 313) argue that the Chinese system of writing necessarily restricts literacy to 'a small and specially trained professional group'. This is factually untrue. Historically the proportion of literate Chinese was far from insignificant by pre-modern European standards and was certainly not limited to the professional mandarinate, though precise figures are hard to come by. In the 1950s the literacy rate in Japan (where the writing system is comparable to but much more complex than the Chinese, as we shall see in the next chapter) was estimated at 97–98 per cent, the same as Canada, higher than France, Belgium, or the USA, and beaten only by the British Isles, Scandinavia, the Netherlands, Germany, Switzerland, Austria, Australia, and New Zealand (UNESCO 1957). Small differences in estimated literacy levels have to be interpreted with care because of the difficulty of ensuring that one is comparing like with like; but the very high figure for Japan suggests strongly that what determines a society's literacy level has very little to do with the nature of its script and almost everything to do with its general educational facilities and level of civilization (cf. Downing 1973, p. 178). The 25 territories placed by UNESCO in the lowest category of 5 per cent literacy or less, which include African countries never colonized by Britain together with Arabia,

Afghanistan, Nepal, and Bhutan, are without exception territories where the script in use is phonographic. If, as Goody and Watt believe, the criterion for literacy in Chinese is that one is familiar with the full repertory of 50,000 *(sic)* graphs, then no Chinese has ever been literate; but this is absurd.

The assumption that a logographic script is more difficult to learn than a phonographic one may be not just false but meaningless, since the truth seems to be that the two kinds of script involve different, and incommensurable, *kinds* of difficulty. A logographic script requires a lot of time to commit the many graphs to memory; a phonographic script requires analytic intelligence to split words into sounds (cf. p. 36). Rozin, Poritsky, and Sotsky (1971) worked with American schoolchildren who had failed to learn to read even words such as *cat* or *pip*, and taught them to read simple stories written in a script which used Chinese graphs to represent thirty English words. 'In . . . about 4 hours we taught children to read . . . Chinese characters that were in many ways more complex than normal English orthography. Yet these same children had failed to acquire the basics of English reading in almost 2 years of schooling.' Experiments by Steinberg and Yamada (1978–9) suggest that beginning readers may find logographs easier to learn than visually-simpler phonographic symbols, because the meaningfulness of the former outweighs their visual complexity as a factor determining learnability. As Ignatius Mattingly puts it (1972, p. 144), anyone with plenty of time to spare can learn to read Chinese; if a script is phonographic there will be 'more reading successes, because the learning time is far shorter, but proportionately' more failures, too, because of the greater demand on linguistic awareness'.

In Japan (where, as we shall see in Chapter 9, the script mixes clearly-logographic and clearly-phonographic elements), Makita (1968) finds that developmental dyslexia is extremely rare by comparison with Western countries. Sasanuma (1974) shows that it is quite common in Japan for acquired dyslexia (i.e. reading difficulties induced by damage to the brain of a person who was previously literate) to affect the processing of the phonographic and not the logographic aspect of the script, but the reverse is very uncommon. (Margaret Snowling (e.g. 1981) has found comparable results with developmentally-dyslexic British children – we shall see in Chapter 10 that English orthography can be regarded as mixing logographic and phonographic elements.)

Logographic Chinese script may be not only easier to learn but easier to read than phonographic script once learned. In reading Chinese script, one has to identify each word as a visual *Gestalt*, a whole with its own distinctive shape; in reading a phonographic script one can do this, or alternatively one can work out the identity of a word letter by letter. (Schoolteachers call these alternative strategies the 'look-and-say' and 'phonic' methods of reading, respectively.) Because the familiar Western languages are written in essentially phonographic scripts, Europeans tend instinctively to assume that the second, 'phonic' method of reading is more natural. The psychological evidence, as we shall see in Chapter 10, suggests just the opposite: that normal language-users read (in any script) most naturally and efficiently by the look-and-say method. It appears to follow that the best script from the point of view of efficient reading will be one in which the visual shapes of words are relatively distinctive. From this point of view Chinese script – the graphs of which are composed of quite a wide variety of distinct basic elements arranged in varying spatial configurations – scores heavily over any alphabetic script in which all words are made up of reshufflings of the same two or three dozen letters in one-dimensional sequences. At an anecdotal level, literate Chinese encountering European script have been known to make comments suggesting that it produces on them the same impression of monotony and lack of distinctiveness which we might experience if faced with pages printed entirely in the dots and dashes of Morse code. (cf. Chiang 1973, pp. 3–4; Geschwind 1973.)

An extreme version of the view that logographic script is inferior as a medium of culture is expressed by the anthropologist Jack Goody (Goody and Watt 1963; Goody 1977). According to Goody and Watt (pp. 314–15) it is in the nature of such scripts to 'reify the objects of the natural and social order', and, by so doing, to 'make permanent the existing social and ideological picture'; by contrast, phonographic writing

. . . symboli[zes], not the objects of the social and natural order, but the very process of human interaction in speech: the verb is as easy to express as the noun . . . . Phonetic systems are therefore adapted to expressing every nuance of individual thought . . . [while logographic writing records] only those items in the cultural repertoire which the literate specialists have selected for written expression; and it tends to express the collective attitude towards them.

They go on to argue (pp. 337–8) that the Chinese writing system militates against adoption of the standards of logic normal in 'literate' societies (by which they mean societies using a phonographic script).[4]

To anyone who respects Chinese civilization this sort of nonsense is rather offensive. It is certainly true that China was traditionally a conservative society, and arguably also one not much interested in logical issues. But the suggestion that either of these cultural traits is a consequence of logographic script is quite untenable. Chinese script provides a graph for virtually every morpheme of the language: words for ideologically-crucial notions and words for banal objects, verbs as well as nouns. (The few exceptional morphemes which cannot be written down are ones occurring only in regional dialects, or slang terms which – like English *bonzer* as opposed to *smashing* – are morphemically unrelated to terms of the standard language: it is implausible to suggest that such gaps in the script had any serious effect on the evolution of Chinese culture.) There is absolutely no way in which, for example, the graphs for /ṣừ/ 'civil servant' or /núŋ/ 'peasant' reflect the favourable roles assigned by official Chinese culture to these groups while the graphs for /ṣāŋ/ 'merchant' or /pīŋ/ 'soldier' reflect the suspicion and contempt to which those classes were exposed. (Women's Liberators might point out the number of cases where words for unpleasant character-traits such as jealousy are written with the 'woman' signific; but the incidence of this sort of thing is no greater than that of comparable sexist assumptions in the spoken English language – cf. *bitch* v. *dog*, for instance.) As for the matter of logic: it might be that properties of Chinese *as a spoken language* militated against awareness of logical considerations[5] (the rich system of inflexion and of particles in Classical Greek drew attention to logical relationships within sentences, while Chinese had virtually no inflexion and a poorer system of particles); but, once the spoken Chinese language is accepted as a given, I see no argument for the view that logical explicitness is affected by the question of whether the language is written down phoneme-by-phoneme or morpheme-by-morpheme. (Goody and Watt give no such argument.) One is familiar with the attitude which automatically dismisses any exotic cultural institution as self-evidently inferior; it is sad to find it expressed by an academic of some eminence.

Certainly there are genuine drawbacks in a logographic script such as the Chinese; but the two drawbacks which seem to me most serious are not ones which laymen are inclined to emphasize.

One of these has to do with printing and, more generally, the use of the script in modern word-processing technology. When telegraphy was introduced to China, a numerical code had to be introduced so that Chinese telegrams could be transmitted as sequences of four-digit numbers representing the various graphs; this obviously introduces problems of encoding and decoding that are absent with alphabetic systems. Likewise, any word-processing machinery using keyboard input is difficult to adapt to Chinese script because the number of graphs is too large for any practical keyboard. Typewriters are manufactured, but they use separate pieces of type (as in letterpress printing) that are picked up by a single arm, rather than a permanent set of a few dozen typebars as on Western machines; writing with them is slow, so they are little used.

This drawback is a real one. However, it is a very recent one; until well into the 20c it probably did not cause an appreciable degree of inefficiency. Printing itself had of course existed long before and was indeed invented in China, but, while the relative cost of labour to capital remains fairly low, it probably matters little to a printing shop using traditional hand-set type whether thousands or only hundreds of 'sorts' are needed. (For that matter the number of sorts may not have been dramatically larger in a Chinese than in a European printing shop of the 19c, since in Europe the number was multiplied by the practice of stocking a large number of different faces, all in various sizes of roman and italic capitals, lower case, and small capitals. The Chinese did not go in for variety of type-faces; they were never interested in typography as an art, probably because the virtues prized in calligraphy – which was a major art-form – were just the properties of spontaneity and unmechanical irregularity which cannot be reproduced in type: cf. Chiang 1973, p. 115.)

More recently still, new technology has again begun to reduce the inefficiencies associated with logographic script. For instance, rather than inputting graphs into a machine by finding the right one among thousands of keys or the equivalent, it is now possible with a small keyboard to specify a few properties of the target graph and choose between the various graphs sharing those properties displayed on a screen. Likewise, lack of typewriters is a nuisance when record-keeping depends on carbon copies, but it becomes much less important when photocopying is available.

Whatever devices are invented to reduce the difficulties, logographic writing will probably always continue to pose somewhat greater technological problems than phonographic writing. But one should not exaggerate this difference; any suggestion that logographic script is incompatible with a high level of modern technological development is obviously refuted by the case of Japan.

The other drawback of the Chinese script is less obvious but, I suspect, more serious. This has to do with foreign words and names.

In an alphabetic script like ours, there is no difficulty about writing borrowed words: *curry*, *boomerang*, *Schadenfreude*, etc., etc. Even names that are unpronounceable in English can be written down easily, and we can give them some conventional mispronunciation: *Nkomo, Tbilisi, Llanllwchaiarn*, etc. In Chinese script, on the other hand, each graph represents a morpheme of the Chinese language. The only way a non-Chinese word can be written is as a series of Chinese morphemes of similar pronunciation; but, since Chinese has a quite limited range of sounds, the imitation usually cannot be very close.

Until quite recently, this limitation also was of little practical importance for the Chinese. For most of its history China was an area of high culture largely cut off from the outside world by geography, and the only non-Chinese peoples encountered by the Chinese were 'barbarians'. The Chinese had little reason to borrow vocabulary from other languages, and did so only to an extremely limited extent. (The main exception within historical times was the borrowing of a number of Sanskrit terms when Buddhism reached China from India; an example is 涅槃 /niè-pʰán/ for *nirvāṇa* – the meaning of the Chinese morphemes, 'opaque place-of-retirement', is vaguely appropriate, but they were chosen essentially for their sound.) Even nowadays, Western technological and other terms are not normally borrowed in their original form; rather, Chinese uses morphemes of its own literary stock to coin compounds rather in the way that we use Latin and Greek roots.

The words for which transliteration is unavoidable are proper names. Chinese names, even personal names, are always composed of meaningful morphemes. Foreign names, on the other hand, are meaningless noises to the Chinese. Names of the leading foreign countries have been Sinicized, in the sense that their Chinese translations follow the pattern of Chinese place-names: thus England is 英國 /īŋ-kuó/ 'the nation of heroes', with /īŋ/ sounding like the beginning of *England,* while France is 法國 /fà-kuó/ 'the nation of law'; and Westerners who live in China or have dealings with the Chinese are given Chinese names. But for the great majority of foreign names such individual treatment is impossible, and they are simply spelled out by long sequences of graphs. The Chinese tend to use a limited subset of their vocabulary for transliteration purposes, and many morphemes in that subset are otherwise almost or wholly obsolete (which is useful in that it makes clear that a given graph-sequence is to be read for its phonetic value rather than its meaning – Chinese script does not normally use any device akin to capitals that would show that a sequence of graphs is meant as a proper name); but these tendencies are by no means absolute.

Some samples of such transliterations, supplemented with literal morpheme-by-morpheme glosses, are the following:

迭更斯 tié-kəŋ-sū 'repeatedly-change-this': Dickens

柴霍甫斯基 zʰái-xuò-fǔ-sū-cī 'firewood-suddenly-begin-this-foundation': Tchaikovsky

里約熱內盧 lǐ-yē-ɽɣ-nèi-lú 'village-agree-hot-inner-brazier": Rio de Janeiro

利奧波德維爾 lì-àu-pō-tɣ-wéi-ɔɽ 'profit-mysterious-wave-virtue-fasten-you': Léopoldville

The results of this system are clumsy, for several reasons. First, the phonetic correspondence with the foreign original is usually very inexact. Secondly, because of the difficulty of adapting Chinese phonology to foreign sounds, the Chinese version of a foreign name is often as long as a whole Chinese sentence. Third and most important, the looseness of fit between original and Chinese equivalent means that there are many possible Chinese transliterations for any given foreign name, which creates obvious practical problems. In practice the Chinese achieve a fair degree of consistency in writing the most famous foreign names, but even in these cases the consistency is very far from complete; for instance, two reference-works on my bookshelf transliterate 'Wordsworth' as 華滋華斯 /xuá-çū-xuá-sū/ 'flowery-flavour-flowery-this' and as 威至威士 /wēi-zù-wēi-ṣù/ 'prestige-arrive-prestige-scholar' respectively. Less well-known names are probably written differently on almost every occasion that they happen to be put into Chinese.

Now that the Chinese have adopted the Roman alphabet for certain internal purposes and have also taken to writing their own script horizontally, the need to use transliterations like these might be eliminated if they were willing to use Roman script in the middle of a Chinese sentence in order to write non-Chinese words. At present the two scripts are felt to be so alien to one another that this is not possible; everything in a Chinese text must be written in Chinese graphs, with at most the Roman version included in brackets after the first introduction of a new foreign word. While this remains the situation, the treatment of foreign words is a real drawback of the Chinese method of writing; and, if it is a drawback for a relatively self-contained and inward-looking culture like that of China, it would be very much more so for a highly international culture such as that of Britain.

However, these drawbacks are outweighed by certain advantages of the logographic system that have not been discussed yet, and which relate to special properties of the Chinese language.

One of the most characteristic features of modern Chinese, which seems very strange if not almost incredible to someone used to European languages, is its extremely high incidence of homophones. It has already been suggested that Chinese has a rather restricted phonology; each Chinese morpheme is one syllable, and there are relatively few different phonologically-possible syllables. Even in the Old Chinese period as reconstructed by Karlgren the system appears to have been 'straining at the seams', as it were: almost every possible syllable corresponded to an actual morpheme, with few unused possibilities akin to English *sluck*, *fran*, *drebble*, and there were even then a fair number of homophones. But the large number of sound-changes that have occurred since the Old Chinese period have involved massive and repeated losses of important phonological distinctions. The consonant clusters which existed in Old Chinese were reduced to single consonants; final stop consonants dropped; the voiced/voiceless distinction was eliminated; the vowel-system was greatly simplified; etc. etc.

This means that there are now many times more morphemes than phonologically-possible syllables. The average syllable in modern Chinese will now stand for perhaps half a dozen different morphemes of the living language (most of which will have developed widely-divergent polysemies), together with a larger number of literary morphemes which are obsolete in the spoken language but which a scholar might easily encounter in his reading. There are scarcely any syllables in modern Chinese which represent a single morpheme unambiguously, as is common in English (/hɪt, rɪp, dɛθ, wid/ etc. stand for one morpheme each). There is a potential misunderstanding here: Europeans who hear about Chinese homophones often say 'But they solve that problem with their tones'. However, when I talk about there being relatively few distinct syllables in Chinese, I mean syllables distinct with respect to their consonants, their vowels, *or their tone* – the tone is as much part of the pronunciation of a Chinese syllable as any other aspect of it, and it is a misapprehension to think of tones as something special that were added to solve a particular problem.

In Figure 26 I list just the living, modern alternative values of two Modern Chinese syllables, ignoring homophonous morphemes found only in literary language. These particular syllables are more ambiguous than average, but not much more – there are plenty which are far worse. (In Old Chinese, on the other hand, even in the few cases where morphemes are shown as homophones they may in fact have been distinguished by pronunciation-features that have not been reconstructed.) Thus modern spoken Chinese is immensely ambiguous. A passage written in Literary Chinese is normally quite incomprehensible when read aloud, even to someone familiar with every one of the morphemes it contains as well as with the obsolete aspects of

Literary Chinese grammar, because each morpheme is homophonous with several others.

graph	gloss	Old Chinese pronunciation	Modern Chinese pronunciation
欺	cheat	*kʰjəg	
期	period	*kjəg	
崎	mountainous	*gʰia	
溪	creek	*kʰieg	
七	seven		
沏	to mash tea	*tsʰjĕt	cʰī
漆	varnish		
妻	wife	*tsʰiər	
悽	grieved		
棲	roost	*siər	
戚	kinsman	*tsʰiok	
研	grind/research	*ŋian	
延	prolong	*djan	
蜒	slug		
檐	eaves	*djam	
炎	flame		
嚴	strict	*ŋjăm	
巖	cliff	*ŋam	jén
言	speak	*ŋjăn	
閻	name of the King of Hell	*djæm	
顏	face/colour	*ŋan	
鹽	salt	*xljam	
沿	along	*dɥan	
焉	there	*ʔjan	

Figure 26

The spoken language has adopted various strategies in practice in order to overcome this ambiguity. Some of these strategies could in principle be imitated in writing, even if the script were phonographic; for instance, very often concepts that were expressed by single morphemes at an earlier stage are expressed by combinations of two morphemes in modern colloquial Chinese, each of which may be quite ambiguous in isolation but which disambiguate one another when taken together. (Thus /jén/ 'research' is ambiguous as shown in Figure 26, and it has a near-synonym /çiōu/ which also has many homophones – morphemes pronounced /çiōu/ have meanings which include 'gather', 'pigeon', 'clutch', 'blame' – so in Modern Chinese one says /jén-çiōu/ for 'research' rather than either morpheme alone. Various other categories of compound are also used.) But one of the important factors in speech for which writing can have no equivalent is the constant negotiation of meaning that occurs in a dialogue; misunderstandings that occur when people speak face-to-face are often cleared up almost unconsciously, as fast as they arise. In writing, on the other hand, what is written must be sufficient to eliminate the possibility of ambiguity in advance, since negotiation with the reader is impossible.

The significant point is that the immense ambiguity of modern Chinese morphemes in their spoken form is entirely eliminated in writing, where each morpheme retains its own distinctive graph – whereas, with a phonographic script, the ambiguities would carry over from speech to writing. Even with the strategies of morpheme-compounding just mentioned, modern spoken Chinese does seem to be a relatively ambiguous language; indeed, when speaking to one another literate Chinese will not infrequently draw a graph in the air to disambiguate a problematic syllable. Yet speech typically involves a more limited set of topics and more predictable ideas than do written documents, so that ambiguity would cause much greater difficulties in writing than in speech. Contemporary Chinese publications concerned with language sometimes include a corner in which a short text of a few paragraphs is written out entirely in *pinyin* romanization, and readers puzzle through it as a *tour de force*, but it seems doubtful whether phonographic writing could be successfully adopted as the normal script of a Chinese-speaking society.[6]

The second special factor has to do with the Chinese 'dialects', so called. I have until now been speaking of 'Modern Chinese' as if it were a single language, and what I have indicated by that term is what is known in the West as 'Mandarin Chinese'. There is some justice in calling Mandarin Chinese simply 'Chinese': it is the speech of about two-thirds of all Chinese (admittedly with regional variation, but variation that does not prevent mutual comprehension), and it is regarded by the present Chinese regime as the only kind of Chinese with official status. Nevertheless, many Chinese speak languages that are very different indeed from Mandarin. Since about the middle of the +1st millennium, what was originally one fairly homogeneous Chinese language has split into six or eight main varieties (each with sub-varieties, sub-sub-varieties, etc.) which have diverged so widely that they are better called 'languages' than 'dialects'. To give just one example of the pronunciation-differences between these divisions of Chinese: the word for 'north', Mandarin /pĕi/, is Cantonese /pak/, Hakka /pɛt/, Suchow /pɯʔ/, and so on. Comparably large differences run throughout the vocabulary. Their consequences for communication are greatly magnified because of the unusually low 'margins of error' in comprehension of Chinese speech which stem from the high level of homophony and the scarcity of possible-but-unused syllables.

As a result, a Pekinese could no more understand a Cantonese (without studying the latter's language) than a Londoner could understand a Berliner. The non-Mandarin varieties of Chinese are not restricted to individuals of low social status; everyone speaks the variety of Chinese current in his home area.

Yet these different languages are spoken in a single nation which has been very civilized and politically very centralized for a long time, and which therefore needed a universal medium of communication. Again the logographic script solves this problem beautifully, since the 'dialect' distinctions have to do mainly with divergent pronunciations of the same morphemes, and these divergences are not reflected at all in the written graphs. Differences in vocabulary and grammar between the 'dialects' are small, so that they can easily be overcome by agreeing on standards of written usage, rather in the way that speakers of regional dialects in Britain are easily able to use a standard English in writing.

In fact, until this century standard written usage represented a stage of the language which had been obsolete for a millennium and more as a spoken norm. Educated Chinese continued to write (for some purposes they still do write) Chinese as it had been before the spoken language was forced to adapt to the problem of ambiguity arising from homophony on a massive scale, and before the 'dialects' had diverged from one another. Because of the difficulty of training the mass of the population to use the grammar and vocabulary of a long-dead stage of Chinese, since the Republican period the grammar and vocabulary of modern Mandarin has been adopted as the written norm. For a Cantonese speaker to accustom himself to the few differences from his native language at these linguistic levels is no great task, whereas for him to learn to *speak* Mandarin, or to understand it written in a phonographic script, would be a major feat of language-learning.

The homophones and the 'dialects' constitute two special reasons for the retention of logographic script in China. It may be that, if these factors had happened not to be present, the logographic principle would have been abandoned. But this is far from obvious. The main point I have tried to make in this chapter is that, independently of the particular properties of the language to be written, the logographic principle for writing is by no means self-evidently inferior to the phonographic principle.

9 A mixed system: Japanese writing

Like the Koreans, the Japanese had no writing of their own when they encountered and began to absorb Chinese civilization in the +1st millennium. Like the Koreans – indeed, under Korean tutelage – the Japanese made shift to adapt Chinese script to a language that was unrelated to, and typologically very different from, Chinese. (The genetic affiliation of Japanese was for a long time unclear. It is now argued (Martin 1966; Miller 1971) that Korean is the language to which Japanese is most closely related, so that Japanese too is an Altaic language, though the surviving common features which suggest a Korean/Japanese relationship are limited and the matter remains controversial (Patrie 1982, p. 700). The standard handbook on the Japanese language is Miller 1967.) Unlike the Koreans, the Japanese never made a clean break to a different kind of script. (I shall discuss factors which made such a break less possible for the Japanese than it was for Koreans.) Everything in modern Japanese orthography derives ultimately from Chinese writing; but, because the two languages are very different, the processes by which Chinese script was adapted to write the Japanese language often had to be highly roundabout, and the end-result is a system typologically quite different from the Chinese system. Chinese writing is to a close approximation a pure logographic script. Japanese writing is a mixed system, partly logographic and partly phonographic.

Japanese writing differs from Chinese not only in type but also in degree of complexity. I argued in the last chapter that Chinese logographic script, although it looks daunting to the uninitiated, is actually a fairly simple system of writing. Japanese script, on the other hand, is a quite astonishingly complicated method of making language visible.

One reason for this complexity has to do with differences between Japanese and Chinese as spoken languages. But there is another relevant factor. Japanese society, during much of the period in which the script was developed, was characterized by the existence of an aristocratic class many members of which lacked political power or indeed any serious employment, so that their only role in life was as definers and producers of cultural norms, ways of civilized living. (One might perhaps draw a distant parallel with France under the *Ancien Régime*.) As a natural result, many aspects of Japanese culture, including its writing, were greatly elaborated, made exquisite and intellectually rich rather than straightforwardly functional. (This contrasts with the case of China, which at most periods of its history was a rather down-to-earth, workaday civilization and where the script, for instance, was shaped in the historical period largely by civil servants who had plenty to keep them busy.) To quote R. A. Miller (1967, p. 99):

> The tiny segment of the population that was at all concerned with reading and writing had in fact little if anything else to do with its time, and so quite naturally it delighted in any device that would make the process as time-consuming as possible.

If Japanese script seems gratuitously complex in the ways it relates sound, meaning, and written symbols, this should not surprise us, since (Miller 1967, p. 100):

> The early Japanese . . . found this kind of writing intriguing and far more rewarding aesthetically than any simple one-to-one phonetic or semantic equivalency system . . . . They and their culture were not interested in evolving an easy system, or one that could be written quickly or read simply and unambiguously. Such values and goals were totally absent from ancient Japanese society . . . .

Japanese society has changed many of its goals and values since the days referred to in these quotations. Correspondingly, the version of the script used in the late 20c has been considerably simplified by comparison with the full panoply of eccentricities it once possessed; some complications which have disappeared leaving little trace on the modern script will be ignored in my description. But although many complexities have been stripped away, many remain. One reason why Japanese script deserves its place in this book is as an illustration of just how cumbersome a script can be and still serve in practice. For, remember, the writing system to be described in this chapter is not nowadays the private plaything of an exquisitely idle élite. As mentioned in the last chapter, Japan has a very high literacy rate: higher than France or the United States of America. And if the complications of Japanese writing may be thought to make for inefficiency in practical life, they have not hindered Japan from becoming in our time perhaps the most technologically advanced nation on this planet.

While Chinese is an 'isolating' language in which each morpheme or word is an invariant syllable, Japanese has a rich system of derivational and inflexional morphology, with associated morphophonemic alternations. So, for example, from the root /mot-/ 'hold', we find among others the following words formed:

moçu	'hold' (plain)
mocimasu	'hold' (polite)
motanai	'not hold' (plain)
mocimasen	'not hold' (polite)
motta	'held' (plain)
mocimaçita	'held' (polite)
motanakatta	'did not hold' (plain)
motō	'be about to hold' (plain)

mocimaçō	'be about to hold' (polite)
moci	'holding' (noun)
motte	'(is) holding'
etc.	

(In transcriptions of Japanese, /ç c ɟ/ will stand for the affricates written /ts tɕ dʑ/ in the IPA alphabet; the macron indicates vowel-length. One of the factors relevant for verbal inflexion in Japanese is the social status of the addressee, hence the glosses 'plain' and 'polite'.)

Japanese words (even those consisting of a single uninflected morpheme) often consist of several syllables, e.g. /taçika/ 'certain'. But syllable-structure is even simpler than in Chinese: to a close approximation, syllables are restricted to a single consonant (or no consonant) followed by a simple vowel; and there are no distinctions of tone.[1]

The Japanese first began to write their own language in the +7c. In order to get an idea of the problems of writing down Japanese in Chinese script, Miller invites us to imagine that we had no writing system of our own and wanted to use Chinese script to write English. Let us suppose, he says, that we wish to write down: 'The bear killed the man'.

Chinese, as it happens, has no word for *the*. The definite article is not a very important word in English, so we give up on this and press on to the word *bear*. 'Bear' translates into Chinese as /çýŋ/, written 熊 – so we write this graph. 'Kill' is Chinese /ʂā/, written 殺 ; but Chinese has no inflexion comparable to English *-ed*. We might indicate that 殺 is to be understood as 'gone past' by adding, say, 去 /cʰỳ/ 'go'. Alternatively, since the English inflexion is pronounced /d/, we might write some graph for a Chinese morpheme having a similar sound – perhaps 的, pronounced roughly like English /-d/, which is a grammatical suffix in Chinese, though in Chinese it forms the genitive of a noun. Now we come to *the* again. Rather than leaving it out as we did before, this time we may be emboldened by our success just now in 'spelling' *-ed* and decide analogously to write *the* with the graph for a Chinese morpheme sounding something like /ðə/. It cannot be *very* similar, though, because this is a quite un-Chinese sort of syllable: perhaps we choose 色 /sɤ̀/ 'colour'. Finally, *man*: here we will probably write 人 , the graph for /ɽə́n/ 'man' in the 'human being' sense. On the other hand, if in context we take the English word *man* to refer specifically to a male, in contrast to *woman*, Chinese has no one word for this. Chinese uses the phrase 男人 /nán-ɽə́n/, literally 'male person', so we might write these two graphs to stand for the single short English word *man*.

Japanese writing uses Chinese script in all these ways.

The term used to indicate a Chinese graph used to represent a Japanese word whose meaning is the same as, or similar to, that of the Chinese word written with the graph in question is *kun*, literally 'instruction'. One says that the graph has a *'kun* reading'. Thus, Japanese /hito/ 'man' is written 人 (see above); Japanese /jama/ 'mountain' is written 山, the graph for Chinese /ʂān/

'hill'. Of course, since Chinese and Japanese were two independent languages, one would not normally expect to be able to find a perfect synonym in Chinese for a given Japanese word, and frequently scribes had to content themselves with a near-equivalent. (I deliberately draw attention to this aspect of the *kun* system in my discussion by giving the pairs of Chinese and Japanese words involved slightly different English glosses, when this is appropriate. The problems arising from lack of semantic isomorphism between the two languages will be discussed at length later in the chapter.)

In early Japanese writing there would occur, interspersed with graphs intended to be given *kun* readings, other cases where graphs were used for their phonetic value, as in the hypothetical use of 色 /sɤ̀/ 'colour' to represent English *the*. For instance, the Japanese genitive particle /no/ was written 乃, Chinese /năi/ 'your'; the Japanese topic-marking suffix /wa/ was written 波, Ch. /pō/ 'wave'. At the period when this sort of writing was practised, rather more than a thousand years ago, these pairs of words resembled one another phonetically more than they do today: the nuclear vowel of Chinese /năi/ and the vowel of Japanese /no/ were probably both somewhat shwa-like then, the suffix /wa/ was earlier pronounced /pa/, the /o/ of Chinese /pō/ was not yet a rounded vowel. Nevertheless, the equivalences often seem to have been quite inexact. (In order to avoid unnecessary philological complications I shall cite Japanese and Chinese forms in their modern pronunciations below.)

This second kind of writing is called in Japanese *man'yōgana*, literally 'phonographic script *(kana)* of the Myriad-Leaf type', because the most famous document exemplifying it is the *Man'yōshū* or 'Myriad-Leaf Collection', an anthology of poetry compiled in the late +8c. (Sir George Sansom (1962, p. 531 n. 1) suggests that the word *kana* derives from the first two elements of a syllabary beginning *ka-na-ta-ra* which the Koreans used before the invention of Han'gŭl – in which case the Japanese word *kana* is neatly parallel to the English word *alphabet*.) Since each Chinese graph stood for a syllable, and Japanese words were of the CVCVCV. . . type, in *man'yōgana* a graph would stand for a CV combination (ignoring any final consonant in the Chinese syllable). Thus a single Japanese word would be represented in *man'yōgana* by a minimum of one but in most cases more than one Chinese graph.

It may be that the principle of *man'yōgana* writing was invented in response to the problem posed by Japanese 'grammatical words' that had no exact semantic equivalents in Chinese. However, once the principle was established, an ordinary lexical word could be, and often was, written in *man'yōgana* as an alternative to *kun*. For instance, the first poem in the *Man'yōshū* spells the word /fukuçi/ 'trowel' as 布久思, Ch. /pù-ciŏu-sū/ 'cloth long-time thought'. To quote Miller (1967, p. 98) again,

The method of writing a given word in any particular instance would depend on scribal preference, the amount of empty space available for inscribing a given text [because *man'yōgana* used more graphs per Japanese word than *kun* writing], or other aesthetic factors, and there is ample evidence that the early Japanese scribes took considerable pleasure in the possibilities for elegant graphic variation which the script afforded them.

At this period, a page of Japanese writing would consist of Chinese graphs of which some were intended to be given *kun* readings and others read as *man'yōgana*, with no indication of which was which. Faced with, for instance, a token of 波, Ch. /pō/ 'wave', the Japanese reader simply had to work out from context that Japanese /nami/ 'wave' did not make sense and the graph must therefore be intended as the topic-maker /wa/ (or vice versa). If the topic-marker /wa/ were always written with 波 rather than with any of the several other graphs whose Chinese pronunciations were roughly similar then it might have been fairly easy to take 波 automatically as topic-marker except on the rare occasions when 'wave' was appropriate. However, the large number of homophones in Chinese and the differences between the phonology of the respective languages (together with the attitudes sketched in the above quotation) meant that the system was much less predictable than this. Sansom (1962, p. 138) quotes the preface of a modern Japanese edition of the *Man'yōshū* as saying: 'the difficulty of giving [the *man'yōgana*] the correct reading is indescribable . . . though they have been studied incessantly from ancient times there are still many obscure passages'.

Sometimes the scribes left readers to fill in for themselves items that were relatively unimportant or hard to write with Chinese graphs, as suggested for the first *the* in our hypothetical transcription of 'The bear killed the man'. For instance, in the first line of poem 255 of the *Man'yōshū*, which runs /tōzuma no koko ni araneba/, 'because of my distant love's not being here', the genitive particle /no/ is omitted and the reader has to fill it in from his knowledge of the language (although in the following line the same Japanese word is represented by the *kun* 之 , a Chinese genitive particle pronounced /z̩ū/, and we have already seen that on other occasions it was written with a *man'yōgana* graph). It may be that /no/ was omitted in the line quoted on the ground that Chinese would not include a genitive-marker in a comparable construction; or this may have been a random decision by the scribe.

So far the discussion has proceeded as if the spoken Japanese language remained independent of Chinese, so that the only issue facing Japanese writers was how to use Chinese script to write a quite un-Chinese language. But Japanese, like Korean, borrowed Chinese vocabulary on a massive scale. Chinese plays something like the same role *vis-à-vis* Japanese as Greek, Latin, and Norman French between them play *vis-à-vis* English: many words came into Japanese from Chinese along with the cultural institutions to which they refer, as English acquired words like *assize, chase, dinner* when the Conquest introduced Norman law, amusements, eating habits, and the like into England, but also when the Japanese needed to coin new terms subsequently they automatically resorted to Chinese roots as we turn to the roots of Latin and Greek. Commonly a modern technical term will involve the same combination of morphemes in Japanese as in modern Chinese, although sometimes the two languages construct divergent neologisms from the common stock of Chinese roots.

Quite naturally, any word borrowed from Chinese continued to be written with its Chinese graph. This implies that a given graph may be read as a Sino-Japanese ('SJ') loan, or alternatively as a native Japanese ('NJ') form; readings of the former kind are called *on* as opposed to *kun*. (Because of the many phonological changes that Chinese has undergone, it is often difficult to recognize the phonological relationship between a Sino-Japanese word and its modern Chinese pronunciation.)

Take, for instance, the well-known word /kimono/, 'clothing'. This is a compound formed from the NJ roots /ki-/ 'wear' and /mono/ 'thing, stuff': clothes in Japanese are 'wearables'. The compound is written with two graphs: 着物. The first of these corresponds to a rather vague Chinese word /z̧áu/, meaning 'to place, put, cause' – the Japanese have used it to represent NJ /ki-/, thinking of 'wear' as 'put on', apparently. The second graph corresponds to Ch. /ù/ 'thing, creature'. But both of these Chinese morphemes also exist as loans in Japanese. The first has the SJ pronunciation /caku/ and occurs for example in the compound 着手/cakuçu/ literally 'put-hand', meaning 'to start' (put one's hand to the wheel, as it were) – the /çu/ likewise being the SJ version of Ch. /şǒu/ 'hand'. Similarly, Ch. /ù/ 'thing, creature' exists in the SJ guise /buçu/ for instance in the compound 動物 /dōbuçu/ 'animal', where /dō/ is the SJ version of Ch.動 /tùŋ/ 'move' – an animal is a 'moving (i.e. animate) object'. One says that the graph 着 has the *kun* reading /ki-/ and the *on* reading /caku/; 物 has the *kun* reading /mono/ and the *on* reading /buçu/. Likewise, the graph 手 'hand' has a *kun* reading as NJ /te/ 'hand', and 動 'move' has a *kun* reading as NJ /ugok-/ 'move, run'. Notice that nothing in the script tells one to read 着物 as (*kun*) /kimono/ rather than as (*on*) */cakubuçu/, or to read着手as (*on*) /cakuçu/ rather than as (*kun*) */kite/. The reader just has to know which of these alternatives is right, by virtue of his knowledge of Japanese vocabulary. This sort of problem is non-existent when Chinese script is used to write Chinese, for each graph (with marginal exceptions) then has one and just one reading.

Since Japanese is phonologically very different from Chinese, SJ morphemes were usually pronounced rather differently from their Chinese originals, whether the comparison is made with Chinese as it was at the time of borrowing (so-called 'Middle' or 'Ancient' – as opposed to 'Archaic' – Chinese) or with modern Chinese. (Compare the fact that a classical Roman would be unlikely to recognize Latin roots as we pronounce them in English words, and nor can a speaker of a modern Romance – i.e. Latin-descended – language such as Italian or French readily recognize Romance roots in English speech – although orthography tends to make the relationships relatively perspicuous.) In a few respects Japanese phonology was expanded so as to admit sounds or sound-combinations occurring in Chinese words: word-initial /r/ was introduced as an approximation to Chinese /l/, in the same way that initial /v/ was introduced into English as a consequence of the borrowing of words such as *vain, valiant* from French, and clusters of consonant plus /j/ were created. But very many of the phonological distinctions of Chinese were lost in the process of adapting Chinese syllables to Japanese habits of pronunciation. All distinctions of tone disappeared, Japanese not being a tone language, and many consonant and vowel contrasts were merged.

It is true that Middle Chinese had more phonological distinctions than modern Mandarin Chinese, and there are a handful of contrasts which are lost in modern Chinese but have been preserved in Sino-Japanese. But such cases are few, whereas there are very many distinctions that are preserved in Chinese but absent in Sino-Japanese. Remember that Chinese is already a language in which a large number of morphemes are shared out between a relatively small number of distinct phonological syllables. When the effect of Japanizing the pronunciation is added, the result is a truly colossal degree of homophony in the SJ vocabulary. This is why I suggested earlier that purely phonographic script, though feasible for Koreans, is not feasible for Japanese: Sino-Korean phonology maintains many of the contrasts lost in modern Chinese, but Sino-Japanese has even fewer contrasts than Chinese.

To illustrate, I give a sample of the different Chinese morphemes which all exist in the (modern, living) Japanese language with the SJ pronunciation /kan/. As can be seen, each morpheme in the list has a distinct pronunciation even in the phonologically-impoverished modern Mandarin version of Chinese; each of the morphemes listed naturally has several Chinese homophones, most of which also exist in Japanese as /kan/, and this list by no means exhausts the range of phonologically-distinct Chinese syllables corresponding to SJ /kan/.

	Chinese pronunciation	meaning	Japanese pronunciation
甘	kān	'sweet'	
感	kǎn	'be affected'	
刊	kʰān	'print'	
慣	kuàn	'be accustomed to'	
観	kuān	'view'	
勘	kʰàn	'investigate'	
緩	xuǎn	'slow'	kan
管	kuǎn	'tube'	
鐶	xuán	'a ring'	
歓	xuān	'enjoy'	
巻	cyàn	'a volume'	
韓	xán	'Korean'	
漢	xàn	'Chinese'	

etc. etc.

With Chinese, although there are very many homophones among morphemes taken singly, two-morpheme compounds are usually unambiguous: if a vocabulary-item consists of a pair of syllables XY it tends to be the case that only one of the various morphemes pronounced X and one of the morphemes pronounced Y fit together as a recognized compound. With the massive level of homophony found in Sino-Japanese, however, even this is far from true. To give just one example: the disyllable /kankō/ is ambiguous as between all of the following SJ compound words (among others); again I give the Chinese pronunciation for comparison:

	Chinese pronunciation	meaning	Japanese pronunciation
甘汞	kān-kŭŋ	'mercurous chloride'	
感光	kǎn-kuāŋ	'expose (photographically)'	
刊行	kʰān-çíŋ	'publication'	
慣行	kuàn-çíŋ	'habitual'	kankō
観光	kuān-kuāŋ	'sightseeing'	
勘考	kʰàn-kʰǎu	'consider'	
緩行	xuǎn-çíŋ	'run slow'	
etc.			

If the Chinese language had developed this degree of homophony in the course of its evolution, no doubt it would have taken measures of one sort or another to solve the problem (as indeed did happen when monomorphemic words in classical Chinese were replaced by compounds in the modern spoken language). But Japanese is, as it were, at the mercy of Chinese – from the point of view of Japanese society, Chinese is the authoritative source both of non-native morphemes and, to a large extent, of the approved ways of compounding them. If the result of adapting this stock of roots to Japanese habits of pronunciation is a vocabulary which is extremely ambiguous in its spoken form, that is just bad luck for the Japanese. There are isolated parallels in English: it is unfortunate for us that the Romans used words for 'mouth' and 'ear', *ōris* and *auris*, which (while sounding quite different in Latin) fall together in the confusing pair of English homophones *oral* and *aural*. Life would be more convenient for us if we decided to use, say, *gaur-* rather than *aur-* as the root for 'ear' in technical vocabulary; but we feel that Latin is a fixed given, so we cannot do this and must tolerate the unfortunate consequences of using the genuine roots. For the Japanese this situation is multiplied thousands of times over. This implies, among other things, that the logographic nature of Chinese writing is even more important for the Japanese than for the Chinese.

So far we have seen that many different Chinese syllables may correspond to the same SJ pronunciation. But the situation is more complicated than that. We have seen that Chinese pronunciation changed over the years, and Chinese vocabulary was borrowed into Japanese in a series of separate waves; in each wave of borrowings, the Japanese pronunciation of a given morpheme would imitate the *current* Chinese pronunciation. Therefore there are different 'layers' of *on*-readings for Chinese graphs. In other words a single graph, having just one pronunciation in any given dialect of Chinese, will often have more than one *on*-reading (as well as one or, possibly, more than one *kun* reading) in Japanese.

The point may be illustrated by analogy. Suppose that Latin had been written with a logographic script; then, say, the adjective *masculus* might have been written ♂. *Masculus* evolved by various sound-changes into French *mâle*. We have both versions of the root in English, the Latin version in e.g. *masculine, emasculate,* and the French version in *male.* So, if we had borrowed a logographic rather than a phonographic script from the Romans, we would be writing both the *mascul-* of *masculine* and the word *male* as ♂; and we might use this graph also for the native Germanic morpheme *groom* in *bridegroom.* Then:

♂ = /mæskjel/   would be 'Roman *on*'
♂ = /meɪl/   would be 'Norman *on*'
♂ = /grum/   would be '*kun*'.

The English reader would have to learn that ⟨♂-ine⟩, for example, is read with Roman *on,* and that ⟨♂⟩ as an independent word is usually read with Norman *on* but is given its *kun* value when it occurs as a noun in the context of weddings.

Japanese has three layers of *on*: in chronological order they are called *go'on, kan'on,* and *tōsō'on. On* means 'sound' or 'pronunciation', so the three terms mean respectively 'the pronunciation of *Go, Kan,* and *Tōsō*'; these are Chinese proper names, akin to 'Roman' and 'Norman' in my hypothetical analogy.

Kan'on is the 'unmarked' layer: most SJ compounds use *kan'on* pronunciations, and conventionally any new term coined in recent times will use the *kan'on* versions of Chinese roots. *Go'on* pronunciations occur in words that were borrowed particularly early, before the +7c; and, since the first important cultural export from China to Japan was Buddhism, most *go'on* words were originally Buddhist terms. Conversely, *tōsō'on* readings (which are the rarest) occur in a group of words which entered Japan much later than the main wave of imports, in the 14c, and many of these words are terms used by late-emerging sects of Buddhism such as Zen.

If the use of *go'on* and *tōsō'on* words had continued to be restricted to Buddhist contexts, then the complications associated with the different layers of *on* would be of little practical relevance nowadays in everyday Japanese life. But words which have entered a language do not remain neatly penned up in the thematic containers in which they were imported. The word *substance* came into English as a philosophical term denoting that which is common to the three Persons of the Christian Trinity; but a 20c Englishman who describes foam-rubber as a spongy substance would be justifiably startled to be told that he was engaging in theological discourse. In Japanese the situation is the same. Thus, for instance, 無 'without' is *kan'on* /bu/, as in e.g. 無事 literally 'without business', SJ /buɟi/ 'peace, quiet', and 限 'limit' is *kan'on* /kan/; but it happens that 無限 'without limit, infinite' is pronounced as *go'on*

/mugen/ rather than *kan'on* */bukan/, because this compound word entered Japanese as part of the technical Buddhist term 'infinite compassion'. Nowadays, however, /mugen/ is simply the ordinary mathematical term for 'infinite', and a caterpillar-tractor is a '*mugen*-track vehicle'. A Japanese reading the graphs 無限 has to know that they are to be pronounced /mugen/ rather than */bukan/, but nothing in the script itself indicates this.

In many cases it is not clear whether the *go'on* v. *kan'on* distinction ever had anything to do with Buddhism. Thus it happens that 定 'fix' is *kan'on* /tei/ in 定價 /teika/ 'fixed price' but *go'on* /jō/ in 定連 /jōren/ 'regular customer'; 説 'discourse' is *kan'on* /zei/ in 遊説 /jūzei/ 'campaign speech' but *go'on* /seçu/ in 社説 /çaseçu/ 'editorial'; and so on.

A few graphs have *on*-readings of all three layers. Thus 行, standing for a Chinese morpheme with a broad range of meanings covering 'move', 'practise', hence 'a practice', 'a commercial firm', in Japanese has the *kun* reading /ik-/, the ordinary NJ root for 'to go', but it also has the following *on*-readings:

go'on /gjō/ in e.g. 修行 (literally 'cultivate-practice'): /çugjō/ 'training'. This word is read in *go'on* because it originally referred to ascetic Buddhist training disciplines, but nowadays it is just the ordinary word for 'training'.

kan'on /kō/ in e.g. 銀行 (literally 'silver-firm'):   /ginkō/ 'a bank'.

tōsō'on /an/ in e.g. 行脚 (literally 'go-foot'): /angja/, originally a Buddhist pilgrimage, but nowadays 'a walking tour'.

Notice how phonetically divergent the various *on*-readings of a particular graph can be. Within the limitations of Japanese phonology one could hardly find a pair of syllables that contrast much more than /tei/ and /jō/, unless it were /gjō/ and /an/. Yet the former pair both derive by different routes from a Middle Chinese pronounciation [dʰèŋ], and the latter from Middle Chinese [ɣǣŋ].

This may be the appropriate place to point out how the system of alternative readings for individual graphs, apart from being complex in itself, throws another difficulty in the path of the Japanese learning to read and write in that it greatly reduces the mnemonic value of the phonetic elements of complex graphs. Since most of the commonest Japanese words belong to the native stock, when a Japanese child learns to read and write, the earliest pronunciation he encounters for a graph will tend to be its *kun* reading, which will obviously be entirely useless for determining the value of the 'phonetic' element of the graph. But, even among *on*-readings, the process of Japanizing Chinese sounds, together with the fact of borrowing from different versions of Chinese, disturb the already shaky phonological relationships among the original Chinese pronunciations of graphs sharing a common 'phonetic'. The signific elements of complex graphs are probably mnemonically about as useful to Japanese as they are to Chinese; but significs are drawn from a small class while phonetics are very diverse, so that most of the 'information' (in the mathematician's sense) is concentrated in the phonetic element of a complex graph. Thus the point just discussed appears to imply a substantial reduction in the learnability of the script.

To return to the issue of alternative *on*-readings: it should be pointed out that even if a Japanese learned to categorize the various readings of graphs as *go'on* versus *kan'on* versus *tōsō'on* this would be only a limited help in deciding how to read compounds, since although the two elements of a SJ compound word will usually both be drawn from the same *on* layer one cannot reliably expect this to be so. Many words are analogous to English *television*, which mixes Greek and Latin roots. For that matter, one cannot even assume that all elements of a compound will be SJ rather than NJ (or vice versa). Thus the graph 宿 Ch. /sù/ 'to lodge', whose *on* reading is /çuku/ as in 宿舍 SJ /çukuça/ 'lodging', has the *kun* readingj /jado/ which occurs not only as an independent word for 'lodging' and in the wholly NJ compound 宿屋 /jadoja/ 'inn', but also in half-native, half-Chinese compounds such as 宿賃 /jadocin/ 'hotel charges', 宿張 /jadocō/ 'hotel register'.

Such phenomena are, obviously, much more awkward for the foreigner trying to master Japanese than for a native speaker of Japanese learning the script, who already knows what is and what is not in the vocabulary in terms of pronunciation. But one would imagine that such complications force even the native speaker to remain constantly on his toes, as it were, when reading. And anyway presumably a Japanese, like an Englishman, picks up much of his vocabulary of less common words from reading rather than from hearing words spoken – in such cases he would have the same problems as the foreigner in knowing how to pronounce a novel compound.

Thus far we have considered only the Japanese use of Chinese graphs in their original form. There is a good deal more to say about that subject; but before moving on to that, let us examine the process by which the Japanese developed categories of graphic symbols of their own, distinct from *kanji* or Chinese graphs.

We have seen how, at an early period, the Japanese used the *man'yōgana* system of spelling out NJ words with Chinese graphs standing for their phonetic values, as an alternative to the *kun* system. As the years went by, the *man'yōgana* system evolved in two respects.

First, the particular graphs used for *man'yōgana* were standardized. In the early days one used any graph whose Chinese pronunciation was roughly appropriate; scribes prided themselves on varying their *man'yōgana*, and even on using complex and rare rather than simple graphs when either would do. Later, a tendency arose always to use one graph or just a small range of alternative graphs for any given Japanese syllable. Secondly, the forms of the graphs used for *man'yōgana* were greatly simplified, and this served two purposes: it made them quicker to write (which was useful in view of the fact that the system required several graphs per word), but – more important – it created a clear visual distinction between symbols used purely for phonographic syllabic values, and graphs in their original form used with *kun* or *on* values.

What happened ultimately was that two sets of syllabic signs evolved, comparable to our minuscules and capitals (though, whereas all our minuscule/capital pairs derive from common ancestral forms, in some cases the sign for a given syllable in one of the two Japanese syllabaries derives from a different Chinese graph than the sign for the same syllable in the other syllabary). The two syllabaries are called *hiragana* ('plain *kana*'), which consist of very simplified cursive outlines of complete Chinese graphs, and *katakana* ('partial *kana*') which consist of carefully-written small distinctive elements of the original Chinese graphs. The term *kanji* is used for Chinese graphs in their full form, as opposed to *kana* of either set. By the late 19c the two syllabaries had been standardized to the point where each contained one and just one distinct symbol for each syllable represented (in all, 49 symbols in each syllabary). In handwriting people still sometimes use non-standard alternative versions of some *kana* (either derived from *kanji* other than the usual one, or abbreviating that *kanji* in an unorthodox way), but such symbols are never now printed. Figure 27 shows the derivation of some of the symbols in the two syllabaries.

	Katakana		Man'yōgana			Hiragana
i	イ	←	伊 i 'he'	以 i 'by'	→	い
ro	ロ	←	呂 ro (a place-name)		→	ろ
ha	ハ	←	八 haci 'eight'	波 ha 'wave'	→	は
ci	チ	←	千 ci 'thousand'	知 ci 'know'	→	ち
nu	ヌ	←	奴 nu 'slave'		→	ぬ
wo	ヲ	←	乎 wo (interrogative particle)	遠 won 'far'	→	を

Figure 27

For much of the period during which *hiragana* and *katakana* have been used, the two systems were somewhat 'incomplete' in the same sense (and indeed in one of the same specific respects) as the Linear B syllabary described in Chapter 4. The chief gap was that the *kana* systems did not mark voicing in obstruent consonants; /b d g z/ were not distinguished from /h t k s/. (Modern Japanese /h/ derives from an earlier */p/.) There was more justification for this in the case of Japanese *kana* than in the case of the similar failing in Linear B, since in (native) Japanese most instances of voiced obstruents were conditioned variants of their voiceless counterparts, though the occurrence of voicing was not fully predictable. (Voice *was* fully distinctive in Sino-Japanese words, but these, as we shall see shortly, were not written with *kana*.) In recent centuries, however, a diacritic has been consistently used to mark voice in obstruents (and another to distinguish modern /p/ from /h/); the two syllabaries are now fully 'complete' as representations of the segmental phonology of a slightly pre-modern version of Japanese. (However, they ignore the pitch-accent mentioned in note 1, p. 217.) Devices have even been added in order to enable *kana* to represent sounds and sound-sequences, such as /v/, /ti/, which are not found in Japanese but do occur in words borrowed from languages such as English.

In modern Japanese writing, *kanji* in their various *kun* and *on* readings are used for the lexical morphemes (proper and common nouns, verb roots, etc.) of the NJ and SJ vocabularies. *Hiragana* are used to spell the grammatical morphemes akin to English *of*, *the*, etc., and also the inflexions of inflected words. *Katakana* are used for lexical words borrowed from foreign languages (i.e. not from Chinese), for foreign names, and sometimes in order to spell out words that used to be written with *kanji* which were so rare that they have been given up.[2] (In other words, *katakana* are used for linguistic forms belonging to the grammatical classes that would normally be written with *kanji* but which happen for one reason or another not to have *kanji* available.) The use of *katakana* to spell foreign words is one of the few respects – but a very important one – in which Japanese writing is more efficient than Chinese.

Hiragana spellings are often slightly archaic – like many other scripts, it has preserved a phonographic system that has not always kept pace with historical sound-changes. Thus, for example, the direct-object suffix /o/ is always written ⟨wo⟩ rather than ⟨o⟩ though /w/ no longer occurs before /o/ in modern Japanese; separate symbols are used for ⟨di⟩ and ⟨zi⟩ although these syllables have now merged as /ɟi/; and so forth. Until recently *hiragana* spellings were much more archaic than they are now; recent *hiragana* usage is very much more 'rational', from the phonetic point of view, than English spelling.

Hiragana used to spell out inflexions are called *okurigana*, 'escorting *kana*'. Broadly they begin where the root part of an inflected word ends, but there are two complications.

First, in (native) Japanese (as in English), roots and grammatical inflexions do not exhaust the morphological structure of words, as there is also derivational morphology, by which complex vocabulary-items are constructed from simple roots. In writing a native Japanese word, derivational morphology may be treated as part of the root or spelled out with *hiragana*, depending partly on whether Chinese happens to provide a graph appropriate to stand as *kun* for the derived form; we shall see examples illustrating this below.

Secondly, since each *kana* symbol stands for a consonant + vowel combination, if the last phoneme of the root is a consonant it must be included in the *okurigana*; a *kana* for a simple vowel can represent only a vowel that has no consonant preceding it. Thus the NJ root /ajum-/ 'to step' is written with the *kun* 歩 (Ch. /pù/ 'a pace'), but forms such as /ajumu/ 'I/you/he steps', /ajumanai/ 'does not step', and so forth are written:

歩む STEP-mu *not** 歩う STEP-u

歩まない STEP-ma-na-i *not** 歩あない STEP-a-na-i

This point is an advantage to the reader, since, by giving the last consonant of the correct reading of the root, the *okurigana* may eliminate other potential readings. The graph 歩 is ambiguous as between two NJ values – it can also represent the near-synonym /aruk-/ 'go on foot'; only the *okurigana* differentiate between the written forms of pairs such as /aruku/ 'goes on foot' and /ajumu/ 'steps':

$$歩く \left\{ {STEP \atop GO\text{-}ON\text{-}FOOT} \right\} \text{-ku} \quad versus \quad 歩む \left\{ {STEP \atop GO\text{-}ON\text{-}FOOT} \right\} \text{-mu}$$

(The same *kanji* also has two *on*-readings, /ho/ and /bu/, but these cannot occur in inflected forms and are therefore irrelevant to the point under discussion.) Cases such as this, where the first consonant of the *okurigana* is crucial for disambiguation, are not too frequent, but quite often the information must be helpful as one clue among others to enable the reader to arrive at the correct reading of a *kanji* relatively rapidly.

As an illustration of the various aspects of modern Japanese script, Figure 28 shows the written form of the sentence /içumo doiçugo no hon o jonde iru jō desu/, 'He always seems to be reading German books'. (A more literal rendering might be 'Always a-matter-of-be-reading-book-of-Germany exists – the subject 'he' is understood, and, because Japanese word-order rules are often the converse of English, the items I have linked with hyphens occur in the reverse order in the Japanese sentence.) The written sentence runs vertically downwards, as is still standard in Japanese script (though the horizontal European system is making inroads).

何時} *kun* for NJ /içu/, 'when'

も *hiragana* /mo/, suffix converting 'when' to 'always'

ドイツ} *katakana* /do-i-çu/, 'German', from *deutsch*

語 *on* for SJ /go/, 'language'

の *hiragana* /no/, genitive particle

本 *on* for SJ /hon/, 'book'

を *hiragana* /wo/, accusative suffix

読 *kun* for NJ /jom-/, 'read'

で *hiragana* (*okurigana*) /de/, '-ing'

居 *kun* for NJ /i-/, 'be'

る *hiragana* (*okurigana*) /ru/, present tense suffix

用 *on* for SJ /jō/, 'business, matter'

です} *hiragana* /de-su/, polite present of NJ /da/, 'exist'

Figure 28

Japanese orthography has no formal method of marking word-boundaries, and simply writes the symbols of the various categories one below another with equal spacing. In this respect, however, the reader is better placed than in the case of Chinese, because the alternation of *kanji* with *kana* goes some way to showing the grouping of symbols into words at a glance. It is roughly true to say that Japanese roots never have prefixes, only suffixes, so a transition from *hiragana* to *kanji* must represent a word-boundary. With Chinese writing the reader is given no visual clues as to how to group the graphs into meaningful blocs, since all are equally salient.

Note the following points relating to individual elements of the sentence in Figure 28. Chinese has no single word for 'when' but expresses the idea by two morphemes, /xɤ ʂɯ́/ 'what time'; therefore the single NJ root /iɕu/ is written with two *kanji*. In the first of the three *katakana* graphs, the double tick is a diacritic of voice, converting ⟨to⟩ to ⟨do⟩; this diacritic reappears in two occurrences of *hiragana* ⟨de⟩, below. (In the word /jonde/ the voicing of /d/ is automatic after the nasal consonant of the root, but since the modern *kana* system has been equipped with a diacritic to indicate voicing it is used even where voicing is predictable.) The *hiragana* spelling ⟨wo⟩ for the accusative suffix, as we have already seen, is archaic: the actual modern pronunciation is /o/ (but it is convenient to have a distinctive graphic shape for such a common grammatical unit). In the root for 'read', the final /m/ becomes /n/ by automatic phonological rule before the alveolar suffix; but since the root is written logographically this variation is ignored. In the word /iru/ it happens that the consonant /r/ is part of the inflexion rather than belonging to the root, but it would have to be represented in the *okurigana* in either case.

As it happens, three of the forms written with *kanji* in Figure 28 – /iɕu/ 'when', the verb-root /i-/ 'be', and the noun /jō/ 'matter' – could alternatively be written in *hiragana*; they are all so common that they are perceived as falling on the borderline between lexical and grammatical elements, despite the fact that the latter two belong to grammatical classes most of whose members are clearly lexical. The tendency nowadays is to prefer *hiragana* rather than *kanji* in such borderline cases; so in that sense the script of Figure 28 is somewhat old-fashioned. However, Figure 28 is not unrepresentative of contemporary Japanese writing in terms of the proportion of *kanji* to *hiragana*. (*Katakana* is much less frequent, because of the specialized functions it serves.) Modern writing typically contains very roughly two *hiragana* graphs to one *kanji*.

The complications in Japanese script which I have discussed so far are essentially difficulties for the reader rather than for the writer: they involve alternative ways of translating a given graph into a morpheme of the language. For a Japanese, who knows his language as a repertory of possibilities, the problems posed by such alternatives will sometimes be less great than my discussion may suggest. In the first place he will commonly know that a particular compound of morphemes is a frequent word of the language, while another compound corresponding to alternative values of the same graphs does not exist in Japanese; but also the general structure of the language supplies various useful clues. For instance, SJ words do not inflect, so that *on*-readings for a graph can be discarded immediately if it is followed by *okurigana* (though the converse does not hold – a word without *okurigana* may be either SJ or NJ). Again, a single *kanji* standing as a word in isolation is more likely to require a *kun* than an *on* reading, since SJ morphemes occur mainly in two-root compounds, though this is only a statistical rather than an absolute rule.

However, parallel to the problems facing the reader there are also analogous problems facing the writer, who will often have to make choices between alternative graphs each of which can represent the same linguistic form.

In one sense, of course, this is already abundantly obvious. If one thinks of the writer's task as being to convert words considered as sequences of phonemes into written marks, we have seen that most Japanese syllables or short syllable-sequences will correspond to very many different SJ and/or NJ homophones, each of which will have its own graph. But that would be a very artificial and inappropriate way of conceiving the activity of writing (in Japanese or any other language). The writer, except in the special case of taking dictation, is aware of the identity at all linguistic levels of the units he is trying to record – he knows their meanings as well as their sounds. So far I have given no reason to suppose that a Japanese who knows what meaningful elements of his language he wants to write will ever be faced with a choice between alternative possibilities. But this is in fact so, for reasons having to do with the lack of semantic isomorphism between Japanese and Chinese.

Consider for instance the NJ verb root /kae-/. This word is polysemous, analogously to its rough English equivalent 'turn' (consider the different senses this word has in phrases 'turn back', 'turn the page', 'turn round', 'turn into a handsome Prince'). But in the semantic field covered by Japanese /kae-/, Chinese happens to have a number of more precise words. Accordingly, different shades of meaning of /kae-/ are written differently. Taking the simple inflected form /kaeru/, I show some of the possibilities below (there are others), with alphabetic transliteration in place of *okurigana* in order not to burden the Western reader unnecessarily:

1 /kaeru/ = 'return home':   帰 -ru   (Ch. /kuēi/)
2 /kaeru/ = 'come again, revert':   返 -ru   (Ch. /fǎn/)
3 /kaeru/ = 'change, vary' (transitive):   変 -e-ru   (Ch. /pièn/)

4 /kaeru/ = 'exchange, substitute': $\begin{cases} 代 \text{-e-ru} & \text{(Ch. /tài/)} \\ 換 \text{-e-ru} & \text{(Ch. /xuàn/)} \\ 替 \text{-e-ru} & \text{(Ch. /tʰì/)} \end{cases}$

etc.

In Chinese there are small semantic differences between /tài/ 'substitute', /xuàn/ 'exchange', and /tʰì/ 'act on behalf of', but it seems that the range of meaning of Japanese /kae-/ overlaps only with the common semantic ground between these Chinese words, or perhaps that these particular semantic distinctions were originally felt by Japanese writers to be too small to maintain. The semantic distinctions between these three words as a group and Chinese /kuēi/, Chinese /fǎn/, and Chinese /pièn/, on the other hand, are systematically observed in written Japanese even though they are not reflected in spoken (native) Japanese. (Furthermore, although three of the *kanji* are interchangeable with respect to their *kun* reading /kae-/, each of them also has at least one *on*-reading and these are of course distinct, non-interchangeable SJ morphemes.)

The case of /kaeru/ in fact includes a special (though not particularly uncommon) complication. Although all the four Japanese words quoted are identical in pronunciation and involve the same NJ root, they are not morphologically identical; 3 and 4 include a transitivity infix /-e-/ (note that the English glosses are transitive for these cases but intransitive for 1 and 2). It happens that by the rules of Japanese phonology /kae-e-/ becomes /ka-e-/, so that with this particular root the infix makes no net difference to the pronunciation. However, the /-e-/ of 3 and 4 is this derivational infix, and is accordingly represented in the *okurigana*, while the /-e-/ of 1 and 2 is part of the root /kae-/ and is therefore covered by the *kanji*.

Not only may a given *kanji* have a range of different *on*-readings because of the different waves of borrowing from Chinese, and a given NJ root have a range of different *kanji* writings because of the lack of semantic isomorphism between the two languages; this lack of semantic isomorphism also has the consequence that a single *kanji* may have a range of several different NJ, *kun* values (creating further problems for the reader).

Take, for instance, the graph 上 (Ch. /ṣàŋ/ 'on, top', /ṣǎŋ/ 'rise' – these are etymologically the same Chinese morpheme, the tone-difference is one of the rare presumed relics of earlier Chinese inflexion mentioned on p. 158). This graph has the *on*-readings /ɟō/ 'first, excellent' and /çō/ 'upper part, government'; but it also has the following *kun* readings:

上	/ue/	'on'
上	/kami/	'top'
上 -ru	/noboru/	'rise'
上 -ga-ru	/agaru/	'go up'
上 -ge-ru	/ageru/	'raise'

(In the last pair of words the NJ root is the same, and *okurigana* are being used to indicate derivational morphology in a slightly different way from the /kaeru/ case. The transitive verb /ageru/ is morphologically /aga-/ + transitivity-marker /-e-/ + inflexion /-ru/, with the final vowel of the root /aga-/ having dropped before /-e-/; /ageru/ is thus naturally spelled with *okurigana* /-ge-ru/. Although the /-ga-/ of /agaru/ is wholly within the root, it is included in the *okurigana* for that word in order to differentiate it positively from its transitive counterpart.)

Of the above words, /ue/ and /kami/ can be written only as 上 ; and context alone will show whether this graph should be read as /ue/ or as

/kami/, since neither word inflects. But /noboru/ can alternatively be written 登-ru (Ch. /tə̄ŋ/ 'ascend') or 昇 -ru (Ch. /ṣə̄ŋ/ 'arise'); while /agaru/ can alternatively be written 揚-ga-ru (Ch. /jáŋ/ 'to lift, display') or 挙 -ga-ru (Ch. /cy̌/ 'pick up') (and /ageru/ can have either of these latter writings with the appropriate change of *okurigana*). When these NJ roots are used as independent words, the context of the sentence will determine which of the alternative *kanji* is appropriate – and compounds involving these roots will use whichever *kanji* fits the meaning of the compound – *in terms of the original Chinese senses of the* kanji. Thus, for example, NJ /ageçio/ 'rising tide' is written 上-ge-潮 (the latter graph being *kun* for /çio/ 'tide') rather than *揚-ge-潮, because one does not lift the tide up with one's hands; conversely, NJ /agemono/ 'fried food' (literally, 'lifted stuff') is written 揚-ge- 物 (the latter graph, as we have already seen, being *kun* for /mono/ 'thing'), and not *上-ge-物, because East Asian frying involves tumbling the pieces of food in the wok with a spatula, and they will not jump up of their own accord.

In other words, to write Japanese correctly it is not sufficient to know the range of correct transcriptions for the various forms of the spoken Japanese language; it is also necessary to know the semantic distinctions which obtained between those symbols in another language, Chinese, from which they were borrowed, although these semantic distinctions are irrelevant to spoken Japanese.

Admittedly, a Japanese might reject this description of the facts. The axiom of Western linguistics according to which a language is primarily a system of spoken forms, and writing is a subsidiary medium serving to render spoken language visible, is very difficult for an East Asian to accept. To speakers of languages as full of homophones as Chinese and Japanese, it seems obvious that speech is a highly imperfect, vague and ambiguous reflection of written language. Therefore a contemporary Japanese would probably deny that *kanji* provide alternative ways of writing the same word. He would perceive, for example, '/aga-/ = 上 ', '/aga-/ = 揚 ', and '/aga-/ = 挙 ' as three different words that sound the same and have closely-related meanings. But historically, at least, he would be wrong.

We have already in passing seen something of the complications in the rules governing *okurigana*. The examples just discussed can be used to explain something more of this. We saw that the /-ga-/ of /agaru/ 'go up' is spelled out in *okurigana* despite being part of the root, in order to differentiate that word clearly from /ageru/ 'raise', which contains the transitive infix /-e-/. But while there is a deverbal noun /agari/ 'a rise, promotion', there is no corresponding noun */ageri/. Therefore /agari/ is written ⟨上-ri⟩, not *⟨上-ga-ri⟩. Here the *okurigana* rule is logical, though one needs to know the language well to be able to apply it correctly. However, in other cases again this logic breaks down. The graph 富 has the *kun* reading /tom-/ 'to be rich', and the present tense /tomu/ 'is rich' is written ⟨富-mu⟩, as expected. But the deverbal noun /tomi/ 'wealth' is written as just ⟨富⟩, not *⟨富-mi⟩.

The explanation here is probably that the *Chinese* word for which the graph originally stood is a noun rather than a verb; but this, clearly, does not make the situation any more regular from the point of view of a Japanese ignorant of Chinese who is learning to write his own language. (The *on*-reading of 富, which is /fu/, does not occur as an independent noun in Japanese.)

The conventions for using *okurigana* have only recently been codified, and, according to Pye (1971, p. 235): 'If the older system of *okurigana* was simply not a system, the modern standardised system is highly complicated, consisting of a mixture of rationality and time-hallowed usage.' Pye refers to an authoritative modern statement of the rules for *okurigana* as occupying 64 pages of a book published by the Ministry of Education in 1960. We shall go into the matter no deeper. (And I should stress that in other respects, too, I am shielding the reader from the full panoply of difficulties in Japanese orthography.)

A number of measures have been adopted in order to reduce the complications of Japanese script.

Until the end of the Second World War it was common in printing for the problems created by the existence of alternative readings for *kanji* to be resolved for the reader by the addition of tiny *hiragana* symbols (called *furigana*, 'nudging *kana*') at the side of most *kanji*. Thus for instance the word /mugen/ 'infinite' (see p. 181) would appear as in Figure 29:

無む WITHOUT mu
限げん LIMIT gen

Figure 29

But in modern Japan *furigana* are used only in books for children and in rare situations posing some quite unusual problem of interpretation.

As in the case of China, the Japanese too have simplified some of their graphs in terms of number of strokes (the Japanese carried out this reform earlier than the Chinese, and in some cases a given graph has been reformed in different ways in the two countries). I suggested in Chapter 8 that this sort of orthographic reform offered little advantage; the Japanese case seems particularly futile, since the changes in shape are often quite slight. (However, since the unreformed graphs are never now used to write Japanese, this chapter uses the new graphs.)

The most important reform measure was the promulgation in 1946 of a limited list of only 1850 *kanji* with their approved *kun* and *on* readings, with a view to excluding other *kanji* (and unusual readings of the approved *kanji*) from the orthography. If this aim could be achieved it would represent a major simplification. A pre-war Japanese newspaper printing works stocked about 7–8000 *kanji,* and the average educated reader was reckoned to be familiar with about 5000 of them. Nowadays, newspapers in particular do aim to limit themselves to the approved list, and if they need to print a lexical morpheme whose *kanji* is not on the list then either they add a *katakana* transliteration in brackets or even give only *kana* in place of the *kanji*. However, according to Pye (1971, p. 5), virtually all publications other than newspapers and official documents go beyond the approved list of *kanji* to some extent; and even these two categories of publication have to go beyond it for proper names, since many important personal and place names use *kanji* not included in the approved list. As for technical and scholarly publishing, this of necessity continues to use a much wider range of *kanji* – to do otherwise would be to accept a crippling impoverishment of its vocabulary. In practice it seems that one of the main functions of the list of 1850 *kanji* is to act as a well-defined goal for Japanese schooling.

The following statistics are true of the 'approved readings' of the 1850 'approved *kanji*': 844 of the *kanji* have only *on*-readings (they have 903 such readings between them); 30 have only *kun* readings (31 *kun*); the remaining 976 *kanji* each have *on* and *kun* readings, having a total of 1103 *on* and 1085 *kun*. Thus the 1850 *kanji* have altogether 3122 approved readings, or rather less than two each on average. Many individual *kanji* have considerably more than this average; all the individual readings mentioned in this chapter are (I believe) included on the approved list.

Even in the limited way that it has been applied, the approved *kanji* list clearly represents a significant measure of containment of the tangled luxuriance of Japanese orthography. But there is no obvious way in which the process could feasibly be taken much further (indeed, the tendency in recent years has been marginally to widen, rather than to narrow, the range of officially-approved *kanji* and their approved readings). It is implausible to suppose that Japanese script is destined ever to evolve into a system significantly simpler than the one described here; certainly, while the spoken Japanese language remains essentially what it is now, adoption of a phonographic script would be quite impractical.

Finally, in case any readers still feel inclined to contest my view that Japanese script is outstandingly difficult, I might briefly draw attention to a factor which could equally well have been discussed in Chapter 8.

Throughout this book so far I have been tacitly assuming that the ability to identify the individual graphs of a piece of writing in any given script can be taken for granted, and that what is interesting is the relationship between graphs and language. Even for alphabetic scripts this assumption is sometimes unwarranted; we all have acquaintances whose handwriting is barely legible. Nevertheless, before printing was invented clarity and regularity of letter-formation was a goal that Western scribes aimed at even if they did not always perfectly achieve it, and now that printing and the typewriter are commonplace bad handwriting matters little in practice since handwritten documents play a minor role in our lives.

For China and Japan, on the other hand, my tacit assumption is seriously misleading. In the first place, in these societies handwriting has a relatively more important role than in the West. Typewriters are not common, and for instance the lettering on a painted signboard, which in Europe will usually imitate the regularity of print, is in East Asia more likely to simulate freehand brush-and-ink work. But also, the social norms and aesthetic standards applicable to handwriting do not value neatness and regularity; quite the reverse. Traditionally, to write neatly to an educated man could actually be seen as insulting, since it suggested that he was thought incapable of reading cursive forms. Normal handwriting (what the Chinese call *xíng shū*, 'running style') is some way removed from the neatness of print, fusing what are printed as separate dots and strokes into continuous, smooth motions of the brush (or pen); but it is not too hard to learn to 'see' the printed shapes below the surface forms of *xíng shū*. The most admired calligraphy, however – not merely for artistic purposes but for everyday use – is so-called *cǎo shū*, 'grass style', which simplifies so radically that graphs involving a dozen or two dozen strokes in their regular printed forms may be reduced to a few hasty hints, and it is difficult even to separate the graphs one from another visually. Figure 30, for instance, shows a page from a Japanese copybook published in the 18c or early 19c as a model for official correspondence. (The degree of cursiveness it represents is far from extreme, and it is in no way obsolete.)

The ability to read grass-style handwriting is a study in itself, one which is mastered by very few Western Orientalists. Yet only provided a Japanese can identify the specific graphs that are lurking behind the visual jumble of a page such as Figure 30 will he be in a position to begin the complex process of decipherment of graphs into linguistic forms that has been described in this chapter.

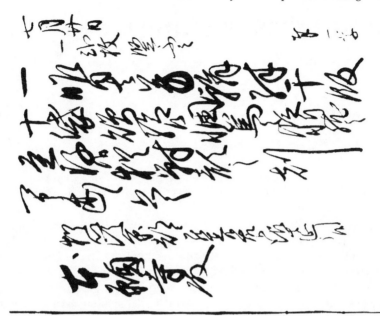

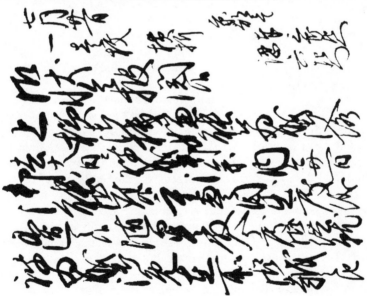

Figure 30

10 English spelling

Where should the conventional orthography used for our own language be located in terms of the spectrum of script-types defined and illustrated in previous chapters?

Like other European scripts, our own descends from the segmental, phonographic Greek alphabet. Most Britons have only a dim awareness that other principles of writing exist, and thus our orthography is commonly assessed by reference to this particular standard. Notoriously, in these terms it falls very far short of the ideal. English, together with French, are remarkable among European languages for the extent to which their spelling-systems depart from the principle of one-to-one correspondence between the sequence of segment-types that occur in a spoken utterance and the sequence of graphemes which appear in its written equivalent.

There is a 'received view' about this state of affairs, shared tacitly at least by a large number of English-speakers, which if set out explicitly would run more or less as follows.

Once, at some remote time in the historical past, English had a 'phonemic' orthography in which words were spelled as they were pronounced. (Here and below, the term 'phonemic' is meant to imply that pronunciation can be predicted by straightforward rules from spelling and vice versa – it is not intended to lay special stress on the distinction between phonemes and allophones.) But pronunciation changed over the centuries, while spelling was conservative. Thus, the orthography we use today is, in essence, a phonemic script for a spoken language that vanished long ago – while, in relation to the contemporary spoken language, our spelling is simply chaotic. And this is a thoroughly bad thing. It may well be one of the bad things that must be endured because they cannot be cured; but, if it were possible by a wave of a magic wand to equip every adult English-speaker with competence in a new, phonemic system of spelling, and to replace the millions of books and papers in our libraries and filing-cabinets by copies written in the new system, then to do so would confer a great boon on future generations of English-speakers. The only loss would be aesthetic: many people feel that our traditional spelling has a beauty which does something to offset its lack of rationality, and which would be lost in a system which spelled *conquer* or *passionate* as ⟨konker⟩, ⟨pashunut⟩.

Spelling reform has in fact been a very live issue at various times in the last hundred years or so. The reason why the science of phonetics that developed in the late 19c and early 20c was a mainly British enterprise, at a time when other aspects of scientific language-study were centred on Germany, had to do with the fact that the early phoneticians were largely motivated by a desire to reform spelling: Germany orthography, as it happens, was already near-phonemic. Henry Sweet's *Handbook of Phonetics* (1877) was subtitled as *Including a Popular Exposition of the Principles of Spelling Reform*. Daniel Jones developed the theory of the 'phoneme' as the unit for which an ideal orthography would provide a grapheme (e.g. Jones 1932).

Many detailed proposals for a revised English orthography have been put forward (see Figure 31). Perhaps the best known, and certainly the most radical, is the 'Shavian' system (MacCarthy 1969) invented by Kingsley Read in 1959 in response to a competition established to fulfil the terms of George Bernard Shaw's will, and consisting of a set of 48 graphemes wholly unrelated in shape to the letters of the Roman or other existing alphabets. The Swede Axel Wijk approached the problem from the opposite direction in his 'Regularized English' scheme (Wijk 1959, 1969): this retains the standard English phoneme/grapheme correspondence rules but removes the exceptions to them, so that more than 90 per cent of words in the vocabulary retain their traditional spelling. Most proposals have fallen between these extremes, keeping the Roman alphabet (sometimes adding a few diacritics or extra letters) but departing from the standard English spelling conventions to attain a simpler relationship between phonemes and graphemes than in Wijk's scheme (in which for instance the diphthong /eɪ/ is represented in different words by ⟨ai⟩, ⟨ay⟩, ⟨ei⟩, or ⟨a . . . e⟩ as in *paste*). Thus for instance the system of 'New Spelling' agreed between the Simplified Spelling Society of Great Britain and the Simpler Spelling Association of the USA in 1956 changes the spelling of all but 10 per cent or less of the vocabulary.

He pauzd for a moement and a wield feeling ov piti kaem oever him.
New Spelling

He pauzed for a moment and a wilde feeling ov pity came over him.
Regularized English

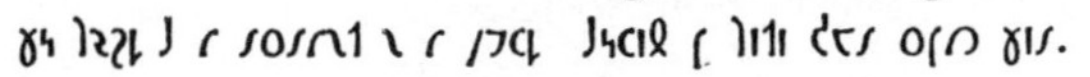

ᛘ ⵏⵣⵜ ᛃ ⸾ ⵣⵓⵏⵏⵏ ⵆ ⸾ ⵏⵣⵇ ᛃⵀⵜⵊⵉ ⸾ ᛁⵏⵏⵏ ⴹⵜⵣ ⵄⵏⵏ ᛘⵏⵣ.
Shavian

hεε pausd for a mœment and a wield fεεliŋ ov pity cæm œver him.
i.t.a.

Figure 31

In the 1980s it seems fair to say that, at least in Britain, spelling reform is not a live issue. One reason for this may be recent British experience with a related orthographic experiment: namely the attempt, initiated in 1960 with Ministry of Education support, to teach children to read using Sir James

Pitman's Initial Teaching Alphabet ('i.t.a.' – see e.g. Downing 1965) as a transition-stage between illiteracy and mastery of traditional orthography. I.t.a. was created as a compromise between the phonemic principle and traditional spelling. It includes many novel graphemes for phonemes which in traditional orthography are commonly spelled by pairs of letters; for instance /eɪ/ is i.t.a. ⟨æ⟩, which is learned and used as a single symbol (as in ⟨ræt⟩ for *rate*) until the time comes for the child to make the change to traditional orthography, whereupon he is taught to divide ⟨æ⟩ into ⟨a . . . e⟩ in regularly-spelled words like *rate* (as well as being taught a list of irregular spellings such as *reign*). Proponents of i.t.a. claim that, by shielding children in the early stages of literacy-acquisition from the confusions of traditional spelling, the system allows them quickly to gain confidence in reading and writing, with the result that children who learn via i.t.a. remain on average ahead of children taught by conventional methods even after making the transition to traditional orthography, and the incidence of severe long-term reading problems in the former group is relatively low. A careful evaluation of the i.t.a. experiment (Warburton and Southgate 1969) suggests that this claim is probably justified (though cf. Haas 1969b); the advantages of the i.t.a. approach to literacy, while perhaps not quite as dramatic as some enthusiasts had originally hoped, are solid enough for the experiment to be regarded as a success. Nevertheless, i.t.a. has by now, for reasons having little to do with its intrinsic merits (Prosser 1982), been almost wholly abandoned; in 1975 it was used by one in every ten British primary schools, seven years later it was used in only 280 schools nationwide.

I.t.a. was designed as a bridge to conventional spelling, rather than as a spelling reform in the ordinary sense. Nevertheless, the i.t.a. movement is obviously linked closely to the spelling-reform question; indeed the director of the experiment, John Downing, as well as being a leading international authority on the psychology of reading, recently became president of the Simplified Spelling Society. Working with i.t.a. familiarizes teachers and parents, as well as children, with the application of phonemic spelling principles to English, and if the i.t.a. experiment had spread it might have opened up the possibility of a relatively painless transition to a reformed orthography (although this would no doubt have needed to use standard Roman letters rather than the novel outlines of i.t.a.). As things are, a generation of Britons have become vaguely aware that educationalists tried mucking about with spelling in the 1960s and gave it up as a bad job; human nature being what it is, this seems likely to inoculate us against the likelihood of reform for some years to come.

That is not to say that the movement for spelling reform is dead everywhere in the English-speaking world. As it happens, it is liveliest at present in Australia, where in particular Harry Lindgren's 'SR1' (Spelling Reform One – Lindgren 1969, p. 19) has made considerable headway. Like many contemporary spelling reformers, Lindgren favours a gradualist approach: rather than sweeping away the whole of traditional orthography overnight (an aim which is always liable to founder on the rocks of prejudice and incomprehension), the suggestion is that one should first agree on a single, limited change which will in itself be easy for the public to grasp and which, if it is successful, may make people receptive to the idea of further rationalization. SR1 is the rule that the phoneme /ɛ/ is invariably spelled ⟨e⟩, as in *hed, lepard, frend, gess.* This simple reform has been adopted widely by Australians. Many general-interest paperbacks and the like are printed in SR1; under Gough Whitlam's Labour government the Australian Ministry of Helth was officially so spelled (though, when Whitlam was replaced by a Liberal administration, it reintroduced orthographic conservatism).

Whatever the eventual fate of SR1, my guess is that Australia represents too small a portion of the English-speaking world to be able to put more thoroughgoing reforms into effect successfully. The influence of outside usage would surely prevent this. And I do not myself believe that radical spelling reforms are likely to occur even in Britain or North America. Nevertheless, even the many people who would in practice object to projects of spelling reform would not, I believe, reject what I outlined some paragraphs ago as the 'received view' of English spelling. More likely, they would concede that a phonemic spelling would be more efficient if universally adopted, but would perhaps argue that efficiency is not everything, or point out the practical difficulties standing in the way of a changeover.

However, the received view is very much open to question. It contains a number of separate components, some factual (e.g. concerning the history of spelling) and others evaluative (concerning the virtues of the phonemic principle); there is probably a measure of truth in each component, but each is also at least partly false. English spelling is not simply a phonographic script overtaken by innovations in English speech; the ways in which it deviates from the phonemic principle have little to do with historical language-change, nor are they randomly chaotic. If we were minded to do so, there would be little practical difficulty in adopting a phonemic reformed spelling. But, even if such a change could be put into effect costlessly, it is not obvious that society would on balance benefit from it; it might quite possibly stand to lose.

In the rest of this chapter I shall argue for these claims in turn. The only component of the received view which I shall not challenge is the aesthetic one, on which I have no special contribution to offer. I, too, find our current orthography more attractive than any proposed alternative; it seems to me that the very familiarity of the standard orthography is an important part of what makes it pleasing, but to say this is not to dissolve the pleasure.

English possessed a standard national written form, based on the speech of Wessex, by the 11c, before the Norman Conquest – it was in fact the only modern European language to do so at that period, since elsewhere Latin was used for all official purposes. This written language embodied a fixed set of spelling conventions which added up to an approximately (though not perfectly) phonemic orthography. However, the fact that English spelling later lost this character was not caused by internal developments within the spoken English language. (The standard history of English spelling is Scragg (1974), on which I draw heavily in the following pages.) Many sound-changes did occur in later centuries, but they could have been accommodated by only minor changes in the spelling-system, such as were already occurring in the 11c. Rather, the unphonemic nature of modern English spelling was caused by external influences, particularly political developments stemming from the Conquest, which introduced rival spelling-conventions that competed with the native conventions and with one another. If the Normans had not prevailed in 1066 it seems likely that 20c English spelling would have been at least as phonemic as that of German or the Scandinavian languages.

The immediate consequence of the Conquest was that for more than three centuries, until the early 15c, English ceased to be a language used for official purposes, which inevitably led to a breakdown in the standardization of its written form. (In addition, the feudal system introduced by the Normans imposed greater regional separatism on speakers of English, which likewise militated against standard national orthographic norms.) The languages of public life were French and Latin. At the time of the Conquest French had not yet acquired fully consistent spelling-conventions; but the partially-regular spelling rules that had emerged were quite different from those of English. Since scribes, even if they were themselves English native speakers, now spent much of their time writing French, they naturally imported French spelling-conventions into the writing of English words – hence, for example, the modern use of ⟨c⟩ rather than ⟨s⟩ in a word like *ice*. In some cases the French conventions took over completely: all the English words which had been spelled with ⟨cw-⟩ came to be written with ⟨qu-⟩, for instance. In other cases the native orthography survived in one word while the French orthography became usual in another: hence, for instance, the fact that the same Middle English and Modern English vowel is written with ⟨ee⟩ in *deed*, *heel* but, following a French convention, with ⟨ie⟩ in *fiend*, *thief*.

Naturally, the many words that were borrowed from French into English after the Conquest were normally spelled according to French conventions. But here an extra complication arose because of the influence of Latin orthography. Educated Englishmen before the Conquest had known Latin, but they had little difficulty in keeping it separate from their own language – English did not descend from Latin, and English scribes even wrote the two languages in different styles of lettering (just as the Germans did until they abandoned gothic script in the 20c, reserving it for their own language and writing Latin loans in roman). French, on the other hand, was a Romance language, so there was a perpetual tension between phonemic spelling of the pronunciations of French words and spelling which reflected their Latin etymologies: e.g. *povre* 'poor' was re-spelled *pauvre* because of its derivation from Latin *pauper*. Independently of changes in spoken French, French spelling became less phonemic as the etymological principle won wider acceptance in the Middle Ages (and this principle has been supported by the French State through the Académie Francaise since the late 17c (Cohen 1958, p. 425)).

Thus, for instance, the Latin /h/ which had dropped out of spoken French was reintroduced in writing, but inconsistently: hence our spellings *honour, hour* versus *ability* (while in modern French the etymological, non-phonemic spelling has become fully consistent in this case: *honneur, heure, habilité*).

In medieval England, then, a given word could commonly be spelled in many ways, each of which was justifiable in terms of one of the accepted conventions. Furthermore, this diversity had positive advantages for some of those professionally concerned with writing. Copyists were paid by the inch, so etymologizing spellings which included redundant letters swelled their income. When printing was introduced in the late 15c, the possibility of varying the length of words was the simplest means of 'justifying' lines of type (i.e. obtaining an even right-hand margin). And printing brought further disturbances to spelling habits. It transferred control of public orthography away from the disciplined worlds of religious house and chancery to the anarchical environment of small business, reducing the possibility of maintaining national norms. Furthermore, Caxton brought printing to England after living for thirty years in the Low Countries; he knew little of current English orthographic conventions, and his compositors were foreigners. The first books printed in England were heavily influenced by the spelling conventions of Dutch; spellings such as the ⟨gh⟩ of *ghost* reflect this influence today.

In contrast to the case in France, in England there was only one period when writers deliberately moved away from the phonemic principle: during the tide of enthusiasm for Classical learning which reached its peak in the early 16c it became common to write words derived from Classical languages with unphonemic spellings reflecting their etymology. But Scragg suggests that this fashion had a disproportionate effect on modern spelling, because it occurred shortly before printers began in the late 16c to accept the convention of a single fixed spelling for each word. Thus, for example, *det* or *dette* (from Latin *dēbitum*) became *debt*, *samon* (from *salmōnem*) became *salmon*, *septre* (from *scēptrum*) became *sceptre*. Many such examples are concealed from us now by the fact that the spelling-changes led to changes in pronunciation. Spellings such as *absolve, captive, corpse* were originally archaizing, Latinate ways of writing words which medieval Englishmen spoke and wote as *assoil, caitiff, corse*; but the new spellings were taken up in speech rather as, in our own time, /wɛskɪts/ are becoming /weɪstkəʊts/ and /fɒrɪdz/, /fɔhɛdz/.

By about 1650 English spellings were fixed: it was accepted that there was a 'correct' way to spell any word (with a small proportion of exceptions such as *gaol/jail*), and since then there have been only trivial changes in spelling. But it was essentially a matter of chance in the case of any particular word which of the alternative spellings available for it became standard: thus *pity* was standardized with one ⟨t⟩ and *ditty* with two, though both words had previously been spelled either way. Sometimes a spelling was adopted that had no justification either in pronunciation or in etymology: *foreign* derived from Old French *forain*, Latin *forānum*, and was given its modern spelling in the 16c apparently in the mistaken belief that it was related to *reign*, from Latin *rēgnum*.

The fact that modern English spellings have resulted from such a variety of causes, rather than from simple conservative refusal to alter a once-phonemic script in face of changes in the spoken language, may well reinforce our impression that current orthography is chaotic, that it fails to display any system whatever.

However, a number of arguments have been put forward to contradict this impression. Certainly there was nothing systematic about the manner in which our orthography evolved, but it is possible to see the product as more rational than the processes which brought it into being.

The most radical view of this sort is undoubtedly that of the generative phonologists, as represented by Noam Chomsky and Morris Halle (Chomsky and Halle 1968). For Chomsky and Halle, as we saw in Chapter 7, our orthography is an almost wholly accurate phonographic spelling-system, but the segments it records are those of the 'underlying' level of lexical storage rather than the 'surface' phonemes which are actually uttered. A generative phonologist of course recognizes that English orthography is very different in kind from Spanish or Finnish orthographies (to quote two cases commonly acknowledged as near-perfectly phonemic). But there are two possibilities available to the generative phonologist for analysing this difference without treating our own orthography as less regular than the others.

On the one hand, it may be that Spanish orthography appears more 'phonemic' because it is a surface rather than deep orthography. For instance, Spanish has a phonological rule whereby the |e| in roots such as |ped-| 'ask' becomes /i/ in stressed positions, yielding surface contrasts such as /pe'dir/ 'to ask', /pe'dimos/ 'we ask' v. /'pido/ 'I ask', /'pide/ 'he asks'. The rule is regular; a deep orthography would write ⟨ped-⟩ in all cases, but Spanish spelling in fact writes *pedir, pedimos* v. *pido, pide*. If this is in general the explanation for the strikingly 'phonemic' nature of Spanish orthography, then for Chomsky and Halle that orthography is inferior, since 'The fundamental principle of orthography is that phonetic variation is not indicated where it is predictable . . . an optimal orthography would have one representation for each lexical entry' (Chomsky and Halle 1968, p. 49). Spaniards ought to write the latter two 'words cited as *⟨pedo⟩, *⟨pede⟩; the fact that they do not makes their spelling useful for 'an actor reading lines in a language with which he is unfamiliar', but not for 'readers who know the language' (ibid.).

Alternatively – or additionally – it may be that Spanish and Finnish, as spoken languages, happen to contain far fewer morphophonemic alternations than English and French. If this were so, then there would be relatively little difference between surface and deep levels of phonology in the former languages, so that their orthographies might come as close as that of English to obeying Chomsky and Halle's 'fundamental principle' and yet they would still be close to phonemic.

Languages certainly differ in the complexity of their morphophonemic alternations: Vietnamese, for instance, has virtually none at all. It may be that Spanish and Finnish are morphophonemically simpler than English or French, though my impression is that the difference in this respect is not as great as the difference in terms of orthography. But I have not investigated the matter carefully, since I find the theory of generative phonology unconvincing on other grounds.

In the first place it seems *a priori* implausible that ordinary users of spoken English could construct the set of morphophonemic rules and 'underlying representations' attributed to them by Chomsky and Halle, since these depend on perceiving relationships between variant forms of roots; in many cases these relationships are obscure even to knowledgeable adults, let alone to average children during the period of language-acquisition. Noam Chomsky's wife Carol has published an article (C. Chomsky 1970) discussing her experience of teaching children to spell guided by the generative-phonological axiom that deep spelling is natural and that schoolteachers merely confuse children by drawing their attention to irrelevant surface pronunciations (cf. N. Chomsky 1970). She includes a revealing anecdote about how she suggested to one 'seventh-grade' (about 12 years old) pupil that she consider the word *signature* in deciding how to spell *sign*, to which the child replied 'so what's one got to do with the other?' The semantic relationship between *sign* and *signature* is relatively obvious compared to many of the relationships on which the generative phonologists' rules depend. In practice speakers often fail to notice relationships between words which are etymologically cognate, and they sometimes suppose such relationships to exist where they do not: thus, in the same article, Carol Chomsky mistakenly takes *prodigal*, from Latin *prōdig-us* 'wasteful', to share a root with *prodigious*, from Latin *prōdigi-um* 'a portent'. The various attempts that have been made to investigate the psychological reality of generative-phonological analyses empirically have yielded fairly uniformly negative results (see e.g. Sampson 1970, §7.5; articles by Hsieh, Skousen, Steinberg and Krohn in Koerner 1975; Simons 1975; P. Smith and Baker 1976).

Furthermore it is factually untrue, as Valerie Yule (1978) has pointed out, that English orthography conforms to the predictions of the generative phonologists' theories. Many of its non-phonemic properties have no connection with morphophonemic alternations. Chomsky and Halle justify the ⟨gh⟩ of *right/righteous* by arguing from synchronic evidence that the root must be underlying |rixt|; but there is no comparable evidence for an underlying |x| in *night* or *light*.[1] No current morphophonemic alternations explain any of the cases where initial /n/ is spelled ⟨kn⟩ or ⟨gn⟩, as in *knee, know, gnash*. And, conversely, there are many cases where a single root displays alternating spellings in different derived forms: *spEAk* v. *spEEch*, *palaCe* v. *palaTial*, *joKe* v. *joCular*, *colliDe* v. *colliSion* – some of these contrasts in spelling represent alternations in surface pronunciation, but these alternations are regular, so there should be no difference in lexical representation. The generative phonologists' account of English orthography was very influential for a number of years, but I conclude with W. N. Francis (1970, p. 51) that it is 'extravagant and unsupported'.

A relatively restrained argument for system underlying the apparent chaos of English orthography has been advanced by K. H. Albrow (1972; and cf. Venezky 1970). Albrow's analysis is cast in terms of J. R. Firth's theory of the 'polysystemic' structuring of language (Sampson 1980a, pp. 215–18). Albrow argues that English spelling displays fairly regular phoneme/grapheme correspondences, but these correspondences form not one but a range of alternative systems which come into play in different types of morpheme.

For instance, one linguistic contrast crucial for English orthography is that between lexical and grammatical morphemes. A lexical morpheme must contain at least three letters, while a grammatical morpheme will where possible have fewer: hence *see*, *bee* v. *me*, *be*, or the unique use (other than in proper names or dialect words) of ⟨gg⟩ for final /g/ in *egg* (contrast *leg*, *dreg*), and the unusual use of ⟨f⟩ for final /f/ in *if* (contrast *stiff*, *cliff*). The vowel /ɪ/ is spelled ⟨i⟩ in a lexical morpheme but, commonly, ⟨e⟩ in a grammatical morpheme: hence /ɪd/ is spelled differently in *solid* v. *wanted*. These contrasting spelling-rules mean that English orthography indicates not only the sounds of words but their status as lexical or grammatical forms. There is evidence that fluent readers make practical use of such cues in order to take in the general structure of a piece of prose at a brief glance (P. T. Smith 1980, pp. 127–8).

Thus far, Albrow's account seems broadly accurate and enlightening (though it is not unproblematic: e.g. Albrow overlooks the word *ox*, which is an exception to his 'three-letter rule'). It is less easy to follow him, however, when he goes on to divide the lexical roots into two classes using different phoneme/grapheme correspondences. For instance, Albrow suggests that one-letter vowel symbols (⟨a⟩, ⟨e⟩, ⟨i⟩ etc. as opposed to ⟨ai⟩, ⟨ee⟩, ⟨ou⟩ etc.), when preceding single consonants in polysyllables, stand for long vowels in 'system 1' but for short vowels in 'system 2': for instance ⟨e⟩ stands for /i/ in *meter* but for /ɛ/ in *merit*. Clearly this does nothing to reduce orthographic confusion unless we are given some independent criterion for deciding whether a given root belongs to system 1 or system 2. Albrow points out that by and large system 1 roots belong to the native Germanic vocabulary, while system 2 roots are French or Classical loans (*meter* derives from the near-obsolete native verb *mete*, 'to measure', *merit* is from Latin *meritum*). The reader will appreciate, in view of earlier discussion, why this difference in etymological origin might be expected to correlate with differences in spelling-conventions. But Albrow suggests that the contrast between two classes of roots, though having a historical cause, lives on as a synchronic fact of modern English: the two root-classes display quite different patterns of derivation, with system 2 roots taking a wide range of suffixes such as *-ic*, *-ical*, *-ous*, *-ity*, *-orious*, etc. etc., while system 1 roots are limited to a smaller range such as *-er*, *-ly*, *-ship*. It is not unreasonable to suggest (though it is not obviously true) that ordinary native speakers of English develop a feeling for what type of dervational affixes are appropriate for a given root; if so, they have the information they need to choose between Albrow's two orthographic systems.

This idea is interesting. One can even offer further evidence in support of it. Earlier I quoted *pity* and *ditty* as a paradigm case of a word-pair whose orthographic contrast (between single and double ⟨t⟩) has no basis in either pronunciation or etymology. The words are perfect rhymes, and both derive from French: *pity* is ultimately from Latin *pietātem*, *ditty* from *dictātum*, and they already rhymed for both ear and eye in Old French. Historically, therefore, one might expect both to be system 2 roots in Albrow's terms, in which case *ditty* ought to be written *⟨dity⟩. But, while *pity* is obviously related to the derived form *piteous*, which thus places it firmly in system 2, *ditty* has no synchronic cognates – one needs to be deeply versed in philology to appreciate the connection between *ditty* and *dictate*. In terms of its current meaning *ditty* is just the sort of informal, homely word which usually has a Germanic origin: so perhaps, after all, it is not accidental that *ditty* has come to be spelled according to the system 1 rule while *pity* has system 2 spelling.

Unfortunately, however, there are many exceptions to Albrow's rules. If *ditty* is classed as system 1, why is *petal* not classified likewise and either pronounced */pitəl/ or spelled *⟨pettle⟩? True, it is a recent loan from Greek; but in modern English it has no commonly-known derived forms, and it is a quite 'homely' term. Albrow mentions as an awkwardness for his theory that *patent* is often pronounced with /eɪ/ rather than /æ/; in fact the /eɪ/ pronunciation is the commoner of the two, and *latent* is always /eɪ/ despite the fact that the *-ent* suffix, together with the derivative *latency*, ought to make it a clear example of system 2. Or again, how would Albrow explain the spelling-difference between *ribald* and *ribbon*? – historically both derive from French, and in terms of modern English both seem equally appropriate candidates for system 1 spelling. It may be that in putting forward these counter-examples I am interpreting Albrow's theory as making stronger claims than its author intended. (In any case Albrow does not claim that the phoneme/grapheme relationships within his separate systems are one-to-one; rather, he suggests (p. 14) that each system enables a pronunciation to be read off near-unambiguously from a given spelling while still permitting a variety of spellings for a given pronunciation.) But, pending some further elaboration of what is presented as an 'interim report', it is difficult to accept Albrow's polysystemic account as a well-founded theory of English orthography.

We may see another kind of method in the apparent madness of our spelling, though, if we avoid letting ourselves be obsessed by the phonographic origins of the Roman alphabet and think of English spelling as at least partly logographic.

The fact that the Roman letters originally stood for segmental sounds would not in principle be any bar to constructing a purely logographic script with them. We could assign arbitrary letter-sequences to the various words of

English without any regard for their pronunciation – say ⟨pzm⟩ for *dog*, ⟨uvcr⟩ for *cat*, ⟨ni⟩ for *horse*, and so on. Obviously no-one would suggest that modern English orthography has lost touch with its phonographic ancestry as completely as this. But our script might be described as a compromise between the phonographic and logographic principles – somewhat akin, in fact, to Japanese script, though with a much higher proportion of phonography and correspondingly less logography than the latter, and without the complication of alternative 'readings' for single written forms. Since (even according to Albrow's theory) the spellings of English words are not predictable from pronunciation, we have to learn the spellings of words case by case, as Japanese have to learn *kanji* individually. Most Japanese *kanji* contain a phonetic element giving a hint of the *on* pronunciation(s), though this hint is much less informative than the clue given by an English spelling to the corresponding pronunciation. In Japanese the highest-frequency vocabulary-items are mostly Native words, corresponding to *kun* readings of *kanji*, and here the shape of the *kanji* is wholly unrelated to pronunciation. In English spelling, Wijk (1969, p. 52) has shown that the overall impression of extreme irregularity stems largely from the fact that many of the commonest words are written quite irregularly. We might compare English words such as *one*, *who* to Native Japanese *kun* values of *kanji* – though here the analogy is weak, since even these English spellings are distantly related to the pronunciations /wʌn, hu/.

In many cases the logographic aspect of English spelling has the result which is important in Japanese of distinguishing homophones visually: if our spelling were purely phonographic, *right*, *rite*, *write*, *wright* (for instance) would necessarily look identical. The incidence of homophones is so much lower in European languages than in Japanese that this advantage of logographic script may seem scarcely a weighty one. On the other hand it is noticeable that even French orthography, which is governed more consistently than ours by the etymological principle, violates that principle by including non-etymological devices to distinguish homophones: for instance, the past participle of *devoir* is written *dû*, with a circumflex accent that has no connection with a historical /s/ (as French circumflexes normally have) in order to differentiate it from *du* = *de le*. (This is not intended to suggest that avoidance of homography has been a motive force in the creation of our irregular spellings; in English most irregularly-spelled words – *bright*, *debt*, *psalm*, etc. – have unique pronunciations, and there are many homonym-pairs, such as *seal* the animal and *seal* as signet, which are not distinguished in spelling.)

From the point of view being argued here, the generative phonologists are partly right in their statement of the 'fundamental principle' to which English orthography conforms. A given English lexical item commonly has a single spelling which remains fixed despite the fact that phonological rules may produce alternative allomorphic realizations – just as, in Japanese, a *kanji* retains a constant shape irrespective of phonological rules that affect its pronunciation. The semantic unit 'telegraph' is pronounced /'tɛlə,graf/ in isolation, /təˈlɛgrəf/ before the suffix -*y*, /ˌtɛləˈgræf/ before -*ic*, but it is always written ⟨telegraph⟩. As in the Japanese use of *okurigana*, phonetic differences between allomorphs of English word-stems tend to be recorded in writing only when they occur at the end of stems, adjacent to suffixes: phonetically the most salient difference between the allomorphs of the root of *Peter, Petrine* is surely between the stressed vowels /i~ɛ/, but the distinction reflected in the spelling is that between the shwa of the former and the consonantal /r/ of the latter word. Since suffixes, unlike root morphemes, have little individuality, it is understandable if the spelling of suffixes in English should approach the purely phonographic; but if phonographic writing is used it must represent phonological units, which perhaps leads to whole syllables being written phonographically when they belong partly to a root and partly to a suffix.

The aspect of generative-phonological theory that is rejected by a logographic account of English spelling is its claim that where spelling deviates from surface phonology it reflects underlying phonology. From the logographic point of view, the ⟨gh⟩ of *right, righteous* is merely an arbitrary mark differentiating the written form of this morpheme from others. Much the same effect would be achieved, from the modern reader's point of view, if the word were spelled, say, ⟨riite⟩ or ⟨qurite⟩. The fact that the distinctive feature of this word is ⟨gh⟩ rather than ⟨ii⟩ or ⟨qu⟩ comes about because, centuries ago, the word was pronounced with an /x/ sound, but that fact has no relevance to the way a contemporary English-speaker processes spoken or written language.

We saw above that there are counter-examples to both aspects of the generative phonologists' account of English orthography. Some morphemes, such as the root common to *speak/speech*, have alternating graphic forms that cannot be explained by analogy with Japanese *okurigana*; and some spelling-contrasts, such as that between *knave* and *nave*, do not correlate with morphophonemic phenomena that might be used to argue for divergent 'underlying pronunciations'. But examples of the latter kind are extremely numerous, while examples of the former kind are fairly rare – there are not enough of them to overthrow the general principle that the spelling of English lexical items normally ignores variation between allomorphs except, sometimes, with respect to their final sounds.

It is more enlightening, I believe, to see the spelling-system which ultimately emerged from the centuries of orthographic confusion that followed the Norman Conquest as a system which has evolved some way from the phonographic towards the logographic type, than simply to dismiss it as meaninglessly chaotic. But to say this is not to say anything about whether that development was a good or a bad thing. We saw in Chapter 8 that Europeans, including Britons, have typically regarded phonographic writing as highly superior to logography, and the special characteristics of the Chinese language which make logographic script particularly convenient for it (high incidence of homophones and large dialect-differences) do not apply to English. From this point of view, then, the evolution of English orthography must presumably be seen as a retrograde movement, and a phonographic spelling reform would be a thoroughly good thing which we have failed to adopt only because of the great practical difficulties involved.

Both halves of this verdict are questionable.

In the first place, I do not believe that serious objective difficulties stand in the way of spelling reform. People often cite the massive bulk of existing documents which would require to be transliterated into the new spelling; but nothing of the kind would be necessary. Except for some small minority-groups such as scholars and lawyers, people rarely consult papers or books which were printed more than ten years or so earlier – people often read literary classics, but almost always in modern editions. When a book was reprinted it would be transliterated into the new script as a matter of course; given a generation of printers who have been brought up on the new spelling, this would not be a major problem, and automatic word-processing techniques are making it simpler with every day that passes. Those people who for professional reasons need to read old documents – and no doubt many cultured members of the general public – would develop a passive familiarity with the old script, something which is far less burdensome than the active ability to produce the correct traditional spelling for any spoken word. There would be plenty of reference-books in which puzzling old spellings could be checked when they mattered.

There is also the problem of training the population. But, if society in general wanted this problem to be solved, it easily could be. The set of individuals who would crucially need to be thoroughly competent in the new system are the primary-school teachers. People nowadays have to qualify for this career by undergoing quite a long training-period, and if we decided to reform our spelling then knowledge of the new orthography would obviously become an important component of this training. Surely it will not be suggested that potential schoolteachers brought up on old spelling would be incapable of mastering a new system? After all, the point of reformed spelling is to be easy.

Once a generation of children had been brought up on the new spelling, it would matter little whether or not the bulk of their elders fell into line. Printers' English spellings were standardized by about 1650, but private spelling did not follow suit until well after Dr Johnson's Dictionary became available in 1755 (Scragg 1974, p. 82). No doubt some newspapers, magazines, and book-publishers would shift to the new standard rapidly and others choose to stick to the old, on straightforward commercial considerations of what their particular readership preferred. Those that made the switch would employ compositors and editors skilled in the new system, who would transliterate the copy of contributors who used the old. Thirty years after the changeover began, the old spelling would linger only in a few self-consciously quaint periodicals.

The reason why all this, at a guess, will never happen has to do with subjective rather than objective factors. Because there has been no change at all within living memory in our rather complex orthography, people imagine that it is unchangeable and dismiss those who take the possibility of reform seriously as cranks. It is very little realized that English and French orthographies, the two least phonemic in Europe, are unusual in not having undergone reform in recent times. The Scandinavian nations, for instance, which use fairly phonemic orthographies, tinker with them every few decades. Paradoxically it seems to be broadly true that those European nations with the most phonemic scripts are the most inclined to reform them. If your script is almost perfectly phonemic, then you see its graphemes as devices for representing sounds and you perceive the respects in which they fail to do so as striking and curable imperfections. An Englishman, on the other hand, does not see his orthography as a system deviating in certain limited respects from an essentially phonographic ideal – and rightly so, since modern English spelling has as much title to be called logographic as phonographic. In Spain recently a non-specialized paperback house published a call for reform of what is possibly the most phonemic of all widely-used alphabetic scripts (Mosterín 1981). It is difficult to imagine a comparable book appearing in Britain at present.

The tradition, common to the English-speaking countries, of minimizing the role of the State in cultural matters means that spelling reform here would be more dependent than in some other European countries on popular demand; governments could facilitate, but they could hardly impose, such a development. And, since the English-speaking world no longer has a single cultural centre, such demand would have to grow in separate publics – there would surely be little to be said in favour of one English-speaking nation switching to a radically novel orthography if others were unwilling to do the same.

I do not believe this sort of demand is likely to grow, because it appears to me that the great majority of influential English-speakers who entertain the notion of spelling-reform as a serious possibility are opposed to it. They find the idea unattractive aesthetically, and unless they have small children they see little to be gained by it; they themselves have already mastered traditional orthography (otherwise they would not be influential). People may consciously or unconsciously resent the idea of spelling reform as a threat to the authority possessed by those who are masters of the traditional system – even poor spellers can share this attitude, as a sinner may hate atheism.

But, to return from these subjective issues to objective matters, it is questionable whether phonographic spelling-reform would in practice be as advantageous as enthusiasts have often assumed. Until quite recently the psychology of reading and writing was a little-investigated area, and the benefits and drawbacks of alternative orthographic systems could be discussed only in relatively untechnical, common-sense terms. In the last few years there has been an explosive growth of research in this branch of psychology. (Downing and Leong 1982 provide an extensive bibliography.) The findings that are beginning to emerge shed new light on, among other things, the question of phonography versus logography.

It must be stressed at the outset that, because this research is so new, few of its results are uncontroversial. But one thesis for which considerable experimental evidence has built up is that the processes of reading and writing are less closely linked than people used to suppose. Key references here are Uta Frith (1979, 1980a) and Bryant and Bradley (1980).

Frith argues that it is most natural for users of an alphabetic script to 'write by ear', that is to spell words phonographically, but to 'read by eye', that is to move directly from visible letter-sequences to the corresponding vocabulary-items stored in memory, without 'phonic mediation' – i.e. without using the correspondences between the phonetic values of the individual letters and the pronunciation of the relevant word as a guide to retrieval of the correct word.

'Reading by eye' – what schoolteachers call the 'look-and-say' as opposed to 'phonic' approach to reading – is itself an ambiguous concept. It may mean that a word is perceived as an unanalysed visual *Gestalt*, a unitary outline not resolved into individual letters. Uta Frith seems to argue that it is reading by eye in this sense which is more natural than phonically-mediated reading (and cf. Monk and Hulme 1983). She discusses an experiment in which subjects read sentences distorted in alternative ways, as exemplified by:

1   A robln hoppeb up to my windcw.
2   A robbin hoppt up to my winndo.

In 1 the appearance of the sentence is fairly well preserved although some letters are replaced by visually-similar ones. In 2 the appearance of the sentence is more heavily distorted, though the phoneme/grapheme correspondence rules of English imply an undistorted pronunciation.[2] Frith finds that 7-year-olds and (more strikingly) adults have more trouble with distortions of type 2 than type 1. However, other psychologists, such as Leslie Henderson (1982), doubt whether 'reading by eye' normally occurs in this *Gestalt* fashion; they argue that reading does involve identifying some or all of the letters making up a written word. But this does not disturb the claim that readers retrieve the intended vocabulary-item directly from the letter-sequence without reference to the pronunciation of the former or the phonetic implications of the latter, just as we would have to do if words were written in an arbitrary coding (⟨pzm⟩ for *dog*, ⟨uvcr⟩ for *cat*, etc.). Likewise, a Chinese reader undoubtedly perceives most complex graphs as composites of familiar elements, rather than as atomic wholes; but this does not imply that he retrieves the morpheme corresponding to such a graph by associating the visual elements with sounds and searching for a word whose pronunciation contains those sounds – Chinese script, being logographic, does not work that way. We must not assume, because European writing usually *could* be read phonographically, that it commonly *is*.[3]

Bryant and Bradley (1980) demonstrate this dissociation between the reading and writing processes in English-speaking children. They find not only that children frequently cannot spell correctly words which they read correctly (in itself no great surprise), but also that children can often spell correctly words which they cannot read, which is more unexpected. Furthermore there is a difference in the kinds of words with which these respective types of failure commonly occur. Examples of words which are read but not spelled correctly are *school, light, train, egg* – all words whose spelling is relatively unpredictable on the basis of pronunciation (we have already seen that the final double ⟨g⟩ of *egg* is unique, p. 202). Examples of words which are spelled but not read correctly are *bun, mat, leg, pat* – words which are phonographically quite regular, but are short and offer little that is visually distinctive in terms of unusual letters or letter-combinations.

Anyone who succeeds in becoming a skilled user of written English must eventually learn to use both 'look-and-say' (or logographic) and 'phonic' strategies in both processing-modes, reading and writing. The phonic strategy must be used in reading when one encounters a new word. An unfamiliar surname, for instance, obviously cannot be recognized as a unit, so a reader who arrives at a pronunciation for it must do so by some method of grapheme/phoneme conversion. On the other hand, a familiar word with a thoroughly irregular spelling must be handled logographically even by the writer: no-one could spell *knight* correctly by 'sounding out' the word and converting phonemes to graphemes. (Indeed, if we are discussing competent users of English orthography rather than learners, then it is not clear whether it makes sense to suggest that they ever write familiar words purely phonographically, since the phoneme/grapheme correspondences of our orthography commonly do not yield unique spellings for words. Andrew Ellis (1984, ch. 6) suggests by implication that the 'writing by ear' half of Uta Frith's slogan is less plausible than 'reading by eye'.) But Frith believes that one strategy in each processing-mode is less natural and efficient than the other; individuals will differ in how early and how successfully they learn to use the 'unnatural' strategy in either processing-mode when it is necessary to do so. Poor spellers, who lack the ability to switch strategies, sometimes have difficulty in reading their own mis-spellings.

Parenthetically, even a 'phonic' reading strategy, when it is used, need not necessarily involve unconscious resort to a fixed, algorithmic set of rules, such as those described by Wijk or Albrow, for converting letter-sequences to sound-sequences. An alternative view holds that an unfamiliar word is read by constructing analogies between its spelling and that of familiar words which can be read logographically, and guessing at the pronunciation of the new word by reference to the known pronunciations of the familiar words. In the linguistics of spoken language this contrast between fixed rules and open-ended analogies as alternative means of executing novel linguistic behaviour has sometimes – I believe mistakenly – been dismissed as a pseudo-opposition. In the psychology of literacy the two principles yield contrasting empirical predictions, and there is some evidence to suggest that analogies rather than rules are used (Baron 1977; Glushko 1979; Henderson 1982, pt 2; though cf. Ellis 1984). If this is correct, then the role of the phonographic principle in reading (and possibly in writing too) is even smaller than suggested above.

These findings imply that a phonographic spelling reform would benefit the competent user of written English, if at all, then only in his role as writer rather than reader. But the implications may well go further. If we find it natural to 'write by ear' then it may be that the best orthography for the writer is phonemic. But if we read logographically, then the best orthography for the reader is presumably one in which the words are highly distinctive. This point was made in Chapter 5 with respect to the shapes of the graphemes, but it applies equally to the patterns of grapheme-sequences: to be read efficiently, words need to be very diverse in terms of their length and the letter-combinations they contain.

Now, an unphonemic alphabetic script is not necessarily a script in which words have distinctive spellings. For instance, if we changed English orthography by spelling the phoneme-sequence /pl/ as ⟨pr⟩ and /pr/ as ⟨pl⟩, the script would become even less straightforwardly phonemic than it is now (since the value of ⟨l⟩ and ⟨r⟩ would depend on whether or not they were preceded by ⟨p⟩), but there would be no gain in visual distinctiveness: English phonology assigns similar privileges of occurrence to the consonant-clusters /pl/ and /pr/, so the range of spellings occurring in the novel orthography would be no more diverse than the range currently used. But the converse entailment does hold: maximizing the distinctiveness of word-spellings requires departure from the phonemic principle. Unphonemic English spellings such as the ⟨kn⟩ and the ⟨gh⟩ of *knight*, the ⟨b⟩ of *debt* and *doubt*, the ⟨sc⟩ of *science* and *sceptre*, and many others, make the words containing them more distinctive than they would be if their spelling was predictable from their sound. Here I am not saying merely that homophones often have distinctive spellings (though that is a corollary of the point I am making). The word /dɛt/ is unambiguous in speech, but the fact that it is spelled *debt* makes it look more different from *bet, net, den* etc. than it would if spelled phonemically. In general, it seems to be true that the 'graphemic grammar' of written English provides a considerably greater variety of possible letter-sequences than the phonological grammar provides possible phoneme-sequences for English words.

That is not to say that all deviations from the phonemic principle in our traditional orthography have this effect. Far from it. For instance, the word *tough* would be more visually distinctive, as well as more phonemic, if spelled *⟨tugh⟩. In general, diversity of spellings for a given sound makes for visual distinctiveness, whereas diversity of sounds corresponding in different words to a given grapheme or grapheme-combination is irrelevant. Yule (1982, p. 19) offers a sobering analysis of the extent to which *both* of these types of deviation from the phonemic principle occur in English orthography.

Nevertheless, it seems fair to say that the former category of deviation is a good deal more widespread.

What I am suggesting, then, is that an 'ideal orthography' may have to be a compromise between the interests of the writer and those of the reader (cf. F. Smith 1973, p. 117ff; Frith and Frith 1980, p. 295). For the writer, a highly phonemic script such as that of Spanish may be ideal. For the reader, a purely logographic script such as that of Chinese, because of its great visual distinctiveness, might be even better than English orthography.

Most people who criticize our current orthography are not motivated by thoughts about the reading or writing processes as executed by competent users of the system, but by problems of literacy-acquisition, whether on the part of children or adult illiterates. It is widely assumed that a more phonemic script would be significantly easier to learn. If spelling were reformed, children would no longer have to waste dreary hours at the schoolroom desk rote-learning senseless orthographic fossils, when they could make better use of the time acquiring more worthwhile and interesting knowledge, or playing outdoors in the fresh air. Adult illiteracy might be reduced or eliminated.

We saw on p. 163 that it is problematic to call a phonographic script 'easier' than a more logographic script; the issues discussed there make it implausible that spelling reform would help adult illiterates. (In any case, what adult illiterates lack may well be motivation rather than ability; pompous academics for whom literacy is the alpha and omega of life, and agents of States who wish their citizens to respond promptly and efficiently to written instructions, are far too ready to assume that all of humanity shares their particular scale of priorities.)[4] We might concede that those children who do succeed in learning to read at the normal age would learn *faster* if our orthography were more phonemic; though even here the gain cannot be quantified, and rests ultimately on faith. One often encounters loose statements about Chinese or Japanese children taking x years more – or Spanish childen taking y months less – than British children to learn to read and write, but such comparisons are meaningless, because there are always many relevant variables other than the differences in orthographic system. Children in different countries begin school at different ages, they inhabit societies with different attitudes to literacy, their schools are run on different lines; and the ease of literacy-acquisition depends not only on the nature of the orthography to be acquired but also on the nature of the spoken language it is used for. (Kyöstiö (1980) illustrates many of these problems as they arise in comparing literacy-acquisition in Finland and in English-speaking countries.) The i.t.a. experiment discussed above was probably the nearest approach there has yet been to a fair test of the claim that phonemic orthography is easily learned, but even here there were enormous problems stemming from interfering variables; for instance, children using i.t.a. may have been at an advantage because their teachers were fired with enthusiasm for an interesting new idea, while on the other hand they may have been disadvantaged by the fact that writing they saw away from the school context was in another script.

Nevertheless, I would not ultimately dispute the claim that, other things being equal, a purely phonemic script is likely to be learned somewhat faster than a more logographic script such as ours. But it does not follow that spelling reform is desirable, since the learners' interests are not the only interests to be considered. There are also the interests of competent users to be taken into account. Any literate adult, even a professional author, reads far more than he writes; so if, as suggested above, the ideal script for a reader is a somewhat unphonemic script, it may be that the interests of the competent user of a script are at odds with the interests of the learner, just as the interests of the writer diverge from those of the reader. From this point of view, those who advocate spelling reform passionately have often been guilty of that error which is so common in political life, of demanding that the interests of one group be fully met while entirely overlooking the countervailing interests of other groups.

All this is not intended to imply that the orthography of English in fact represents the ideal compromise between the demands of learnability and readability. Some English spellings, such as the ⟨ou⟩ of *tough*, are both unphonemic and undistinctive. Such examples may not be numerous; but, leaving them aside, we have no way of calculating where the ideal balance of advantage lies. The spelling reformers may be right in arguing that society would stand to gain from the adoption of a more phonemic script. Equally, it may be that the advantages of distinctive spelling to the reader are so significant that we would have been fortunate had we inherited an even greater wealth of silent letters, alternative spellings for given phonemes, and the like. The situation is one of those described as typical of the social as opposed to the physical domain by the sociologist Friedrich Hayek (e.g. 1955), where we can see in outline what the relevant countervailing considerations are that jointly determine a best solution, but cannot go on to specify what that best solution will be.

At most, if the reader will allow me to close on a highly speculative note, one might be able to say something about the direction in which the balance of social advantage has shifted over history.

Consider, first, the idea that the reader's interests favour graphically-distinctive (and hence at least partly logographic) scripts, while the writer's interests favour phonographic scripts. It is clear that the invention of printing, and its increased cheapness as technology has progressed, must have caused the average number of occasions on which a given text is read to grow enormously over the half-millennium since Gutenberg, while each text is still written only once. There are texts, such as ephemeral personal letters, which receive only one reading; but since the invention of the telephone the number of these per head of population may have decreased, and in any case nowadays they exist side by side with a mass of texts such as written road-signs, daily papers, advertising material, and the like, which may receive millions of readings each – cases such as these scarcely existed two or three centuries ago. This implies that the balance of advantage has been tending to move towards the reader and away from the writer: extra trouble in writing a single text can now be massively repaid by increased efficiency of very many acts of reading that text. Thus the ideal orthography should now be more logographic, less phonographic than before.

Consider also the opposition of interests as between learner and mature user. Another set of social changes that have taken place since the Middle Ages are that life expectancy has increased (although what is relevant is the life expectancy of individuals at the age when they have mastered an orthography, and this has increased much less dramatically than life expectancy at birth), and that literacy-acquisition takes place younger (adults learning to read and write are now the exception where once they were the rule). This must tend to shift the balance of advantage away from learner and towards mature user: it is worth spending more time nowadays to learn an orthography, if the extra time is the cost of acquiring a system that is relatively efficient once mastered, because the period during which the average individual will enjoy mastery of an orthography is now longer than it used to be. Again, on the assumptions stated earlier these changes favour a more logographic, less phonographic script.

Thus it may be no accident that modern English spelling is so much less regular than its forerunner of nine centuries earlier. Rather than representing a dogged and anti-social conservatism on the part of the literary élite, this phenomenon may well amount to an appropriate (though, certainly, unplanned) response to the changing balance of social forces. Our orthography is possibly not the least valuable of the institutions our ancestors have bequeathed to us.

Notes

Chapter 1   Introduction

1   Dell Hymes (1961) and John Honey (1983) are unusual in regarding this assumption as open to question.
2   According to Updike (1922, vol. 2, p. 229, n. 1), the long *s* was first given up in roman type by John Bell in about 1775. It would obviously be difficult to establish when it finally died out in handwriting, though a clue is offered by Winifred Holtby's novel *South Riding* (1936) in which one of the older characters is described as the last man to make the distinction.
3   On problems that arise with the concepts 'grapheme' and 'allograph', see Bazell (1956) and Minkoff (1975, pp. 195–6).

Chapter 2   Theoretical preliminaries

1   In fact the conventional pronunciation of a passage of Literary Chinese varies from one part of China to another, but this is not relevant to the point being made here.
2   From the theoretical point of view, it is misleading to describe phonetic features as elements of segments; rather, features overlap with one another and co-occur with sequences of other features in complex ways within a syllable (Sampson, 1980a, pp. 217–18). But we need not enter into this matter here.

Chapter 3   The earliest writing

1   As it happens, other aspects of the translation of this particular inscription are now regarded as doubtful: cf. Edzard 1968, pp. 167–8; but this does not affect our understanding of the general nature of the script.
2   Arno Poebel (1923, pp. 10–11) suggests that the role of the phonographic principle in Sumerian Cuneiform was much greater than this, but his interpretation has not found favour with more recent authorities. Civil (1973, pp. 26–7) gives statistical details of the relative proportions of logographic and phonographic writing in various Sumerian texts.

Chapter 4 A syllabic system: Linear B

1 Since short vowels are much commoner than long vowels in Greek, when quoting examples I shall mark long vowels but leave short vowels unmarked in this chapter and in Chapter 6. In a few cases length is unknown (Allen 1968, pp. 86–9).

Chapter 5 Consonantal writing

1 Evidence from the site of Ugarit, near modern Latakia on the coast of Syria (Diringer 1968, pp. 150–2, Jensen 1970, pp. 118ff.), suggests that the very earliest Semitic alphabet may have contained several extra letters for Proto-Semitic consonants which in Hebrew merged with other phonemes.

2 Gelb argues that the history of all scripts involves a progression from logographic through syllabic to segmental, and that it is 'unthinkable' that the middle stage could be skipped. Yet he acknowledges that most Egyptologists think it.

3 Probably the best analysis of Biblical Hebrew vowel phonology, though it is not claimed to be a definitive solution, is that by J. Cantineau (1950), who gives a 'polysystemic' account (Sampson 1980a, p. 215ff.). See also Z. S. Harris (1941) and Morag (1962).

4 'Focus' is used loosely here. What is relevant is not simply whether the lens is accommodated to focus letters on the retina but whether given letters are brought within the two-degree portion of the whole visual field that focuses on the very sensitive retinal area called the fovea. See e.g. Downing and Leong 1982, pp. 136–7.

5 On the analogous problems which arise for Arabic readers, see e.g. Mahmoud (1979).

Chapter 6 The Graeco-Roman alphabet

1 Some scholars attribute the invention of G to Appius Claudius Caecus (late −4c) rather than Spurius Carvilius.

2 Terms such as 'gothic', 'roman', and 'humanist' are written with small letters when they refer to varieties of the Roman alphabet.

3 There has recently been an attempt to replace the somewhat vague and variable terms for type styles with artificial, internationally-agreed names: Old Face becomes 'Garalde', Modern Face 'Didone', and Sans Serif 'Lineale'. In my experience the new names are rarely used, and I shall ignore them.

Chapter 7   A featural system: Korean Han'gŭl

1   My formulation is based on Martin (1954, p. 18); for a different account, see e.g. Chang (1982, p. 30).
2   See Martin (1954, pp. 21–2) for complications omitted here.
3   I know of one case where phonographic writing is claimed to have begun 'deep' and evolved towards a shallower approach, namely in Sumerian Cuneiform (Civil and Biggs 1966, pp. 14ff.); but the fact that this script was principally logographic makes it questionable whether this development offers much support to generative phonology.

Chapter 8   A logographic system: Chinese writing

1   It is true that the grammar and vocabulary of written Chinese diverge from that of spoken Chinese, as is the case with many languages (p. 27), and indeed before the written norms were reformed early in the 20c the divergence was extreme. But Literary Chinese was no more a 'logical' or 'philosophical' language than modern spoken Chinese is.
2   There is an element of circularity at this point, since graph-structure is one of the categories of evidence used to reconstruct Old Chinese. Other kinds of evidence are also available; but it must be stressed that Karlgren's reconstructions are tentative, and many revisions are proposed in the specialist literature. In particular, there may well have been further phonological contrasts in Old Chinese which are now beyond our ken.
3   Gelb (1952, p. 104) misunderstands the relationship between phonetic and signific elements in Chinese graphs, suggesting that the phonetics were added in order to disambiguate the significs rather than vice versa. Historically this is certainly incorrect (see e.g. Forrest 1948, p. 37); and indeed a writing system in which individual symbols were ambiguous as between all the words that share a common signific in the Chinese script would be unusable. Gelb may be misled by a false analogy with Sumerian script (cf. p. 55).
4   Similarly bizarre statements about Chinese script are retailed by Marshall McLuhan (1962, p. 27), and cf. Havelock (1976, p. 85).
5   Graham (1959, pp. 110–12) argues that this aspect of Chinese has been exaggerated.
6   The reader may wonder how Koreans manage to understand Sino-Korean vocabulary written in phonographic Han'gŭl script. The answer is twofold: first, Sino-Korean pronunciation was fixed at a period when Chinese preserved many more phonological contrasts than it does now; second, Sino-Korean vocabulary reflects the compounding characteristic of Modern Chinese. The shallow/deep issue in Korean orthography discussed on pp. 136ff. is also relevant here: the morphophonemic rules of spoken Korean reduce the range of contrasts found in the underlying forms of Sino-Korean words, so it could be argued that the move from shallow to deep spelling is a price that Koreans had to pay in order to avoid using

Chinese graphs. (We saw that Lee Ki-moon prefers the traditional shallow spellings; but Lee is unusual among contemporary Korean linguists in continuing to use Chinese graphs rather than Han'gŭl to write Sino-Korean elements.)

Chapter 9   A mixed system: Japanese writing

1   Three further points should be mentioned for the sake of completeness. In recent centuries a contrast between single and geminate has developed in non-initial obstruent consonants, and a range of syllables with final /-n/ has emerged. Also, while Japanese is not a tone language, it does have a system of 'pitch accent' akin to those of Ancient Greek and Korean; since this has no relevance in connection with the writing system, I ignore it in what follows.

2   *Katakana* also sometimes replace *hiragana* in very formal documents, or as an equivalent to italicization.

Chapter 10   English spelling

1   Indeed, the fact that *delight, delicious* follow the pattern of *expedite, expeditious* in their pronunciation rather than of *right, righteous* seems to imply that by Chomsky and Halle's own arguments *delight* does *not* contain an underlying |x|. The truth of the matter is that *delight* is spelled as it is because in the 16c somebody mistakenly thought it was related to the word *light,* which in turn has been spelled with ⟨gh⟩ ever since the time when it contained the sound /x/ in its pronunciation.

2   So at least Frith supposes, though it might be argued that ⟨hoppt⟩ and ⟨winndo⟩ violate the regular spelling-conventions while ⟨hopped⟩, ⟨window⟩ are regularly-spelled words.

3   Feldman and Turvey (1983) argue that European languages differ in the extent to which phonic mediation is normal in reading them.

3   A recent British survey of literacy and numeracy among adults (ALBSU 1983) found that over 70 per cent of those with literacy problems denied that these caused any difficulties in their everyday lives.

References

Place of publication is omitted for books published in London.

Abercrombie, D. (1967), *Elements of General Phonetics*, Edinburgh University Press (Edinburgh)

Albrow, K. H. (1972), *The English Writing System: Notes towards a Description*, Longman for the Schools Council

ALBSU (1983), *Literacy and numeracy: evidence from the National Child Development Survey*, Adult Literacy and Basic Skills Unit

Allen, W. S. (1965), *Vox Latina*, Cambridge University Press

Allen, W. S. (1968), *Vox Graeca*, Cambridge University Press

Amiet, P. (1966), 'Il y a 5000 ans les élamites inventaient l'écriture', *Archeologia*, vol. 12, pp. 16–23

Baron, J. (1977), 'What we might know about orthographic rules', in S. Dornič, (ed.), *Attention and Performance VI*, Erlbaum (Hillsdale, NJ)

Barr, J. (1976), 'Reading a script without vowels', in Haas (1976b)

Bazell, C. E. (1956), 'The grapheme', reprinted in Hamp *et al.* (1966)

Bradley, Lynette and Bryant, P. E. (1983), 'Categorizing sounds and learning to read – a causal connection', *Nature*, vol. 301, pp. 419–21

Brady, M. (1981), 'Toward a computational theory of early visual processing in reading', *Visible Language*, vol. 15, pp. 183–215

Breasted, J. H. (1926), *The Conquest of Civilization*, Harper and Brothers

Bryant, P. E. and Bradley, Lynette (1980), 'Why children sometimes write words which they do not read', in Frith (1980b)

Bryden, M. P. and Allard, F. (1976), 'Visual hemifield differences depend on typeface', *Brain and Language*, vol. 3, pp. 191–200

Burt, C. (1959), *A Psychological Study of Typography*, Cambridge University Press

Cantineau, J. (1950), 'Essai d'une phonologie de l'hébreu biblique', *Bulletin de la Société de Linguistique de Paris*, vol. 46, fasc. 1, pp. 82–122

Chadwick, J. (1958), *The Decipherment of Linear B*, Cambridge University Press

Chadwick, J. (1976), *The Mycenaean World*, Cambridge University Press

Chang, Namgui (1982), *Phonological Variations in 15th Century Korean*, Project on Linguistic Analysis (Berkeley, Calif.)

Chao, Yuen-Ren (1934), 'The non-uniqueness of phonemic solutions of phonetic systems', reprinted in M. Joos (ed.), *Readings in Linguistics*, American Council of Learned Societies (New York), 1957

Chao, Yuen-Ren (1968), *Language and Symbolic Systems*, Cambridge University Press

Cheng, Chin-chuan *et al.* (1977), 'In defense of teaching simplified characters', with responses by Leong and others, *Journal of Chinese Linguistics*, vol. 5, pp. 314–54

Chiang Yee (1973), *Chinese Calligraphy* (3rd edn), Harvard University Press (Cambridge, Mass.)

Chomsky, Carol (1970), 'Reading, writing, and phonology', *Harvard Educational Review*, vol. 40, pp. 287–310

Chomsky, N. (1970), 'Phonology and reading', in Levin and Williams (1970)

Chomsky, N. and Halle, M. (1968), *The Sound Pattern of English*, Harper & Row

Chou En-lai *et al.* (1958), *Reform of the Chinese Written Language*, Foreign Languages Press (Peking)

Civil, M. (1973), 'The Sumerian writing system: some problems', *Orientalia*, vol. 42, pp. 21–34

Civil, M. and Biggs, R. D. (1966), 'Notes sur des textes sumériens archaïques', *Revue d'assyriologie et d'archéologie orientale*, vol. 60, pp. 1–16

Cohen, M. (1958), *La grande invention de l'écriture et son évolution* (2 vols.), Klincksieck (Paris); page references are to the Text volume

Derrida, J. (1967), *Of Grammatology*, English translation published by Johns Hopkins University Press, 1976

Diringer, D. (1968), *The Alphabet* (2 vols.), Hutchinson; page references are to vol. 1

Downing, J. (1965), *The Initial Teaching Alphabet Explained and Illustrated* (5th, revised, edn), Cassell

Downing, J. (ed.) (1973), *Comparative Reading*, Collier-Macmillan

Downing, J. and Leong, C. K. (1982), *Psychology of Reading*, Collier-Macmillan

Driver, G. R. (1954), *Semitic Writing, From Pictograph to Alphabet* (2nd edn), Oxford University Press

Dunn-Rankin, P. (1978), 'The visual characteristics of words', *Scientific American*, January 1978, pp. 122–30

Edzard, D. O. (1968), *Sumerische Rechtsurkunden des III. Jahrtausends aus der Zeit vor der III. Dynastie von Ur* (*Bayerische Akademie der Wissenschaften, Philosophisch-Historische Klasse, Abhandlungen*, new series, vol. 67), Verlag der Bayerischen Akademie der Wissenschaften (Munich)

Eisenstein, Elizabeth L. (1979), *The Printing Press as an Agent of Change* (2 vols.), Cambridge University Press

Ellis, A. W. (1984), *Reading, Writing and Dyslexia: a cognitive analysis*, Lawrence Erlbaum

Feitelson, Dina (1967), 'The relationship between systems of writing and the teaching of reading', in Marion D. Jenkinson (ed.), *Reading Instruction*, International Reading Association (Newark, Delaware)

Feldman, Laurie B. and Turvey, M. T. (1983), 'Word recognition in Serbo-Croatian is phonologically analytic', *Journal of Experimental Psychology: Human Perception and Performance*, vol. 9, pp. 288-98

Forrest, R. A. D. (1948), *The Chinese Language*, Faber & Faber

Francis, W. N. (1970), 'Linguistics and reading: a commentary on chs. 1 to 3', in Levin and Williams (1970)

Frith, Uta (1979), 'Reading by eye and writing by ear', in P. A. Kolers, M. Wrolstad, and H. Bouma, (eds.), *Processing of Visible Language, I*, Plenum (New York)

Frith, Uta (1980a), 'Unexpected spelling problems', in Frith (ed.) (1980b)

Frith, Uta (ed.) (1980b), *Cognitive Processes in Spelling*, Academic Press

Frith, Uta and Frith, C. (1980), 'Relationships between reading and spelling', in Kavanagh and Venezky (1980)

Gelb, I. J. (1952), *A Study of Writing*, University of Chicago Press

Gelb, I. J. (1958), 'New evidence in favour of the syllabic nature of West Semitic writing', *Bibliotheca Orientalis*, vol. 15, pp. 2–7

Geschwind, N. (1973), letter to the Editor, *Science*, vol. 173, p. 190

Gibson, E. J. and Levin, H. (1975), *The Psychology of Reading*, MIT Press

Glushko, R. J. (1979), 'The organization and activation of orthographic knowledge in reading aloud', *Journal of Experimental Psychology: Human Perception and Performance*, vol. 5, pp. 674–91

Goodman, K. S. (1967), 'A psycholinguistic guessing game', *Journal of the Reading Specialist*, vol. 6, pp. 126–35

Goody, J. (1977), *The Domestication of the Savage Mind*, Cambridge University Press

Goody, J. and Watt, I. (1963), 'The consequences of literacy', *Comparative Studies in Society and History*, vol. 5, pp. 304–45

Graham, A. C. (1959),' "Being" in Western philosophy compared with *shih/fei* and *yu/wu* in Chinese philosophy', *Asia Major*, vol. 7, pp. 79–112

Gray, W. S. (1956), *The Teaching of Reading and Writing* (*Monographs on Fundamental Education*, X), UNESCO (Paris)

Green, M. W. (1981), 'The construction and implementation of the Cuneiform writing system', *Visible Language*, vol. 15, pp. 345–72

Grumach, E. (1976), 'The Cretan scripts and the Greek alphabet', in Haas (1976b)

Haas, W. (ed.) (1969a), *Alphabets for English*, Manchester University Press (Manchester)

Haas, W. (1969b), 'From look-and-say to i.t.a.', *Times Educational Supplement*, 28 November 1969

Haas, W. (1976a), 'Writing: the basic options', in Haas (ed.) (1976b)

Haas, W. (ed.) (1976b), *Writing Without Letters*, Manchester University Press (Manchester)

Halliday, M. A. K. (1967), *Intonation and Grammar in British English*, Mouton (The Hague)

Hamp, E. P. *et al.* (eds.) (1966), *Readings in Linguistics II*, University of Chicago Press

Harris, Z. S. (1941), 'Linguistic structure of Hebrew', *Journal of the American Oriental Society*, vol. 61, pp. 143–67

Hartley, J. (ed.) (1980), *The Psychology of Written Communication*, Kogan Page

Hartley, J. and Rooum, D. (1983), 'Sir Cyril Burt and typography: A re-evaluation', *British Journal of Psychology*, vol. 74, pp. 203–12

Havelock, E. A. (1976), *Origins of Western Literacy*, Ontario Institute for Studies in Education (Toronto)

Havelock, E. A. (1978), *The Greek Concept of Justice*, Harvard University Press

Hayek, F. A. (1955), *The Counter-Revolution of Science*, Collier-Macmillan

Henderson, L. (1982), *Orthography and Word Recognition in Reading*, Academic Press

Hochberg, J. and Brooks, Virginia (1976), 'Reading as an intentional behavior', in H. Singer and R. B. Ruddell (eds.), *Theoretical Models and Processes of Reading* (2nd edn), International Reading Association (Newark, Delaware)

Honey, J. (1983), *The Language Trap: Race, Class, and the "Standard English" Issue in British Schools*, National Council for Educational Standards

Householder, F. W. (1969), Review of Langacker, *Language and its Structure, Language*, vol. 45, pp. 886–97
Hymes, D. (1961), 'Functions of speech: an evolutionary approach', in F.C. Gruber (ed.), *Anthropology and Education*, University of Pennsylvania Press
Jeffery, L. H. (1961), *The Local Scripts of Archaic Greece*, Clarendon Press (Oxford)
Jensen, H. (1970), *Sign, Symbol and Script* (3rd edn), George Allen & Unwin
Johnson, A. F. (1966), *Type Designs* (3rd edn), André Deutsch
Jones, D. (1932), 'The theory of phonemes, and its importance in practical linguistics', reprinted in Hamp *et al.* (eds.) (1966)
Justeson, J. S. (1976), 'Universals of language and universals of writing', in A. Juilland (ed.), *Linguistic Studies Offered to Joseph Greenberg on the Occasion of his Sixtieth Birthday*, vol. 1, Anma Libri (Saratoga, Calif.)
Karlgren, B. (1957), *Grammata Serica Recensa*, reprinted from the *Museum of Far Eastern Antiquities Bulletin 29* (Stockholm)
Kavanagh, J. F. and Mattingly, I. G. (eds.) (1972), *Language by Ear and by Eye*, MIT Press
Kavanagh, J. F. and Venezky, R. L. (eds.) (1980), *Orthography, Reading, and Dyslexia*, University Park Press (Baltimore)
Kim, Chin-Wu (1965), 'On the autonomy of the tensity feature in stop classification', *Word*, vol. 21, pp. 339–59
Kim, Chin-Wu (1968), 'The vowel system of Korean', *Language*, vol. 44, pp. 516–27
Kim-Renaud, Young-Key (1975), *Korean Consonantal Phonology*, T'ap Ch'ulp'ansa (Seoul)
Kiparsky, P. (1979), 'Metrical structure assignment is cyclic', *Linguistic Inquiry*, vol. 10, pp. 421–41
Knowlson, J. (1975), *Universal Language Schemes in England and France 1600–1800*, University of Toronto Press (Toronto)
Koerner, E. F. K. (ed.) (1975), *The Transformational-Generative Paradigm and Modern Linguistic Theory*, John Benjamins (Amsterdam)
Kramer, S. N. (1963), *The Sumerians*, University of Chicago Press
Kratochvíl, P. (1968), *The Chinese Language Today*, Hutchinson
Kyöstiö, O.K. (1980), 'Is learning to read easy in a language in which the grapheme-phoneme correspondences are regular?', in Kavanagh and Venezky (eds.) (1980)
Labat, R. (1963), *Manuel d'épigraphie akkadienne*, Imprimerie Nationale (Paris)
Labov, W., *et al.* (1972), *A Quantitative Study of Sound Change in Progress*, US Regional Survey (Philadelphia)
Lambdin, T. O. (1973), *Introduction to Biblical Hebrew*, Darton, Longman, & Todd
Le Brun, A. and Vallat, F. (1979), 'L'origine de l'écriture à Suse', *Cahiers de la délégation archéologique française en Iran*, vol. 8 (dated 1978), pp. 11–59
Ledyard, G. (1966), *The Korean Language Reform of 1446*, PhD thesis, University of California, Berkeley
Lee, Ki-moon (Yi Ki-mun) (1963), English resumé of *Kugŏ p'yogipŏp ŭi yŏksajŏk yŏn'gu* (A study on the history of the Korean writing system), Han'guk Yŏn'guwŏn (Seoul)
Lee, Ki-moon (Yi Ki-mun) (1977), *Geschichte der Koreanischen Sprache*, Dr Ludwig Reichert Verlag (Wiesbaden)
Lee, Ki-moon (Yi Ki-mun) (1981), 'Chu Si-gyŏng: a reconsideration of his linguistic theories' (in Korean), *Ŏhak Yŏn'gu*, vol. 17, pp. 155–65
Leong, Che Kan (1973), 'Hong Kong', in Downing (ed.) (1973)

Levin, H. and Williams, J. P. (eds.) (1970), *Basic Studies on Reading*, Basic Books (New York)

Lieberman, S. J. (1980), 'Of clay pebbles, hollow clay balls, and writing: a Sumerian view', *American Journal of Archaeology*, vol. 84, pp. 339–58

Lindgren, H. (1969), *Spelling Reform: A New Approach*, Alpha Books (Sydney)

Love, N. (1980), *Generative Phonology: A Case-Study from French*, John Benjamins (Amsterdam)

Lowenstamm, Jean (1981), 'On the maximal cluster approach to syllable structure', *Linguistic Inquiry*, vol. 12, pp. 575–604

MacCarthy, P. A. D. (1969), 'The Bernard Shaw alphabet', in Haas (ed.) (1969a)

McCawley, J. D. (1970), 'Some tonal systems that come close to being pitch accent systems but don't quite make it', in *Papers from the Sixth Regional Meeting, Chicago Linguistic Society*, Chicago

McLuhan, M. (1962), *The Gutenberg Galaxy*, Routledge & Kegan Paul

Mahmoud, Y. (1979), 'On the reform of the Arabic writing system', *The Linguistic Reporter*, September 1979, p. 4

Makita, K. (1968), 'The rarity of reading disability in Japanese children', *American Journal of Orthopsychiatry*, vol. 38, pp. 599–614

Marrou, H.-I. (1965), *Histoire de l'éducation dans l'antiquité* (6th edn), Editions du Seuil (Paris)

Martin, S. E. (1951), 'Korean phonemics', *Language*, vol. 27, pp. 519–33

Martin, S. E. (1954), *Korean Morphophonemics*, Linguistic Society of America (Baltimore)

Martin, S. E. (1966), 'Lexical evidence relating Korean to Japanese', *Language*, vol. 42, pp. 185–251

Martin, S.E. (1968), 'Korean standardization: problems, observations, and suggestions', *Ural-Altaische Jahrbücher* 40, pp. 85–114

Mattingly, I. G. (1972), 'Reading, the linguistic process, and linguistic awareness', in Kavanagh and Mattingly (eds.) (1972)

Miller, R. A. (1967), *The Japanese Language*, University of Chicago Press

Miller, R. A. (1971), *Japanese and the Other Altaic Languages*, University of Chicago Press

Minkoff, H. (1975), 'Graphemics and diachrony: some evidence from Hebrew cursive', *Afroasiatic Linguistics*, vol. 1, pp. 193–208

Monk, A. F and Hulme, C. (1983), 'Errors in proofreading: evidence for the use of word shape in word recognition', *Memory and Cognition*, vol. 11, pp. 16–23

Morag, S. (1962), *The Vocalization Systems of Arabic, Hebrew, and Aramaic*, Mouton (The Hague)

Morison, S. (1972), *Politics and Script*, Clarendon Press (Oxford)

Morison, S. (1973), *A Tally of Types*, Cambridge University Press

Mosterín, J. (1981), *La ortografía fonémica del español*, Alianza Editorial (Madrid)

Myers, Prue W. (1984), 'Handwriting in English education', *Visible Language*, vol. 17, pp. 333–56

Norman, D. A. (1972), brief contribution in Kavanagh and Mattingly (eds.) (1972, p. 156)

Palmer, L. R. (1963), *The Interpretation of Mycenaean Greek Texts*, Clarendon Press (Oxford)

Paterson, D. G. and Tinker, M. A. (1932), 'Studies of typographical factors influencing speed of reading: X. Style of type face', *Journal of Applied Psychology*, vol. 16, pp. 605–13

Patrie, J. (1982), review of R. A. Miller, *Origins of the Japanese Language, Language*, vol. 58, pp. 699–701

Poebel, A. (1923), *Grundzüge der sumerischen Grammatik*, Selbstverlag des Verfassers (Rostock)

Poulton, E. C. (1965), 'Letter differentiation and rate of comprehension in reading', *Journal of Applied Psychology*, vol. 49, pp. 358–62

Powell, M. A. (1981), 'Three problems in the history of Cuneiform writing: origins, direction of script, literacy', *Visible Language*, vol. 15, pp. 419–40

Prosser, Margaret (1982), 'A sound idea which did not work', *Times Educational Supplement*, 27 August 1982

Pulleyblank, E. G. (1979), 'The Chinese cyclical signs as phonograms', *Journal of the American Oriental Society*, vol. 99, pp. 24–38

Pye, M. (1971), *The Study of Kanji*, Hokuseido Press (Tokyo)

Rabin, C. (1977), 'Acceptability in a revived language', in S. Greenbaum (ed.), *Acceptability in Language*, Mouton (The Hague)

Rayner, K. and McConkie, G. W (1977), 'Perceptual processes in reading: the perceptual spans', in Reber and Scarborough (eds.) (1977)

Reber, A. S. and Scarborough, D. L. (eds.) (1977), *Towards a Psychology of Reading*, Erlbaum (Hillsdale, NJ)

Reischauer, E. O. (1960), ch. 10 of E. O. Reischauer and J. K. Fairbank, *East Asia: The Great Tradition*, Houghton Mifflin (Boston)

Rosén, H. B. (1977), *Contemporary Hebrew*, Mouton (The Hague)

Rozin, P. and Gleitman, Lila R. (1977), 'The structure and acquisition of reading II: the reading process and the acquisition of the alphabetic principle', in Reber and Scarborough (eds.) (1977)

Rozin, P., Poritsky, S. and Sotsky, R. (1971), 'American children with reading problems can easily learn to read English represented by Chinese characters', *Science*, vol. 171, pp. 1264–7

Ruijgh, C. J. (1967), *Etudes sur la grammaire et le vocabulaire du grec mycénien*, Adolf Hakkert (Amsterdam)

Sampson, G. R. (1970), 'On the need for a phonological base', *Language*, vol. 46, pp. 586–626

Sampson, G. R. (1975), 'One fact needs one explanation', *Lingua*, vol. 36, pp. 231–9

Sampson, G. R. (1980a), *Schools of Linguistics*, Hutchinson and Stanford University Press

Sampson, G. R. (1980b), *Making Sense*, Oxford University Press

Sansom, G. B. (1962), *Japan: A Short Cultural History*, Appleton-Century-Crofts (New York)

Sasanuma, Susumo (1974), 'Impairment of written language in Japanese aphasics: *kana* versus *kanji* processing', *Journal of Chinese Linguistics*, vol. 5, pp. 141–58

Schmandt-Besserat, Denise (1978), 'The earliest precursor of writing', *Scientific American*, June 1978, pp. 38–47

Schmandt-Besserat, Denise (1979a), 'An archaic recording system in the Uruk-Jemdet Nasr period', *American Journal of Archaeology*, vol. 83, pp. 19–48, 375

Schmandt-Besserat, Denise (1979b), 'Reckoning before writing', *Archaeology*, May/June 1979, pp. 22–31

Schmandt-Besserat, Denise (1981), 'From tokens to tablets: a re-evaluation of the so-called "numerical tablets"', *Visible Language*, vol 15, pp. 321–44

Scragg, D. G. (1974), *A History of English Spelling*, Manchester University Press (Manchester)

Scribner, Sylvia and Cole, M. (1981), *The Psychology of Literacy*, Harvard University Press

Shannon, C. E. and Weaver, W. (1949), *The Mathematical Theory of Communication*, University of Illinois Press (Urbana, Ill.)

Shimron, J. and Navon, D. (1980), 'The distribution of visual information in the vertical dimension of Roman and Hebrew letters', *Visible Language*, vol. 14, pp. 5–12

Simons, H. D. (1975), 'Transformational phonology and reading acquisition', *Journal of Reading Behavior*, vol. 7, pp. 49–59

Smith, F. (1973), 'Alphabetic writing – a language compromise?', in F. Smith (ed.), *Psycholinguistics and Reading*, Holt, Rinehart & Winston

Smith, P. T. (1980), 'In defence of conservatism in English orthography', *Visible Language*, vol 14, pp. 122–36

Smith, P. T. and Baker, R. G. (1976), 'The influence of English spelling patterns on pronunciation', *Journal of Verbal Learning and Verbal Behavior*, vol. 15, pp. 267–85

Snowling, Margaret J. (1981), 'Phonemic deficits in developmental dyslexia', *Psychological Research*, vol. 43, pp. 219–34

Sommerstein, A. H. (1973), *The Sound Pattern of Ancient Greek*, Blackwell (Oxford)

Spencer, H. (1969), *The Visible Word* (2nd edn), Lund Humphries

Steinberg, D. D. and Yamada, J. (1978–9), 'Are whole word Kanji easier to learn than syllable Kana?', *Reading Research Quarterly*, vol. 14, pp. 88–99

Stratton, J. (1980), 'Writing and the concept of law in Ancient Greece', *Visible Language*, vol. 14, pp. 99–121

Stubbs, M. (1980), *Language and Literacy: The Sociology of Reading and Writing*, Routledge & Kegan Paul

Trubetzkoy, N. S. (1958), *Principles of Phonology*, English translation published by University of California Press, 1969

Twyman, M. (in press), 'Articulating graphic language: an historical perspective', to be in P.A. Kolers *et al.* (eds.), *Processing of Visible Language*, vol. 3, Plenum Press

Ullendorff, E. (1971), 'Is Biblical Hebrew a language?', *Bulletin of the School of Oriental and African Studies*, vol. 34, pp. 241–55

UNESCO (1957), *World Illiteracy at Mid-Century: A Statistical Study* (*Monographs on Fundamental Education*, XI), Paris

Updike, D. B. (1922), *Printing Types: Their History, Forms, and Use* (2 vols.), Harvard University Press

Vachek, J. (1973), *Written Language: General Problems and Problems of English*, Mouton (The Hague)

Venezky, R. L. (1970), *The Structure of English Orthography*, Mouton (The Hague)

Ventris, M. and Chadwick, J. (1956), *Documents in Mycenaean Greek*, Cambridge University Press (2nd edn, 1973)

Vos, F. (1964), papers on Korean studies in J. K. Yamagiwa (ed.), *Papers of the CIC Far Eastern Language Institute, The University of Michigan*, Committee on Far Eastern Language Instruction of the Committee on Institutional Cooperation (Ann Arbor, Michigan)

Warburton, F. W. and Southgate, Vera (1969), *i.t.a.: An Independent Evaluation*, John Murray

Watts, Lynne and Nisbet, J. (1974), *Legibility in Children's Books: A Review of Research*, NFER Publishing Co. (Windsor)

Weir, Ruth (1967), 'Some thoughts on spelling', in W. Austin (ed.), *Papers in Linguistics in Honor of Léon Dostert*, Mouton (The Hague)

Wells, J. and Colson, Greta (1971), *Practical Phonetics*, Pitman

Wheatley, P. (1971), *The Pivot of the Four Corners*, Edinburgh University Press (Edinburgh)

Wijk, A. (1959), *Regularized English*, Almqvist & Wiksell (Stockholm)

Wijk, A. (1969), 'Regularized English: the only practicable solution of the English spelling reform problem', in Haas (ed.) (1969a)

Xolodović, A. A. (1958), 'O proekte reformy korejskogo orfografii 1949 g.', in *Voprosy Korejskogo i Kitajskogo Äzykoznaniä (Učenye Zapiski Leningradskogo Ordena Lenina Gosudarstvennogo Universiteta imeni A. A. Ždanova, no. 236)*, Leningrad University (St Petersburg)

Yi Ki-mun, see Lee, Ki-moon

Yule, Valerie (1978), 'Is there evidence for Chomsky's interpretation of English spelling?', *Spelling Progress Bulletin*, vol. 18, no. 4, pp. 10–12

Yule, Valerie (1982), 'An international reform of English spelling and its advantages', *Revista Canaria de Estudios Ingleses*, no. 4, pp. 9–22

Zachert, H. (ed.) (1980), *Hun Min Jeong Eum: Die richtigen Laute zur Unterweisung des Volkes (1446)*, Otto Harrassowitz (Wiesbaden)

INDEX

Frequently-used technical terms are indexed only for passages bearing on their definition. Entries for adjectives such as 'Hebrew', 'Japanese' cover the various entities named by that adjective (spoken language, script, nation) in a single sequence.